Multiplayer Game Development with Unreal Engine 5

Create compelling multiplayer games with C++, Blueprints, and Unreal Engine's networking features

Marco Secchi

BIRMINGHAM—MUMBAI

Multiplayer Game Development with Unreal Engine 5

Group Product Manager: Rohit Rajkumar

Publishing Product Manager: Vaideeshwari Muralikrishnan

Senior Editor: Hayden Edwards

Technical Editor: Simran Udasi

Copy Editor: Safis Editing

Project Coordinator: Sonam Pandey

Proofreader: Safis Editing

Indexer: Sejal Dsilva

Production Designer: Jyoti Kadam

Marketing Coordinators: Namita Velgekar and Nivedita Pandey

First published: October 2023

Production reference: 1300823

Published by Packt Publishing Ltd.
Grosvenor House
11 St Paul's Square
Birmingham
B3 1R

ISBN 978-1-80323-287-4

www.packtpub.com

To my parents, Bruno and Alessandra, for giving me the gift of life...,
... and to my lovely wife, Ambra, for making it wonderful.

– Marco

Contributors

About the author

Marco Secchi is a passionate game programming teacher based in Milan, Italy. Previously, he was a freelance programmer, focusing on game and application development; currently, he is a lecturer and lead game advisor at Nuova Accademia di Belle Arti (NABA). Marco continues to hone his programming skills in the research and development department at NABA, while also working on personal projects, involving game development and cultural heritage.

I want to thank the people who have been close to me and supported me while writing this book, especially the amazing people at Packt (they made writing this book much easier than I thought).

About the reviewers

Gonçalo Marques has been an active gamer since the age of six. He has used Unreal Engine since 2016 and has done freelance and consulting work using the software. Gonçalo also released a free and open source plugin called UI Navigation, which has garnered extremely positive reception, with over 100,000 downloads, and still receives frequent updates and fixes. Thanks to the development of this plugin, he became an Epic MegaGrants recipient. He now works at Funcom ZPX, a game studio in Lisbon that has contributed to games such as Conan Exiles, Mutant Year Zero, and Moons of Madness. Gonçalo is currently working on a new Funcom game in the Dune universe.

Punya Aachman is a talented gameplay programmer and technical artist with four years of experience in the gaming industry. He has worked on game titles, simulations, and other various projects, bringing to life engaging gameplay mechanics, immersive experiences, and efficient game development tools on various platforms, such as PC, Oculus Rift, and PlayStation VR. His expertise includes game engines such as Unreal Engine and digital content creation software such as Blender, as well as programming languages such as C++ and Python. Aachman has also contributed to the open source tools community for Blender. With a drive to innovate and a passion to push the boundaries of what's possible in games, Aachman is a valuable asset to any project.

Table of Contents

3

Testing the Multiplayer System with a Project Prototype   31

Part 2: Networking and Multiplayer Games in Unreal Engine

4

Setting Up Your First Multiplayer Environment   63

5

Managing Actors in a Multiplayer Environment   83

6

Replicating Properties Over the Network   117

Part 3: Improving Your Game

8

Introducing AI into a Multiplayer Environment   163

9

Extending AI Behaviors   181

Part 4: Deploying Your Game Online

12

13

14

Preface

Since their first appearance, multiplayer games have revolutionized the gaming industry, providing players with a new way to experience gaming. Unlike traditional single-player games, multiplayer games allow players to engage and interact with each other in real time, providing a dynamic and engaging social experience.

In recent years, advancements in technology have made multiplayer gaming more accessible than ever before, and as a result, it has become one of the most popular genres in the world, with millions of players participating in multiplayer games every day across various platforms.

Game engines, such as Unreal Engine, have become increasingly popular among game developers because they provide many tools and features specifically designed to support high-quality multiplayer experiences, such as cross-platform multiplayer support and advanced lag compensation techniques.

Unreal Engine also has a large and active community of game developers, providing support, resources, and opportunities for collaboration and networking, meaning that, if you are interested in networked game development, there's no reason why you shouldn't give it a try!

Who this book is for

If you are a game programmer or specifically an Unreal Engine developer, with little or no knowledge of video game networking systems, and want to delve deep into this topic, then this book is for you.

Developers who are proficient in other game engines and are interested in understanding the principles of the Unreal multiplayer system will also benefit from this book; however, a basic knowledge of Unreal Engine and C++ is strongly recommended.

A passion for multiplayer games will help you get the most out of this book.

What this book covers

In *Chapter 1*, *Getting Started with Multiplayer Game Development*, you will be gently introduced to the world of multiplayer game development from a developer's point of view.

In *Chapter 2*, *Understanding Networking Basics*, you will explore the basic concepts of network programming in order to get started with multiplayer development in Unreal Engine.

In *Chapter 3*, *Testing the Multiplayer System with a Project Prototype*, you will be guided through the creation of a simple multiplayer prototype, starting from a project template setup, to test some of the basic multiplayer features.

In *Chapter 4*, *Setting Up Your First Multiplayer Environment*, you'll get the foundations to develop a multiplayer C++ project in Unreal Engine.

In *Chapter 5*, *Managing Actors in a Multiplayer Environment*, you'll start creating a multiplayer character and get the basics on how to handle it in a multiplayer environment.

In *Chapter 6*, *Replicating Properties Over the Network*, you'll learn how to handle properties in a multiplayer environment and synchronize them across clients.

In *Chapter 7*, *Using Remote Procedure Calls (RPCs)*, you'll start calling functions over a networked environment, from the server to clients and from a client to the server.

In *Chapter 8*, *Introducing AI into a Multiplayer Environment*, you'll create an enemy character and add a simple AI to it in order to make it work in a multiplayer system.

In *Chapter 9*, *Extending AI Behaviors*, you will add more features to the AI to make it more engaging.

In *Chapter 10*, *Enhancing the Player Experience*, you will add more features to the game, such as animations and non-player characters.

In *Chapter 11*, *Debugging a Multiplayer Game*, you'll learn the basic principles of debugging and profiling a networked game.

In *Chapter 12*, *Managing Multiplayer Sessions*, you'll be introduced to game sessions and their peculiarities.

In *Chapter 13*, *Handling Data During a Session*, you'll learn how to handle data during a multiplayer session.

In *Chapter 14*, *Deploying Multiplayer Games*, you'll be introduced to the basics of building a dedicated server for a multiplayer game.

In *Chapter 15*, *Adding Epic Online Services (EOS)*, you will get an overall introduction to the Epic Games Developer Portal and Epic Online Services, a powerful suite of services designed to help you create the most immersive online experiences possible.

To get the most out of this book

To get the most out of this book, it is strongly recommended to have a good understanding of Unreal Engine and its main features. Some experience with C++ programming will also be an advantage.

A strong passion for gaming – in particular, multiplayer games – will help you a lot in understanding the most advanced topics. It is recommended that you familiarize yourself with multiplayer games by playing titles such as *League of Legends*, *Fortnite*, and *Call of Duty*.

Software/hardware covered in the book	Operating system requirements
Unreal Engine 5.1	Windows 10 64-bit version 1909 revision .1350 or higher/versions 2004 and 20H2 revision .789 or higher, Ubuntu 22.04, or the latest macOS Ventura
Visual Studio 2019 or 2022 and JetBrain Rider 2023+	

As this book is focused on a networked environment and not on graphics, you won't need a high-spec computer to follow all the chapters. However, to properly run Unreal Engine, a good PC with a good graphics card is highly recommended.

Download the example code files

You can download the example code files for this book from GitHub at `https://github.com/PacktPublishing/Multiplayer-Game-Development-with-Unreal-Engine-5`. If there's an update to the code, it will be updated in the GitHub repository.

We also have other code bundles from our rich catalog of books and videos available at `https://github.com/PacktPublishing/`. Check them out!

Conventions used

There are a number of text conventions used throughout this book.

`Code in text`: Indicates code words in text, database table names, folder names, filenames, file extensions, pathnames, dummy URLs, user input, and Twitter handles. Here is an example: "Next, you will find some declarations, such as `UCLASS()`, `GENERATED_BODY()`, `UPROPERTY()`, and `UFUNCTION()`, that are used by UE and each has a precise function."

A block of code is set as follows:

```
#include "US_GameState.h"
AUS_GameMode::AUS_GameMode()
{
    GameStateClass = AUS_GameState::StaticClass();
}
```

When we wish to draw your attention to a particular part of a code block, the relevant lines or items are set in bold:

```
#include "US_Character.h"
```

```
#include "Components/SphereComponent.h"
```

Bold: Indicates a new term, an important word, or words that you see on screen. For instance, words in menus or dialog boxes appear in **bold**. Here is an example: "From the **Games** section, select the **Blank** template."

> **Tips or important notes**
> Appear like this.

Get in touch

Feedback from our readers is always welcome.

General feedback: If you have questions about any aspect of this book, email us at customercare@packtpub.com and mention the book title in the subject of your message.

Errata: Although we have taken every care to ensure the accuracy of our content, mistakes do happen. If you have found a mistake in this book, we would be grateful if you would report this to us. Please visit www.packtpub.com/support/errata and fill in the form.

Piracy: If you come across any illegal copies of our works in any form on the internet, we would be grateful if you would provide us with the location address or website name. Please contact us at copyright@packtpub.com with a link to the material.

If you are interested in becoming an author: If there is a topic that you have expertise in and you are interested in either writing or contributing to a book, please visit authors.packtpub.com.

Share Your Thoughts

Once you've read *Multiplayer Game Development with Unreal Engine 5*, we'd love to hear your thoughts! Scan the QR code below to go straight to the Amazon review page for this book and share your feedback.

https://packt.link/r/1803232870

Your review is important to us and the tech community and will help us make sure we're delivering excellent quality content.

Download a free PDF copy of this book

Thanks for purchasing this book!

Do you like to read on the go but are unable to carry your print books everywhere?

Is your eBook purchase not compatible with the device of your choice?

Don't worry, now with every Packt book you get a DRM-free PDF version of that book at no cost.

Read anywhere, any place, on any device. Search, copy, and paste code from your favorite technical books directly into your application.

The perks don't stop there, you can get exclusive access to discounts, newsletters, and great free content in your inbox daily

Follow these simple steps to get the benefits:

1.   Scan the QR code or visit the link below

https://packt.link/free-ebook/9781803232874

2.   Submit your proof of purchase

3.   That's it! We'll send your free PDF and other benefits to your email directly

Part 1: Introducing Multiplayer Games

In the first part of book, you will receive a beginner-friendly introduction to the realm of multiplayer game development. Once you have a solid understanding of its key concepts, you will proceed to construct a functional prototype of a multiplayer game.

This part includes the following chapters:

- *Chapter 1, Getting Started with Multiplayer Game Development*
- *Chapter 2, Understanding Networking Basics*
- *Chapter 3, Testing the Multiplayer System with a Project Prototype*

1

Getting Started with Multiplayer Game Development

Welcome to the wonderful world of multiplayer game development in Unreal Engine! I am really excited that you have selected me and my book as a guide to this sometimes scary technology; I promise that I'll do my best to make this journey as easy and as entertaining as possible.

Throughout the book, you will learn how to create an **Unreal Engine** multiplayer game from scratch, handle client/server logic, manage AI opponents, test and profile the network, and take advantage of available cloud services. By the end, you will be proficient in creating a networked video game and have a deep knowledge of many of the pitfalls and how to avoid them.

In this chapter, you will get an overview of what a multiplayer game is, its origins, and the different types of multiplayer games that are available today. Additionally, you will explore how the technology used in multiplayer games has been applied in contexts outside of gaming.

In this chapter, I will discuss the following topics:

- Introducing multiplayer games
- Understanding multiplayer game categories
- Exploring gameplay twists
- Is multiplayer technology just for games?

Technical requirements

As you may already know, the Unreal Engine Editor may be very demanding in terms of hardware prerequisites but don't be scared. Luckily, this book is more focused on game programming than on real-time visual effects.

Here, let's look at the hardware and software requirements, as well as some pre-requisite knowledge you will need to follow this book.

Pre-requisite knowledge

Before you get started, it is my duty to remind you that this book is meant for people who already have some knowledge about Unreal Engine development. As such, you should already be familiar with the following topics:

- The Epic Games Launcher and the Unreal Engine Editor
- Blueprint classes and Blueprint programming
- C++ programming with your IDE of choice
- A minimum level of understanding of C++ programming with Unreal Engine.

Hardware requirements

The following are some basic requirements officially recommended by Epic Games at the time of writing this book; if you have at least this hardware, you should be guaranteed a nice experience throughout the chapters:

- **Windows OS**:
  - **Operating System**: Windows 10 64-bit version 1909 revision .1350 or higher, or versions 2004 and 20H2 revision .789 or higher
  - **Processor**: Quad-core Intel or AMD, 2.5 GHz or faster
  - **Memory**: 8 GB RAM
  - **Graphics Card**: DirectX 11- or 12-compatible graphics card
- **Linux**:
  - **Operating System**: Ubuntu 22.04
  - **Processor**: Quad-core Intel or AMD, 2.5 GHz or faster
  - **Memory**: 32 GB RAM
  - **Video Card**: NVIDIA GeForce 960 GTX or higher with the latest NVIDIA binary drivers
  - **Video RAM**: 8 GB or more
- **macOS**:
  - **Operating System**: Latest macOS Ventura
  - **Processor**: Quad-core Intel, 2.5 GHz or faster

- **Memory**: 8 GB RAM
- **Video Card**: Metal 1.2-compatible graphics card

In my case, I've been writing this book with the following hardware:

- **Desktop**:

  - **Operating System**: Windows 10 64-bit version
  - **Processor**: Intel Core i9 9900K @3.60GHz
  - **Memory**: 64 GB RAM
  - **Graphics Card**: NVIDIA GeForce RTX 3090ti

- **Laptop**:

  - **Operating System**: Windows 10 64-bit version
  - **Processor**: Intel Core i7 9750H @ 2.60GHz
  - **Memory**: 16 GB RAM
  - **Graphics Card**: NVIDIA GeForce RTX 2070

Software requirements

This book assumes you have the Epic Games Launcher and Unreal Engine 5 installed and fully working on your computer.

> Note
>
> At the time of writing this book, the latest version of Unreal Engine is 5.1.1 but you will be able to follow along with any version more recent than 5.1.1.

Additionally, you'll need an IDE supporting C++ and Unreal Engine. If you already have some past experience, chances are you have already installed Visual Studio 2019/2022 or JetBrains Rider; if you don't, you will need to install one of them by the start of *Chapter 4, Setting Up Your First Multiplayer Environment*.

> Note
>
> This book assumes you have Visual Studio 2019 or 2022 installed and fully functional; however, it's totally fine to use JetBrains Rider.

Setting up Visual Studio for Unreal Engine development

Once you have Visual Studio installed, you'll need the following extra components to make it properly work with Unreal Engine:

- **C++ profiling tools**
- **C++ AddressSanitizer**
- **Windows 10 SDK**
- **Unreal Engine installer**

To include these tools, follow these steps:

1. Open **Visual Studio Installer**.
2. Select **Modify** from your own Visual Studio installation, selecting the version you will be using, as shown in *Figure 1.1*:

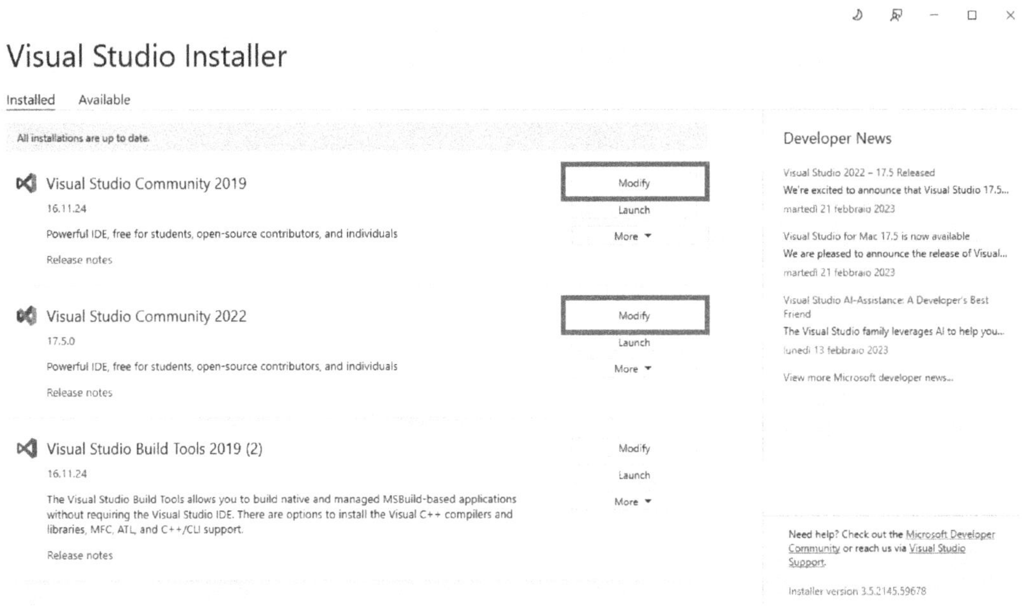

Figure 1.1 – Visual Studio Installer

3. Once the **Modifying** modal window opens, in the top bar, make sure you are in the **Workloads** section.
4. Then, activate the **Game development with C++** option by clicking the checkmark.
5. Next, if it is closed, open **Installation details | Game development with C++ | Optional** from the right sidebar.

6. Select **C++ profiling tools**, **C++ AddressSanitizer**, the latest **Windows 10 SDK** version available, and **Unreal Engine installer**, as shown in *Figure 1.2*.

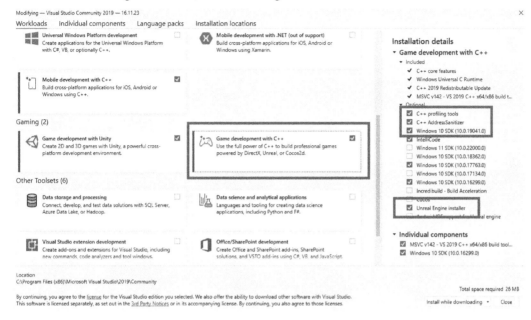

Figure. 1.2 – Visual Studio with Unreal Engine installer activated

7. Click the **Install while downloading** button (or the **Download all, then install** button) to start the installation process.

Once the download and installation process is finished, you will be ready to develop your own C++ games with Unreal Engine.

IDE support for Unreal Engine

Microsoft has recently introduced a new Unreal Engine integration extension for Visual Studio 2022 called *IDE Support for Unreal Engine*. This tool adds some new features such as Blueprint references, Blueprint assets, and CodeLens hints on top of Unreal Engine classes, functions, and properties.

To include this tool, follow these steps:

1. Open the **Workloads** section if it has been closed.

2. Activate the **Game development with C++** option by clicking the checkmark.

3. If it is closed, open **Installation details | Game Development with C++ | Optional** from the right sidebar.

4. Select **IDE support for Unreal Engine**, as shown in *Figure 1.3*.

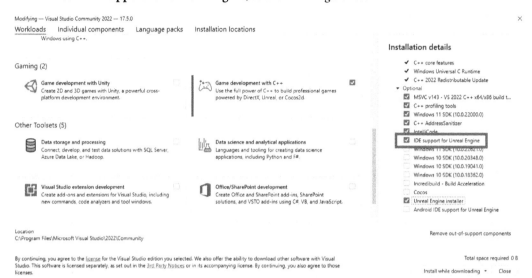

Figure 1.3 – Installing the IDE support

5. Now install the tool.

Now that your IDE is properly configured, it's time to gain some understanding of where multiplayer games come from. In the next section, you'll learn a little bit of video game history.

Introducing multiplayer games

Multiplayer games are probably one of the most attractive forms of entertainment available today. There are several reasons why these types of games have become so popular and engaging over the years.

First, playing with other people adds elements of competition (or cooperation) that can be incredibly motivating and fun. Whether it's a game such as the hyper-realistic *Counter-Strike: Global Offensive* (`https://www.counter-strike.net/`) or some crazy setting such as *Rubber Bandits* (`https://www.rubberbandits.game/`), there is something magical about playing in virtual environments that makes it exciting and enjoyable.

Having someone else to play with also means introducing a lot of opportunities for creative problem-solving and many possibilities for social interaction between people from different backgrounds and countries who may never have met otherwise!

But how did it all begin?

In the early 70s, the **PLATO time-sharing system** developed by the University of Illinois and Control Data Corporation enabled students at multiple locations to access online lessons. Soon after the introduction of PLATO IV, students began utilizing the newly introduced graphical capabilities to create multiplayer video games. By the end of the 70s, PLATO had introduced different games, spanning from dungeon crawlers to space battles to tank combat.

However, multiplayer games didn't really take off until the mid-90s: at this time, internet access became widely available and gamers could finally connect to each other throughout the world.

The popular *Doom* is considered the very first online game as it allowed up to four players at once and featured a deathmatch mode where you could compete for points.

Over the decades, technology has massively improved and we are now able to play together around the globe in amazing immersive virtual worlds without (hopefully!) any lag or connection issues: it's no wonder so many people are drawn toward these types of experiences!

What's more, gamers have developed creative ways to communicate during gameplay, such as using online services including Skype and Discord, which deliver an even more immersive experience.

With the advent of real-time streaming platforms such as Twitch and YouTube, a new phase of multiplayer games has begun. Gamers can play and live broadcast at the same time, letting millions of people enjoy their experience.

Becoming a network programmer in video games

If you are reading this book, chances are you want to understand the basic principles of networking and apply your soon-to-be strong knowledge in multiplayer video game programming to the next big hit. As a multiplayer programmer, you will be able to create fun and interactive games for others to enjoy: this will be an incredibly rewarding experience!

But be aware – network video game programming can be quite challenging, with long work hours and potential stress. It is important to be aware of this before pursuing this type of career.

To avoid these kinds of pitfalls, it's essential to have a solid understanding of how networks work in order to let players have an enjoyable and flawless experience.

Understanding a multiplayer game also means understanding how to troubleshoot computer issues and handle them whenever they pop up.

And rest assured...they *will* pop up sooner or later!

In the following section, you will learn about the major types of multiplayer games, as well as the distinctions that set them apart.

Understanding multiplayer game categories

There is a wide array of game categories available to choose from, ranging from first-person shooters to role-playing; often, a game incorporates more than one genre, giving the player exactly what they are looking for. Here you will find a non-exhaustive list of the most popular game types available nowadays, describing them from a multiplayer point of view.

First-person shooters

First-person shooter (**FPS**) titles are probably some of the most exciting and immersive video games available on the market and involve, as the name suggests, playing from a first-person perspective using various types of weapons.

Players will experience virtual worlds through the eyes of the character with mechanics such as running, taking cover, aiming, shooting (and often reloading your weapon!); this means having fast reflexes or you'll be out of business really quickly!

Multiplayer FPS games offer several game modes that can be played as co-op campaigns, such as *capture the flag* or deathmatches.

There are countless multiplayer FPS games available, but *Apex Legends* (`https://www.ea.com/games/apex-legends`) and *Call of Duty* (`https://www.callofduty.com/`) are good examples of this popular genre.

Third-person shooters

Third-person shooter (**TPS**) games are very similar to FPS games but players can battle each other from a third-person perspective. While FPS games tend to be more focused on shooting opponents and completing objectives, TPS games offer the player a wider view of the surrounding world, making them a good choice for more strategically oriented users.

One of the most popular features with both FPS and TPS games is the ability to change the skin of your character, allowing the creation of unique avatars that will stand out from the crowd.

Fortnite (`https://www.fortnite.com/`) by Epic Games (the developer of Unreal), is one of the most played TPS games, with millions of players around the world every day.

Real-time strategy

Real-time strategy (**RTS**) games combine elements of competition and strategy in a multiplayer experience. Usually, players must build an army and interact with other players online, often involving managing resources, forming pacts with other people (while trying to outsmart them!), and obviously, attacking them when it's clear that there can be only one left standing!

One of the most successful and popular RTS games of all time is *StarCraft* (`https://starcraft.com/`), where players control one species and must battle the others for power and dominance.

Massively multiplayer online role-playing games

In a **massively multiplayer online role-playing game** (**MMORPG**), the classic role-playing game is augmented with networked features allowing thousands (or even millions) of players to interact in real time.

One of the most exciting things about MMORPGs is the ever-changing flow of the story as players will influence it with their own actions; they will buy equipment, hone their skills, and form alliances while looking for the next adventure.

World of Warcraft (`https://worldofwarcraft.blizzard.com/`) is undeniably one of the most popular and longest-running games in this genre.

Multi-user dungeons

Multi-user dungeon (**MUD**) games can be considered the progenitors of MMORPGs and are text-based adventures where each player takes the role of an adventurer in a virtual world. MUDs usually include elements of role-playing, strategy, and hack-and-slash games.

Although they may seem a bit old-fashioned, MUDs are still widely played thanks to their active communities, where players form strong relationships over the years.

Sometimes, MUDs are created by groups of fans of a fictional genre such as *DiscWorldMUD* (`https://discworld.starturtle.net/`), a game based on the *DiscWorld* saga created by Terry Pratchett.

Multiplayer online battle arena

Multiplayer online battle arena (**MOBA**) games are a strategy subgenre where two teams compete against each other: each player controls a character trying to defeat the opposing team, usually by destroying the enemy base. Arenas are predefined, letting teams plan their strategies in advance.

MOBAs also usually feature **non-player character** (**NPC**) minions controlled by **artificial intelligence** (**AI**) that will help characters achieve their goals.

One of the most played MOBA games is *League of Legends* (`https://www.leagueoflegends.com/`), which has been around since 2009 and is still a favorite among players around the world.

> **Note**
>
> The game examples I have provided here have obviously been developed by dozens (if not hundreds) of people, and creating these kinds of games is obviously outside the scope of this book. Additionally, some genres – such as MMORPGs – are some of the most complex and ambitious video games to make. With this in mind, you should exercise caution before attempting to create an intricate multiplayer game – first of all, ensuring that you possess the necessary skills and confidence to handle its vast scope.

Now that we have looked at the different multiplayer genres available, in the next section, you will discover how these genres can be enhanced with creative additions that can completely transform the way they are played.

Reviewing gameplay twists

Given all the aforementioned options available, it is simply a matter of personal preference which multiplayer game genre a player chooses. However, as a developer, you need to be aware of different types of gameplay and technologies to make your project work properly. In this section, I will present a couple of twists applied to regular gameplay.

Asymmetrical gameplay

In **asymmetric multiplayer games**, two or more teams of players compete in gameplay where the mechanics are different for each group. These games usually require players to set their strategy depending on their chosen side.

One of the best examples is *Among Us* (`https://www.innersloth.com/games/among-us/`), which is set on a spaceship where some player takes the role of an impostor whose aim is to let all other crewmates die in some "unexpected" accident before their true identity is revealed.

Hide-and-seek gameplay

There are some games that are meant to be open-ended, letting players explore worlds with considerable freedom and achieve more objectives compared to other more linear adventures.

In multiplayer games, this has led to some **hide-and-seek** variants, where players try to avoid each other (or the main storyline), whether the game officially supports them or not.

An example of this kind of twist is *Secret Neighbor* (`https://www.secretneighbor.com/`), a multiplayer social game where a group of adventurous kids is trying to sneak into their mysterious neighbor's home to uncover evidence that suggests he is keeping children captive.

Asynchronous gameplay

An **asynchronous multiplayer game** will let players interact with each other without the need to be connected at the same time. These games are usually played in turns, where each player will make their move and will wait for the opponent to complete the next one.

And yes...online chess is an asynchronous game!

Now that you have a strong understanding of the main networked game genres, you may be wondering whether game engines' multiplayer technologies are just for gaming. In the next section, I will provide some examples that demonstrate the opposite.

Is multiplayer technology just for games?

As you have read so far, multiplayer networking is an incredibly powerful tool for creating immersive and entertaining games. However, you may be wondering whether this technology is just about gaming.

The short answer is no.

The networking technology available in game engines such as Unreal Engine can be an incredibly useful tool beyond just gaming. Collaborating remotely in real time can have a huge impact on productivity and can be applied to almost any type of project, ranging from educational purposes to architecture, up to cinematography.

Cinematography

Multiplayer technology has become more and more important in movie productions with the advent of **virtual production (VP)**.

VP is a workflow that combines **computer-generated imagery (CGI)**, motion capture, and real and virtual assets combined in a real-time visualization. VP enables content creators (usually filmmakers) to have more efficient and cost-effective productions.

One of the best examples of multiplayer technology used in a VP pipeline is **virtual scouting**, which is the process of exploring and evaluating potential shooting locations without leaving their own studios. This is usually leveraged by a mix of **augmented reality (AR)** and **virtual reality (VR)**.

A good example of using Unreal Engine in VP can be found in *The Mandalorian* series for the streaming service Disney+.

Architecture

Unreal Engine can be used in architecture to create real-time interactive visualizations of architectural projects. These simulations can be run on a multiplayer networking system providing online collaboration capabilities between architects. During the design process, architects can use **Building Information Modeling** (**BIM**) technology in a networked system to access the same model and make changes simultaneously, being more collaborative and efficient.

Real-time rendering software with multi-user capabilities helps designers and architects connect with stakeholders in every phase of the **Architecture, Engineering, and Construction** (**AEC**) life cycle, enabling faster, better communication.

Reflect (`https://unity.com/products/unity-reflect`), a service developed by Unity Technologies, is a good example, letting users experience virtual environments with a mix of 3D rendering, VR, and AR.

Education

Unreal Engine's multiplayer capabilities can be an amazing tool for educators and students, providing immersive and interactive learning experiences. Any teacher with some practical knowledge of the game engine can create a virtual classroom where students can interact with each other in real time.

Games such as *Fortnite* and its *Fortnite Creative* version (`https://www.fortnite.com/creative`) have been used lately as an educational tool in many schools, letting students develop problem-solving skills and engaging them in a fun way.

Unreal's Collab Viewer template

The Unreal Engine Editor has a couple of excellent templates that can be immediately applied as a networked collaborative environment: **Collab Viewer for Architecture** and **Collab Viewer for Automotive, Product Design and Manufacturing**.

In *Figure 1.4*, you can see **Collab Viewer for Architecture** selected and ready to be generated:

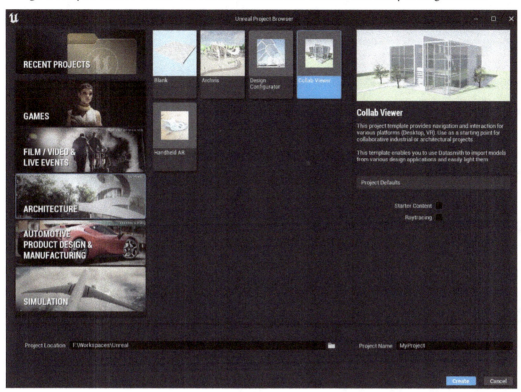

Figure 1.4 – The Collab Viewer template selected in Unreal Editor

These project templates provide an amazing starting point for collaborative industrial and architectural projects; everything has already been set up (even a login panel to access the application), so all you have to do is add your own environment and export the application.

As a teacher, I have often used these Unreal Engine templates as a quick way to create multiplayer educational experiences such as virtual museums or for displaying students' projects.

Figure 1.5 shows the application in action emulating three users on a single machine (don't worry, we will get back to this very soon!).

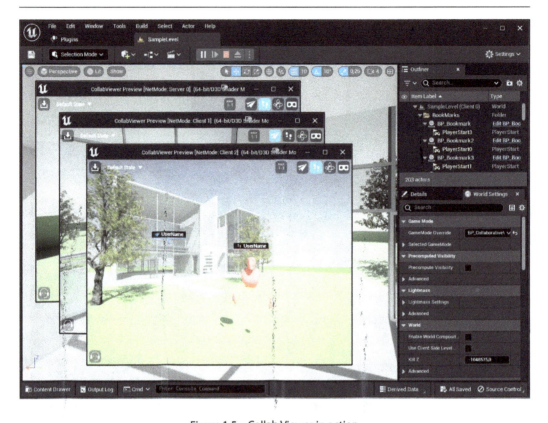

Figure 1.5 – Collab Viewer in action

Knowing how to use Collab Viewer and its many features (VoIP, real-time annotations, VR mode, etc.) is beyond the scope of this book, but if you are interested in this topic, Epic Games has an exhaustive section in the Unreal Engine documentation: `https://docs.unrealengine.com/5.1/en-US/collab-viewer-templates-in-unreal-engine/`.

Summary

In this chapter, you have been introduced to the main categories of multiplayer games and why it is so important to have a solid understanding of networking in the present day. What's more, you were provided with a brief overview of practical examples that extend the concept of something that is traditionally considered a game-only field.

In the next chapter, I will guide you through the basic principles of networking. Although you will encounter a substantial amount of information (which may seem somewhat theoretical), rest assured that it will all become clear as you progress to *Chapter 3*, *Testing the Multiplayer System with a Project Prototype*, where you will start creating your first multiplayer prototype.

2

Understanding Networking Basics

Having a strong knowledge of networking is the foundation of any successful multiplayer game development, as it provides a basic understanding of how the different components that make up a network work. Networking can be divided into three main areas: logical architecture, protocols and standards, and physical infrastructure.

As it's important for anyone interested in networked games to have at least some basic understanding of these concepts, the primary goal of this chapter is to introduce you to these components and the main issues that may pop up during multiplayer application development. By the end of the chapter, you will also get a grip on how the Unreal Engine multiplayer framework is organized in order to be prepared for the next step: creating your first multiplayer game prototype.

So, in this chapter, we will cover the following topics:

- What is computer networking?
- Introducing network protocols
- Understanding network issues
- Introducing the Unreal Engine multiplayer system

Technical requirements

There are no technical requirements to follow in this chapter.

What is computer networking?

We live in a world where we are constantly communicating with each other through computers, smartphones, smart homes, and a plethora of different devices. Computer networks are the backbone of modern technology.

Most people probably don't even care about device communication and how it works; the most important thing is that... well, it works. But what exactly does *network* mean? And most importantly, as multiplayer game developers, what do we need to know about network systems?

Computer networking involves two or more (most of the time, a lot more!) devices that are connected together with the common goal of sharing data and resources as fast and as reliably as possible.

A network can use cables (wired) or radio waves (wireless) and can cover a self-enclosed area or be available at a greater scale. Even if all these technologies share the same purpose, their structure and capabilities will vary significantly.

Once devices are physically connected, they must establish a "contract" in order to communicate securely; without such a contract, data could be sent to the wrong person and put important information at risk.

After the contract is established, each device can send data to another one using a "digital envelope" that identifies the sender and the receiver. This ensures that the data is only received by the intended recipient.

Dispatching data over the network can be very complex, especially when dealing with large files (think about an email with a 150 MB 3D model as an attachment and you'll probably get the idea!). As a consequence, data must be "fragmented" into small pieces by the sender and, once it arrives at its destination, it will be re-packaged by the receiver, ready to be used.

This brings us to the last stage: losing information. Despite the advancements in technology, data loss is still a possibility in our imperfect world. Data can be corrupted or lost during transfer; therefore, it is important to take measures to ensure the safety of data and prevent such losses.

If things sound difficult, that's because they are! But don't be afraid, that's exactly how I felt when I started learning about this type of technology; as you make your way through this book, you will find that many of the topics have been handled by the UE multiplayer system, leaving you free to explore higher level topics.

In the next section, you will learn how a network, or a group of networks, is organized from a structural and operational perspective.

Types of computer networks

As you already know, a computer network provides a way for multiple devices to communicate by sharing information with each other. Some well-known examples are as follows:

- Sending emails
- Streaming videos
- ...and guess what? Playing online games!

But how are these devices connected? There are several different types of computer networks available that have different capabilities and purposes; depending on your needs (and your budget!), you'll have to find a solution that will grant you reliability and trustworthiness.

Local Area Networks

Local Area Networks (**LANs**) are probably the most common type of computer network. A LAN usually consists of a telecommunication network that connects devices that are situated at a close distance (usually no more than 1 kilometer). This type of network usually takes advantage of the fast connection over short distances granted by Ethernet cables.

A LAN can be of two types:

- A client/server LAN, where several devices (i.e., the clients) are connected to a centralized computer (i.e., the server)

- A peer-to-peer LAN, where each device shares the network functionalities equally

Figure 2.1 illustrates a typical small-sized LAN where devices are connected through Wi-Fi or Ethernet cables.

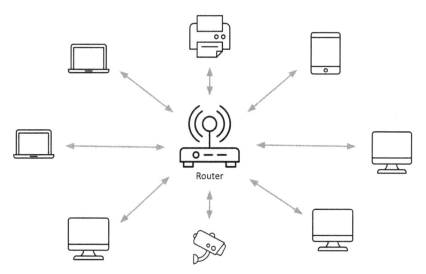

Figure 2.1 – A LAN setup

One of the main advantages of a LAN over a **Wide Area Network** (**WAN**) is the lower level of maintenance and reduced implementation costs. Also, since a LAN is limited to a relatively small distance and to a limited number of connected devices, it ensures a higher level of security.

Some good examples where LANs are used are academic campuses (sometimes called **Campus Area Networks**), hospitals, or offices with multiple departments.

A LAN can become a **Wireless Local Area Network** (**WLAN**) when connections between devices are only made wirelessly, and it is typically used in homes or public spaces (for example, libraries, airports, and cafes) where devices must connect without the need for physical cables.

Wide Area Networks

The primary difference between a LAN and a WAN is that a WAN covers a much larger area and is essentially a collection of LANs connected together.

Similarly for the LAN, a WAN can be as follows:

- A client/server WAN, where multiple devices are connected to a central computer

- A peer-to-peer WAN, where each device shares an equal responsibility in the network functionalities

As there is usually a loss in speed over long distances, a WAN is typically slower than a LAN. However, the main advantage of a WAN is the capability to be publicly owned: a good example is the internet, where no entity has full ownership.

Figure 2.2 shows several LANs connected together through a WAN:

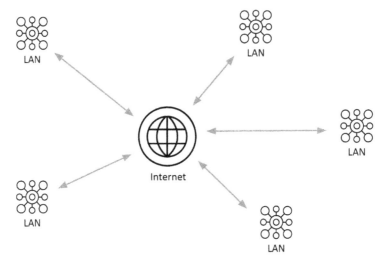

Figure 2.2 – A WAN setup

A **Metropolitan Area Network** (**MAN**) is a smaller WAN usually managed by cities, regions, or governments; it typically includes a high-speed backbone network, which connects multiple LANs. As an example, it may connect multiple campuses belonging to the same academic institution (and that's how it works where I am teaching right now!).

Virtual Private Networks

A **Virtual Private Network (VPN)** is a secure connection over the internet from a device to a network. By using secure encryption, data sent over a VPN is protected, preventing unauthorized tracking, protecting privacy, and bypassing geo-restrictions.

Figure 2.3 shows an example where a device connected to a LAN is communicating over the internet with another device through a VPN.

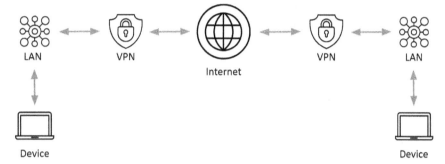

Figure 2.3 – A VPN example

In this section, you have been introduced to the fundamental principles of computer networking. You have explored how computer networks are structured and organized. In the following section, you will delve deeper into these topics to understand how devices communicate using rules and protocols, and how these rules guarantee the reliability and accuracy of the data that is exchanged.

Introducing network protocols

To manage communication between two or more computers, we need some rules that will dictate how data is sent and received, as well as security measures that need to be taken to ensure reliability. These rules are called **protocols**.

Putting it simply, a protocol is like an international language: everyone needs to know the same words to communicate with one another. More specifically, a **network protocol** is a set of directives that rules how to *format, transmit,* and *receive* data so that devices in the same network can interact.

But before transmitting data over the network, it should be carefully packaged and structured so that the receiver can recognize and reassemble it.

Packet switching

Packet switching refers to the method of sending data to a network in the form of small portions (or **packets**). This process involves dividing data into small segments and adding an extra portion of information about the packet's content, origin, and destination. This extra information is called a **header** and is typically placed at the front of each packet. In some cases, the packet may also include additional information at its end, referred to as a **footer**.

These packets are then sent over the network and reassembled at their destination. Along the way, they are processed by intermediate nodes, which can store incoming data and forward it to the next node closer to the final receiver.

Some of the advantages of using packet switching include efficiency in terms of bandwidth and reliability as the receiver can detect missing packages. Another advantage is cost-effectiveness due to relatively cheap implementation.

As an example, *Figure 2.4* shows a **Transmission Control Protocol** (**TCP**) packet composed of its header and data sections:

- The header is made of blocks of bits, each one with its own meaning (as an example, the *header length* tells the header data offset in order to specify where actual data will start in the sequence)
- The data can be of varying lengths and holds the actual content included in the packet

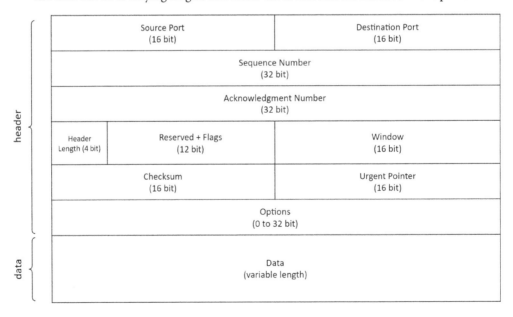

Figure 2.4 – A TCP packet

The collection of protocols that rule how data should be packaged and forwarded through the network is now known as the **Internet Protocol Suite** or the **TCP/IP suite**.

TCP/IP suite

The TCP/IP suite is made of different logical levels, or **layers,** that are stacked one above the other. These include the following:

- The application layer
- The transport layer
- The internet layer
- The data link layer

Figure 2.5 shows the layers of the TCP/IP suite with some of the most commonly used protocols, along with the physical layer, which we will discuss later in this section:

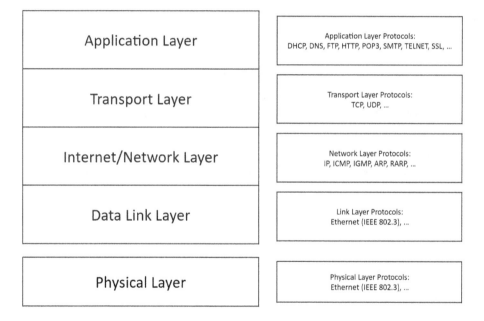

Figure 2.5 – TCP/IP layers

Each layer has an important role to play in supporting the needs of the one above it. As an example, this may involve accepting a block of data from the layer above, processing it according to the current layer's protocols, and then sending it to the layer below.

Let's take a look at each of these layers now.

The application layer

The **application layer** provides the interface for communication between applications running on different machines on the network. It stands at the very top of the TCP/IP suite and allows the sharing of data through the use of protocols, such as the **File Transfer Protocol** (**FTP**) and the **HyperText Transfer Protocol** (**HTTP**), which are used to upload files to the internet and download web pages on your favorite browser.

The transport layer

The **transport layer** is responsible for providing reliable data delivery and flow control and provides services that allow applications to communicate securely over the network.

While TCP is commonly used for its reliability, there are situations where other protocols are preferred for their speed, such as the **User Data Protocol** (**UDP**), which won't ensure packet delivery but will be faster as it doesn't require the overheads associated with establishing and maintaining a connection.

This layer is typically responsible for detecting issues and verifying data integrity; one way is through **checksums**, or sequences of numbers and letters used to check data for errors.

The internet layer

The **internet layer** (or, more generically, the **network layer** in the TCP/IP suite) is responsible for providing the means to route data between different networks and ensure that packets are delivered correctly. This layer also provides various services such as addressing, routing, congestion control, and flow control.

The internet layer is responsible for providing a logical addressing system that allows hosts to be easily replaced, groups of hosts to be organized into subnets, and distant subnets to be able to communicate with one another.

The most common protocol used to implement these features is **Internet Protocol Version 4** (**IPv4**), which is a 32-bit address that identifies a device on a network. The most recent release, **Internet Protocol Version 6** (**IPv6**), is based on a 128-bit address and is designed to replace IPv4, as that one is running out of available addresses.

The data link layer

The **data link layer** is responsible for providing a method for communication between physically connected hosts. This means this layer must provide a method through which a source host can package up information and transmit it through the physical layer.

Figure 2.6 depicts a typical communication flow between two devices, a client and a server, and the data passing through the different layers:

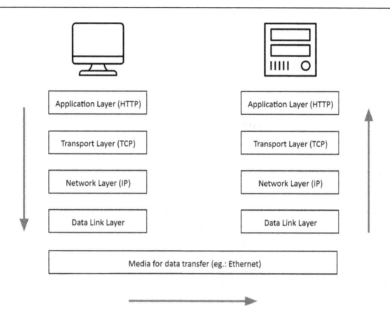

Figure 2.6 – The communication between a client and a server

The physical layer

Underneath all of the previous layers is the **physical layer**, which is responsible for actually sending raw data (bits) over a physical medium, such as a cable, an optical fiber, a Wi-Fi connection, or even a Bluetooth communication.

This layer defines how signals are sent and received, as well as how these signals are modulated and demodulated into usable digital information.

Though we have discussed the physical layer here, it is not actually included in the TCP/IP suite, which is why it is slightly separated from the other layers shown in *Figure 2.5*.

Now that you know how data is packaged and how the TCP/IP suite is organized, you will learn about the main problems and pitfalls that can happen over the network in the next section.

Understanding network issues

With so much data involved and moving around physical media, there is a significant risk of running into serious issues. As such, it is important to be aware of these potential problems and how to best avoid them or limit their impact.

Security

The first issue to consider when dealing with computer networking is **security**. Without proper security protocols in place, it's possible for malicious people to gain access to sensitive information.

Getting your credit card information stolen while in-app purchasing the latest skin for your character or your login credentials stolen from your Steam account is something you definitely don't want to experience!

Packet loss

Packet loss occurs when data packets sent from one device to another are lost or corrupted and is a major issue that can cause significant disruption to any network. This type of disruption can lead to a slow or even complete breakdown in communication, resulting in a negative gaming experience for players.

Consider, for instance, if your perfect shoot at a berserker opponent who is trying to leap at you is lost over the network: you would be in a great deal of trouble at that moment!

Latency

Latency in computer networking is represented by the time it takes for a data packet to travel from one designated point to its destination and is usually measured in milliseconds. This can be caused by a variety of factors, such as slow internet connections, outdated hardware, or congested networks.

In a multiplayer game, latency should be kept as low as possible as it can have a significant impact on the performance of the game you are playing. As an example, in a first-person shooter game where fast reflexes are essential, having your character killed due to a slow connection can ruin all the fun!

> **Note**
> While dealing with security and data loss are not topics discussed in this book, you'll learn about latency and how to handle it in *Part 4* of this book. However, if you are interested in delving deeper into the topics of network security and data loss, Packt offers an extensive collection of books on the subject.

Now that you have a basic grip on the main issues when managing data over the network, it's time to move into Unreal Engine and get an introduction to how this software handles networking.

Introducing the Unreal Engine multiplayer system

As we already saw in the previous sections, in a networked system, it is essential to consider what data is sent and how it is sent, as this can drastically influence the performance and overall experience of the game.

Unreal Engine features a powerful networking framework, which is used in some of the most popular online games in the world. This section provides an overview of the concepts that power the Unreal Engine multiplayer framework, as well as their usage in multiplayer gameplay.

Network modes and server types

In Unreal Engine, a computer's relationship to a multiplayer session is referred to as a **network mode**. An Unreal game can be set as one of the following network modes:

- **Client**: In this mode, the computer will act as a client, connecting to a server in a network multiplayer session.

- **Standalone**: This mode is strictly used for non-networked games (single players or local multiplayer) and will not accept any connections from remote clients.

- **Dedicated Server**: In this mode, the computer will run as a server hosting a network multiplayer session and will accept connections from remote clients. As a dedicated server, everything will be optimized for persistent and secure management, so will ignore any player-oriented features, such as graphics, audio, or input.

- **Listen Server**: In this mode, the computer will run as a server accepting remote clients, but also local players. This means it will sacrifice some performance, but will allow a computer to act both as a server and as a client. This mode can be thought of as a combination of the client and dedicated server modes, allowing you to participate in a game as a client while simultaneously hosting the network.

> Note
>
> Listen servers have gained popularity due to their ease of setup and ability to provide both casual and competitive multiplayer gaming in a LAN. As players hosting the session will be playing directly on the server, they will usually have an advantage over the other players. However, as servers are also run as clients, they are not suitable for highly competitive games or games with a large amount of data involved. Additionally, listen servers, which allow a client to host a game and have other clients join to play, create potential vulnerabilities for all clients on the network. This is because the client hosting the network may engage in malicious actions, such as cheating or granting themselves an unfair advantage over other players.

The replication system

In UE, the process of reproducing game state information between the server and clients is called **replication**. The replication system allows for high-level abstraction and low-level customization, making it simpler to manage any scenarios that may arise when creating an Unreal Engine project intended for multiple users at once.

If replication is enabled on an Actor, all instances of the game running on different machines will be synchronized. On the other hand, if replication is disabled, the Actor will only update its functions on the machine where it was spawned.

Some of the most common elements that you will probably replicate during a multiplayer game development may be creation/destruction, movement, variables, and components.

There are, however, other elements that should not be replicated at all as they will be running separately on the client, such as skeletal and static meshes, materials, particle systems, and sound emitters. Usually, the server does not need to know about these kinds of things, considering the nature of these elements (i.e., purely aesthetical).

Network role

When playing a game online with multiple players, it is important to understand which device is in control of each Actor. This is determined by the network role of the Actor itself.

The device with an **authoritative** Actor role is the one that has control of the Actor's state, and it is responsible for replicating information about the Actor to other players in real time.

A copy of the same Actor located on a remote machine that is not authoritative is defined as a **remote proxy** and will receive all replicated information from the authoritative one.

In UE, the authority is typically held by the server, meaning that information is usually *from* the server *to* the clients. This model is known as **server-authoritative**.

Pawns and PlayerControllers

As you may already know, in UE, a Pawn (or, more often, a Character) can be owned by a PlayerController. This is also true for multiplayer games, where a PlayerController is created for each connected player.

During gameplay, any Actor that has been assigned to a particular Pawn is automatically associated with that Pawn's owning client. As an example, a Pawn may possess an item such as a rifle or a sword Actor, and this item will be held owned by the same connection that owns the Pawn.

Relevance and priority

To determine whether it is beneficial to replicate an Actor during a multiplayer game, **relevance** is taken into account. Actors that are deemed not relevant will be excluded during replication. This method is used to reduce the amount of data that is sent over the network, thereby increasing the efficiency of data replication.

When bandwidth is limited, the most important Actors are selected first when replicating data. Each Actor has an assigned **priority** value, which is used to determine the order of replication.

Remote Procedure Calls

During a multiplayer session, a function can be replicated through a **Remote Procedure Call** (**RPC**). RPCs can be invoked from any machine connected to the network, but their implementation will take place on a particular machine that is part of the network session.

An RPC can be sent from the server, the client, or to multiple clients (**multicast**). An RPC can either be guaranteed to reach its destination (**reliable**) or not (**unreliable**).

In this section, I provided some of the key definitions regarding the UE multiplayer system. The information here may seem quite dense and things may seem a bit overwhelming. But don't be afraid – you just finished the second chapter and the entire book is available to help you learn it all!

Summary

In this chapter, you learned about the fundamental concepts of computer networking and the key players involved in successful network communication. Additionally, you were introduced to the Internet Protocol and the layers that make up the TCP/IP suite with the main issues that may arise during a network connection. Finally, you were presented with the Unreal multiplayer system and the key features offered by the framework.

In the next chapter, you will start to gain practical experience with UE by building a prototype of a multiplayer game and testing its features on your computer.

Credits

The diagrams in this chapter were created with the help of *Made Lineal* icons from Flaticon (`https://www.flaticon.com/`).

3

Testing the Multiplayer System with a Project Prototype

Now that you know how networks work and how computers communicate remotely, it's time to test some of the basic functionalities of the Unreal Engine networking framework. The best way to understand how different elements interact within the UE environment is by using one of the available project templates and enabling its multiplayer capabilities.

The main goal of this chapter is to serve as a gentle introduction to the main UE multiplayer framework features and how to test them on a single device, such as your computer. By the end, you will have created your first multiplayer prototype and will be ready for the next step, which is creating a fully working networked game from scratch.

So, through the next few sections, I will present you with the following topics:

- Creating a multiplayer game prototype
- Testing a multiplayer game locally
- Updating properties over the network
- Executing functions over the network

Technical requirements

For this first prototype, you will just need UE 5 to be installed. For this chapter, you won't be programming in C++, as the prototype will be Blueprints only.

To make things more interesting, I'll be using some assets from Quixel Megascans by using the integrated plugin, but this is not mandatory.

The finished project can be found in this book's project template on GitHub, in the **Chapter 3** section: https://github.com/PacktPublishing/Multiplayer-Game-Development-with-Unreal-Engine-5.

> **Note**
>
> Starting from this chapter, I will use the terms "Blueprint" and "Blueprint Class" interchangeably. If a distinction needs to be made, I will use the appropriate term, such as "Anim Blueprint."

Creating a multiplayer game prototype

For this project, gameplay will not be the primary focus; I want you to concentrate on the core components of the multiplayer framework. Accordingly, the game will be quite simple and abide by the following basic rules:

- Each player should control their character
- The server will spawn item pickups at random positions
- Players will capture pickups and gain points from that
- The game will go on indefinitely

Using a pre-made project such as a template is a great opportunity for you to gain hands-on experience with the main multiplayer capabilities in UE without having to waste time creating a project from scratch. Here, you'll start by creating your own multiplayer game prototype by using the **TopDown** template.

Setting up the project from a template

When you are ready, launch UE 5 from the Epic Games Launcher. Then, follow these steps:

1. Select **Games** | **TopDown** from the available templates.
2. Set the project to **Blueprint**.
3. Name your project (for instance, TopDown_Multiplayer).
4. Leave the other settings as their default values.
5. Click the **Create** button.

Figure 3.1 shows the finished settings for the project:

Figure 3.1 – Project setup

Once the project has been created, you are ready to import some content.

Adding Quixel Megascans

In this project, I want to use something a bit crazy for my pickups: I am going to choose some fruit and vegetables from the Quixel Megascans library (https://quixel.com/megascans)!

Quixel Megascans is a free library that contains high-resolution 3D scans: it is fully integrated with UE; you will just need to use your Epic Games account. To access the models from UE, you will need to use Quixel Bridge, a plugin that's already installed in the Unreal Engine Editor.

To add some Megascans to the project, just do this:

1. Open Quixel Bridge by clicking **Quickly add to the project | Quixel Bridge**.

2. From the **3D Assets** section, look for some fruit or vegetables – or anything that will spark your imagination!

3. Download the assets and add them to your project by clicking the **Download** button.

Figure 3.2 depicts Quixel Bridge with some of my selected models during the download phase:

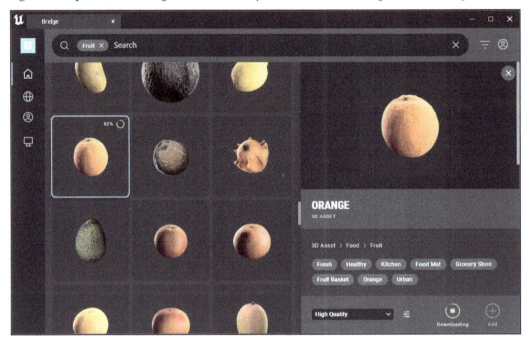

Figure 3.2 – Quixel Bridge

Once you have obtained your assets, they will likely be of various sizes. However, you will need to resize them to create a visually appealing and functional pickup. To do so, follow these steps:

1. From the main menu, create an empty level by selecting **File | New Level** and selecting the **Basic** option. Then, add a reference character (I used the **SKM_Quinn** model located in the `Content | Characters | Mannequins | Meshes` folder).

2. Add your models next to the reference.

3. Scale them so that they are about a third of the size of the reference.

Figure 3.3 shows the models once they have been resized:

Figure 3.3 – The resized models

Since the pickups will be created from a common Blueprint parent, the best thing to do is to set the scale of the models to 1, which we can achieve through the **Modeling Tools** available in UE. Open the **Modeling Tools** panel by selecting it from the **Mode Selection** dropdown in the **Main Toolbar** area, as shown in *Figure 3.4*:

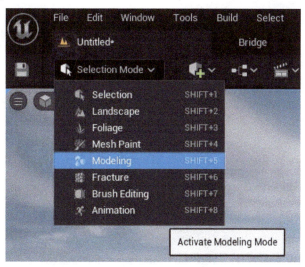

Figure 3.4 – Activating the Modeling Tools panel

Once the **Modeling Tools** panel has been enabled, execute the following steps for each of the models:

1. Select the model.

2. Select **Transform | BakeRS** to activate the **Rotation and Scale** baking tool.

3. In the **New Asset Location** drop-down menu at the bottom of the tool, select **AutoGen Folder (Global)**.

4. Click the blue **Accept** button to start the baking process.

Figure 3.5 depicts the **BakeRS** tool open and ready to process a model:

Figure 3.5 – The BakeRS tool

At the end of this process, all three models will be of equal size, but each scaled to a value of 1.

The last thing you must do is generate a collision for each of the models:

1. Open each of the static meshes in the project.

2. Open the **Collision** drop-down menu.

3. Select **Add 26DOP Simplified Collision** to add a collision area to the mesh.

4. Save the modified assets to apply the changes.

This scene can be safely closed as you won't be using it anymore. Open **TopDownMap,** which is located in the Content | TopDown | Maps folder. By doing this, your assets will be ready to use as pickups in the game.

The next step will be to modify the Player Controller so that you can handle the Pawn movement.

Modifying the Player Controller

The Player Controller from the template is already operational and works properly, but to make the game a bit more exciting (it's a multiplayer game, after all!), you'll need to make some minor adjustments.

At the moment, character movement is controlled by a single click on a point on the map. However, we want players to be able to move their character by keeping the mouse button pressed and moving it around the level.

Follow these steps to modify the Player Controller Blueprint:

1. Navigate to **Content | TopDown | Blueprints** and open the **BP_TopDownController** Blueprint.

2. Then, open the Event Graph by clicking the **Event Graph** tab.

3. Delete the **Set Destination Input – Touch** group as you won't be using it.

4. In the **Set Destination Input – Gamepad and Mouse** group, delete all the nodes connected to the **Canceled** and **Completed** execution pins.

5. Connect the **Ongoing** execution pin to the same **Branch** node as the **Triggered** execution pin.

The modified graph should look like this:

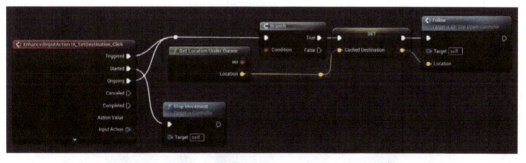

Figure 3.6 – The modified graph for the Player Controller

Now that the Player Controller has been modified, if you try playing the game as is, you should be able to move your character around whenever you keep the left mouse button pressed. This is the normal behavior you would expect when playing a standalone game.

In the next section, you'll learn how to set up UE so that it simulates a multiplayer session on your computer.

Testing a multiplayer game locally

Testing a multiplayer game can pose a problem as it requires the game to be available across multiple devices. Luckily, UE allows you to simulate this scenario on a single computer, making it much easier for developers to create and test multiplayer games. In this section, you will learn how to use your editor as a server and launch other game instances locally.

Playing as a Listen Server

It's time to start testing how the game works in a multiplayer environment. You'll be doing this by using UE's **Net Mode** feature:

1. Open the **Change Play Mode and Play Settings** menu by clicking the hamburger button next to the **Play** button, as shown in *Figure 3.7*:

Figure 3.7 – The hamburger button

2. In the **Number of Players** field, enter the number of players you want to simulate; for instance, 3.

3. Then, select **Net Mode | Play As Listen Server**, as shown in *Figure 3.8*:

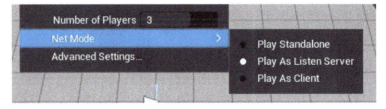

Figure 3.8 – The Net Mode settings

> **Note**
>
> When you are testing a game in the Editor as a **Listen Server**, the Editor acts as a server and a client. Depending on the number of players selected, additional instances will be opened for testing purposes. As a side note, launching the game in **New Editor Window (PIE)** mode will designate one of the screens as the server and the other screens as clients. This distinction can be identified by examining the title bar of the launched windows.

You can now click the **Play** button, after which the Editor will open one window for each additional player, as depicted in *Figure 3.9*:

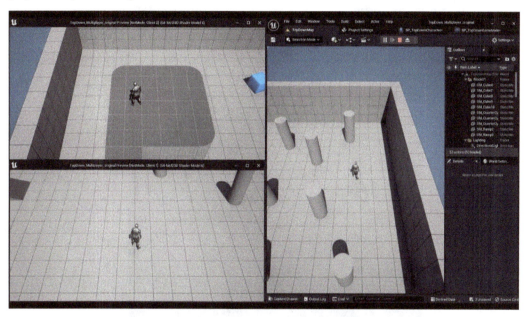

Figure 3.9 – Testing the game as a Listen Server

Focusing on each window will let you play each independent character.

> **Note**
>
> If you check the **Outliner** window while in Play Mode, you will notice that there are three **BP_TopDownCharacter** instances (one for each player), but just one **BP_TopDownController** – this is the one you will need for the local player.

Updating over the network

At this point, you may be wondering how characters can be synchronized across different clients, given that we have not done anything related to the network.

The answer is **replication**, which I explained in the previous chapter, and is demonstrated in this prototype: Character Actors are replication-enabled, so some of their properties, such as **Location** and **Rotation**, are updated across clients during gameplay.

To see whether an Actor replicates, do the following:

1. Open the **BP_TopDownCharacter** Blueprint by going to **Content | TopDown | Blueprints**.
2. Open the **Details** panel by clicking the **Class Defaults** tab.
3. Find the **Replication** category and notice that the **Replicates** attribute has been selected. Additionally, notice that **Replicate Movement** is selected, as depicted in *Figure 3.10*:

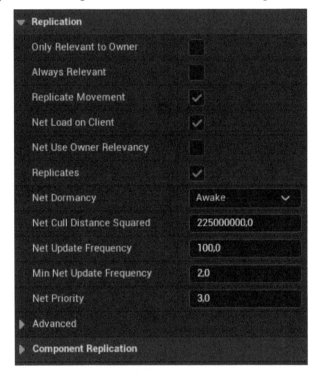

Figure 3.10 – The Replication category

One of the best parts of activating the **Replicates** attribute is that properties will be updated automatically over the network: you won't need to do anything else. Later, you will learn how to execute functions by calling them over the network.

Adding additional character spawn points

As you may have noticed, the three players have been spawned next to each other: this is because we have a single Player Start Actor in the level.

To fix things up, you will be adding some more spawn points:

1. Add several **Player Start** objects, up to the number of players you want to test – you can do this by clicking the **Quickly Add To The Project** button, then selecting **Basic | Player Start**.

2. Place them anywhere on the map that you deem suitable for your game. In *Figure 3.11*, you can see my choice for the three spawn points:

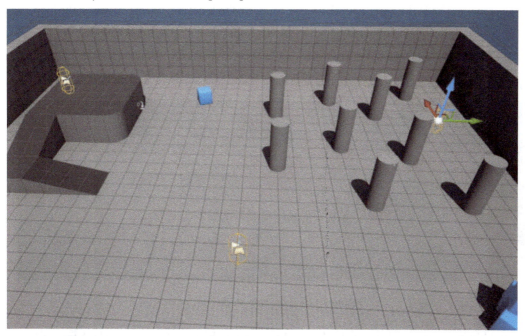

Figure 3.11 – Adding more spawn points

If you test your game at this point, you will notice that players are now randomly spawning at the **Player Start** positions, but sometimes, two or more characters still end up at the same spawn point. This can easily be fixed by checking positions that have already been taken and excluding them from the selection when a new player joins the session. To do this, follow these steps:

1. Open the **BP_TopDownGameMode** Blueprint by going to **Content | Topdown | Blueprints**.

2. Then, open the Event Graph.

3. In **My Blueprints | Functions**, add an override to the **ChoosePlayerStart** function by clicking the **Override** option.

4. Add a **Get All Actors Of Class** node and connect its incoming execution pin to the execution pin of the **Choose Player Start** node. Then, set the **Actor Class** drop-down attribute to **Player Start**.

5. Add a **For Each Loop** node to cycle through all the **Out Actor** properties you found in the previous node.

6. Connect the **Loop Body** execution pin to a **Branch** node.

7. Click and drag from the **Array Element** pin for the loop to get a **Player Start Tag** node and connect its outgoing pin to a not equal (**!=**) node. Assign the comparison value of this node to **Used**. Connect the outcome of this check to the **Condition** pin of the **Branch** node.

8. Connect the **True** execution pin of the **Branch** node to a **Set Player Start Tag** node with a value equal to **Used**. The **Target** pin should be connected to the **Array Element** area of the loop.

9. Connect the outgoing execution pin of the **Set** node to the graph's **Return Node**.

10. The **Return Value** pin of **Return Node** should be set to the **Array Element** property of the loop.

The resulting Blueprint is shown in *Figure 3.12*:

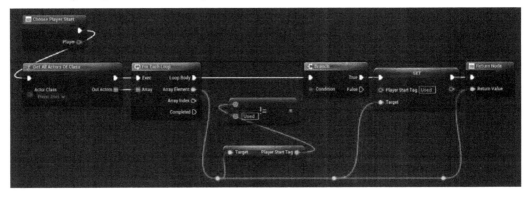

Figure 3.12 – The Game Mode graph

What this graph does is cycle through all of the **Player Start** objects in the level and look for one that has not been tagged as **Used** (that is, it has not been taken already). Once a good candidate has been found, it is tagged as **Used** and its value is returned, ready to be used as a spawn point for the character.

Run the game – each character should now be spawned at unique locations. With that, your players are now ready to interact with the level!

Play around and test your game: check that everything runs as expected and that players are correctly synchronized over all clients.

In the next section, you will learn how to update attributes across multiple clients by adding some pickups and assigning points to the characters as they get them.

Updating properties over the network

Now, it's time to add some gameplay and properly synchronize elements at runtime. In the next few subsections, you'll work on the following features:

- Creating the pickup Blueprint
- Adding pickup variants
- Adding a points counter to the characters

Let's add these features now.

Creating the pickup Blueprint

The first thing we are going to create is a pickable item that will grant points to the character that picks it up by sending them a message.

To create this type of communication, you'll need to create an interface:

1. In your `Blueprint` folder, right-click and select **Blueprints | Blueprint Interface**.
2. Name the interface `PointsAdder`.
3. Open the **Blueprint Interface**.
4. Rename the default function `AddPoints`.
5. Add an **Input** parameter called `Value` that's of the **Integer** type.

The interface you have just created should be the same as the one shown in *Figure 3.13*:

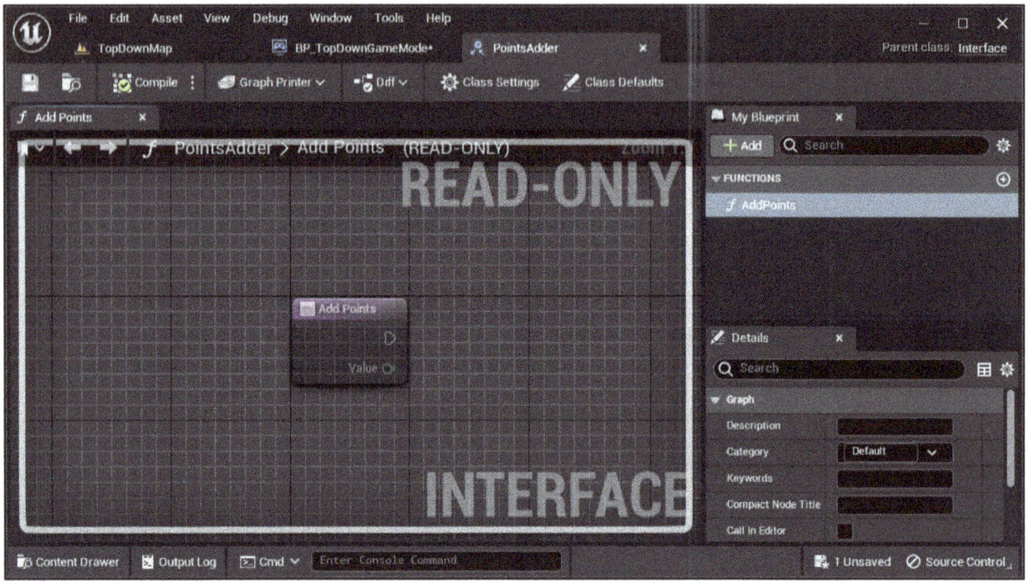

Figure 3.13 – The PointsAdder interface with the AddPoints declaration

Once the interface is ready, you'll need to create the pickup Blueprint that will use it:

1. In your `Blueprints` folder, add a Blueprint Class that inherits from **StaticMeshActor**, and name the Blueprint `BP_BasePickup`.

2. Open the Blueprint. Then, select the **Class Defaults** tab and add a mesh of your choice to the **Static Mesh** field.

3. In the **Physics** section, enable the **Simulate Physics** attribute and check that the **Enable Gravity** attribute has been enabled.

4. Add a **SphereCollision** component to the Blueprint components hierarchy.

5. Name the component `Trigger` and ensure that the **Generate Overlap Events** attribute has been enabled.

6. Set the **Sphere Radius** attribute of the **SphereCollision** component to a value that is a little bigger than the static meshes you'll be using (for instance, **50**).

Now, you need to add some code logic to the Blueprint. First, let's add a points value for the picking character:

1. Open the Event Graph.

2. Add a variable of the **Integer** type and call it `Points`.

3. Make it **Instance Editable** by clicking the eye button next to the variable type.

4. After compiling, set the variable's **Default Value** to **1**.

The Blueprint Viewport should look the same as what's shown in *Figure 3.14*:

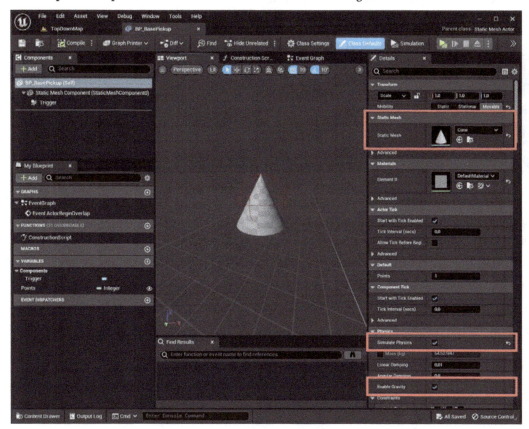

Figure 3.14 – The pickup Viewport

Now, it's time to set the overlap event behavior for the Blueprint:

1. Delete the **Event BeginPlay** and **Event Tick** nodes as you won't be using them.

2. Add a **Cast To Character** node and connect its incoming execution pin to the outgoing pin of **Event ActorBeginOverlap**, to check that the actor is of the required type (that is, a Character).

3. If the check succeeds, then add an **AddPoints (Message)** node: this is the function you previously declared in the interface.

4. Connect the **As Character** pin of the cast to the **Target** pin of the function node.

5.   Add a **Get Points** node to the graph and connect the pin to the **Value** pin of the **Add Points** function node.

6.   Finally, connect the outgoing execution pin of the **Add Points** node to a **Destroy Actor** node to remove the pickup once it has been taken.

The final graph should be similar to the one shown in *Figure 3.15*:

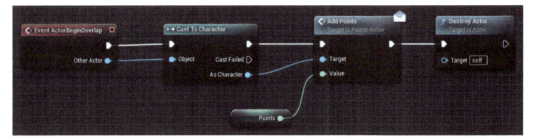

Figure 3.15 – The pickup Event Graph

What this graph does is pretty straightforward: whenever an actor overlaps with the pickup, the pickup will send an **AddPoints** message through the interface and then destroy itself. If the overlapping actor won't implement the interface, the message will simply be lost without dispatching any errors.

Now, it's time to take the most crucial step in the process: enabling replication. To do this, do the following:

1.   In the **Components** tab, select the **BP_BasePickup (self)** element.

2.   Then, in the **Details** panel, look for the **Replication** category and enable the **Replicates** attribute.

Now that you have a base pickup, you can create variants, ready to be used in-game.

Adding pickup variants

Creating a variant for the pickup Blueprint is quite easy:

1.   Right-click on your **BP_BasePickup** item in the Content Browser.

2.   Select **Create Child Blueprint Class**, give your new pickup a name, and open it.

3.   Open the **Class Defaults** tab. Then, assign a mesh to the **Static Mesh** field (in my case, a fruit Megascan).

4.   Assign a value of your choice to the **Points** attribute, as shown in *Figure 3.16*:

Figure 3.16 – The settings for the orange pickup

Repeat these steps for each of your pickups and you'll be ready to go!

Before you implement the **AddPoints** interface for the Blueprint character, you are free to add some of the brand-new pickups and test the game as a listen server multiplayer game.

> **Note**
>
> If your pickups seem to have different rotations through the clients, this means that you probably didn't enable replication. Please make sure that the **Replicates** and **Replicate Movement** fields are checked for your Blueprints!

Adding a points counter to the character

Now that you know how to replicate Actors across the network, it is time to learn how to replicate single variables and how to intercept changes at runtime.

You'll be doing this by keeping track of the points that have been gained by each player by displaying them next to the gaming Actor. Follow these steps:

1. Open **BP_TopDownCharacter**, which is located in your `Blueprints` project folder.

2. Add a **Points** variable of the **Integer** type.

3. In the **Details** panel of the **Points** property, look for the **Replication** field and, from the drop-down menu, select **RepNotify**.

You will notice that, once the **RepNotify** field has been selected, a function named **OnRep_Points** has been added to your Blueprint – this function will be called on the clients every time the variable is updated by the authoritative Actor.

> **Note**
>
> The difference between the **RepNotify** and **Replicated** values is that in the second case, the variable will be updated over the network without executing any notification function. It should also be noted that the **OnRep_XXX** function is called from the server on each client, and will not be executed on the server itself.

You are now going to add a text component to the character to display the points they have gained during the match:

1. Add a **TextRenderer** component to the character and name it `PointsLabel`.

2. Place the component anywhere you deem appropriate. I opted for these **Transform** values: **Location (-120, 0, -80)** and **Rotation (0, 90, 180)**.

3. Enhance the characteristics of the components according to your wishes. I opted for the settings shown in *Figure 3.17*:

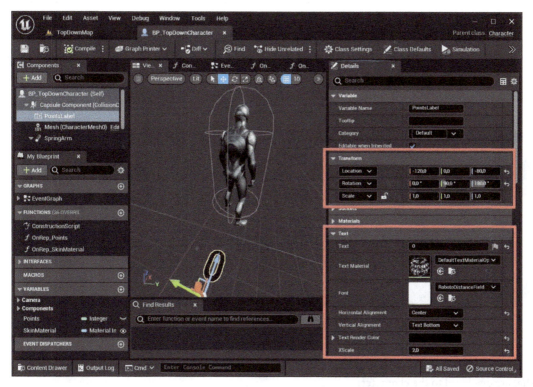

Figure 3.17 – The PointsLabel component

It's finally time to let pickups communicate with the character. We will do this by implementing the interface we defined some time ago:

1. With **BP_TopDownCharacter** open, select the **Class Settings** tab.

2. In the **Details** panel, click the **Add** drop-down button on the **Implemented Interfaces** field and select the **PointsAdded** interface.

3. A new function named **AddPoints** will be added to the **Interfaces** section of the **MyBlueprint** tab. Right-click on the function's name and select **Implement Event** – this will add the corresponding node to the Event Graph and select it.

4. Drag the **Points** variable into the Event Graph and select the **Set** option.

5. Drag the **Points** variable again, this time selecting the **Get** option.

6. Add the outgoing **Value** pin from the event to the **Get Points** node by using an **Add** (+) node.

7. Connect the execution pin of the **Event** node to the **Set** node.

8. Connect the result pin of the **Add** node to the **Points** pin of the set node.

> **Note**
>
> You will notice that both the **Set** and **Get** nodes you added to your graph now have an icon in the top-right corner. In addition, the **Set** node is decorated with text stating **w/Notify**: this means that the **Points** variable is replicated with a function notification.

Figure 3.18 shows the final graph for the **AddPoints** event:

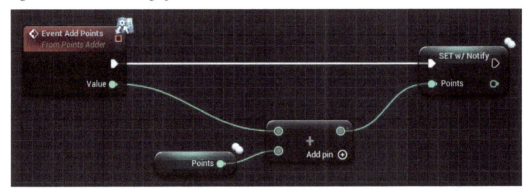

Figure 3.18 – The AddPoints event

The last thing we need to do is implement the notification function so that we can update the points that are displayed to the character:

1. Double-click on the **OnRep_Points** function to open it.

2. Drag a **Get** node from the **PointsLabel** component in the Event Graph.

3. From its outgoing pin, add a **Set Text** node, and connect its incoming execution pin to the outgoing execution pin of the **On Rep Points** node.

4. Drag a **Get** node from the **Points** variable in the Event Graph and connect its pin to the **Value** pin of the **Set Text** node. Unreal will automatically add a **To Text** conversion node.

The final graph should be pretty similar to the one depicted in *Figure 3.19*:

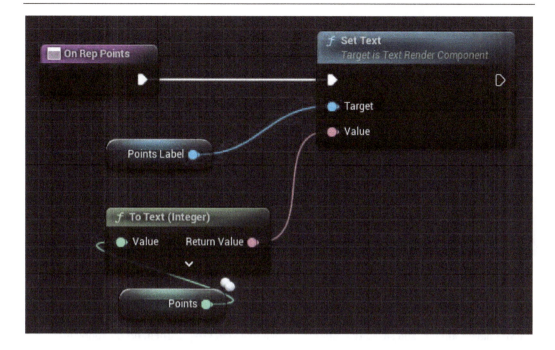

Figure 3.19 – The On Rep Points graph

Now, if you test the game, you should be able to see all the clients update whenever a player gets a pickup in the level.

With that, you've learned about how objects are updated during a multiplayer session. Specifically, you gained insight into how Actors are replicated and how to detect changes in variables through replication notifications. In the next section, you will work on enhancing your prototype by adding a spawn area for your pickups and making some aesthetic improvements to your characters so that they can easily be identified. You will achieve this by calling functions over the network.

Executing functions over the network

In this section, you will learn how to properly call functions over the network and what the word "authority" really means for the UE multiplayer system. In particular, you will get some insight into which entity should execute a function when it has been called: a client or the server.

Spawning Actors

It is time to start adding pickups at runtime. You are going to achieve this by adding a spawn area Blueprint to the level.

This Blueprint should be able to do the following:

- Choose a random position every time it spawns something
- Spawn random pickups at predefined intervals
- And obviously... behave correctly over the network!

Let's get started.

Choosing a random spawn position

Let's start by creating the Blueprint and setting its parameters:

1. Create a new Actor Blueprint and call it BP_Spawner.
2. Add a **Box Collision** component, name it SpawnArea, and make it the **Scene Root** component by dragging it onto the default one.
3. Add an **Array** variable of the **Actor (Class Reference)** type and name it SpawnableObjects, making it **Instance Editable**.

Once you have compiled and saved the Blueprint, open its Event Graph. Then, do the following:

1. Create a function named Spawn and open it.
2. Connect the execution node of the function to a **SpawnActor from Class** node.
3. Add a **Get** node for the **SpawnableObjects** variable and connect its outgoing pin to a **Random Array Item** node.
4. Connect the outgoing **Actor Class Reference** pin of **Random Node** to the **Class** pin of the **Spawn** node.

To get a position for the spawned item, we will get a random location inside the **Box Collision** component:

1. Right-click on the **Spawn Transform** pin of the **SpawnActor** node and select **Split Struct Pin**.
2. Drag the **SpawnArea** component into the function graph and connect its pin to a **Get Scaled Box Extent** node.
3. Add a **Get Actor Location** node and connect its outgoing pin to a **Random Point in Bounding Box** node.
4. Connect the outgoing pin of the **Get Scaled Box Extent** node to the **Half Size** pin of the **Random Point in Bounding Box** one.
5. Connect the **Return Value** pin of the **Random Point in Bounding Box** node to the **Spawn Transform Location** pin of the **SpawnActor** one.

The final graph can be seen in *Figure 3.20*:

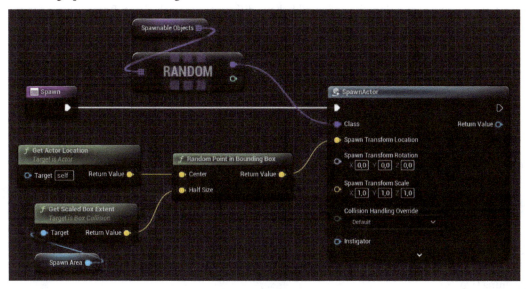

Figure 3.20 – The Spawn function graph

The **Spawn** function selects a random Blueprint Class from a given list of elements and generates an instance of it at a random position within a defined area.

Spawning random pickups at predefined intervals

You are now going to add a timer to spawn pickups at predefined intervals:

1. Open the Event Graph section of the Blueprint and delete the **Actor BeginOverlap** and **Tick** events.
2. Add a **Set Timer by Event** node and connect its incoming execution pin to the outgoing one of the **BeginPlay** event.
3. Set the **Time** value equal to **1** and check the box in **Looping**.
4. Connect the **Event** pin to a **Custom Event** node and call it OnTimer.
5. Connect the execution pin of the custom event to the **Spawn** function.

What you have just done may seem pretty straightforward and correct, but it is actually wrong... or, at least, it's missing something: the code will behave differently on each client. Bear with me for a minute while we test this wrong behavior:

1. Delete all the pickups you may have previously added to your game level.

2. Add an instance of **BP_Spawner** to the level.

3. Place the instance approximately at the center of the scene and change the **Box Extent** values of the **SpawnArea** component so that the box will cover the entire play area; if you are using the default scene, something such as **(1300, 1600, 32)** should be fine.

4. Place the **SpawnArea** component above the ground – pickups should be dropped from above and fall to the ground.

5. Add all the pickups you have created to the **Spawnable Objects** array.

6. Run the multiplayer simulation.

You will notice that things will seem totally out of sync between clients: in particular, the UE instance (that is, the server) will spawn a single pickup at each interval, while the additional client will be spawning two.

What did we do wrong? Put simply, at the moment, every spawner in every client is spawning items, but only the server (the one who has the authority) is spawning items across the network. This means that the server will get only one pickup at a time, but the clients will get two: one spawned by the server, and one created by themselves for which the server has no knowledge at all.

Using Actor authority to correctly spawn pickups

To fix the spawning issue, we just have to tell the spawner to generate pickups only if they have the authority to do so (that is, that it is the server):

1. Add a **Switch Has Authority** node in between the execution pin of the **BeginPlay** event and **Set Timer by Event**.

2. Connect the **Authority** execution pin to the incoming pin of the **Timer** node.

The corrected graph is shown in *Figure 3.21*:

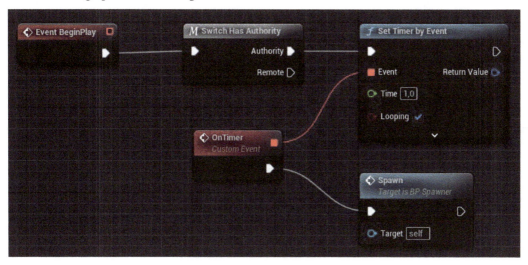

Figure 3.21 – The spawn timer graph

When you test the game now, it should behave correctly: the same object should be spawned at the same time in each client instance.

The prototype is almost finished, but I want you to create one last networked feature: a personalized skin for your characters.

Skinning characters

Playing the game with two or more identical characters may soon become very confusing. The best option for a prototype is to quickly create some colorized materials and assign them to the characters as soon as they are spawned. We will do this in a networked environment.

Let's start by creating some material instances:

1. In the Content Browser, navigate to **Content | Characters | Mannequins | Materials | Instances | Manny**.

2. Duplicate **MI_Manny_01** several times to equal the number of connections you set in the **Play as a Listen Server** section (that is, **3**).

3. Name the new materials with your own preferred conventions; I used MI_Manny_01_ [ColorName].

4. Open each new instance and change the **Tint** property to a color that you like.

5. Save all the material instances and close them.

Now, let's open the character Blueprint and add another replicated variable:

1. Open **BP_TopDownCharacter**.

2. Add a new variable called **SkinMaterial** of the **Material Interface Object Reference** type and make it **Instance Editable**.

3. Set the drop-down menu for the **Replication** field to **RepNotify**. This will create a function called **OnRep_SkinMaterial**.

Next, open the **OnRep_SkinMaterial** function to add the skin change logic. Then, do the following:

1. Drag a reference for **Mesh** from the **Components** panel in the Event Graph.

2. Drag a **Get** node for the **SkinMaterial** variable.

3. Connect the function execution pin to a **Set Material** node.

4. Connect the **Mesh** reference to the **Target** pin.

5. Connect the **SkinMaterial** reference to the **Material** pin.

The graph for this function is shown in *Figure 3.22*:

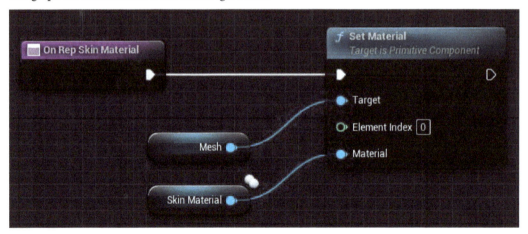

Figure 3.22 – The function for the replicated SkinMaterial variable

1. Whenever the **SkinMaterial** variable is changed, **OnRep_SkinMaterial** will take care of assigning it to the first material of the character.

Now, you need to change the material for each character once it has been added to the level:

1. In the `Blueprints` folder, open **BP_TopDownGameMode**.

2. Add an **Array** variable of the **Material Interface Object Reference** type; name it `SkinMaterials`.

3. Once you have compiled the Blueprint, add all the materials you previously created to the **Default Value** field in the **Details** panel.

4. Add a variable of the **Integer** type named `SkinCount`; this variable will be used as an index counter for selecting the skins.

You may have noticed that we are not replicating the **SkinCount** variable; in this case, we don't need to do this as this variable only exists in the server and it is used to handle the skin of the character as soon as they are spawned in the game. Knowing what variables to replicate and when is a topic I'll cover in *Chapter 6, Replicating Properties Over the Network*.

Next, you must get a count of the used skins. Then, every time a new connection is created, you will assign the next available skin to the character. To achieve this, you'll be using an event named *OnRestartPlayer* that is executed every time a player is restarted (including when it is spawned for the first time):

1. In the Event Graph, add an **Event OnRestartPlayer** node.

2. From **New Player**, connect a **Get Controlled Pawn** node.

3. Cast its outgoing pin to a **BP_TopDownCharacter** node.

4. Connect the event execution pin to the **Cast** node.

5. Connect the outgoing **As BP Top Down Character** to a **Set Skin Material** node (note the w/ **Notify** label that was added to indicate the notification call when the value is changed).

6. Connect the successful execution pin of the cast node to the **Set Skin Material** node.

7. Add a **Get** node for the **SkinMaterials** array and a **Get** node for the **SkinCount** variable.

8. Connect the outgoing **Skin Materials** pin to the **Get (a copy)** node.

9. Connect the **Skin Count** pin to the **Get** index.

10. Connect the outgoing pin of the **Get** node to the **Skin Material** pin of the **Set Skin Material** node.

11. Finally, connect the outgoing execution pin of **Set Skin Material** to an **Increment (++)** node. The **Skin Count x** variable should be incremented; this will keep track of the selected skin in the array.

Figure 3.23 depicts the Game Mode graph:

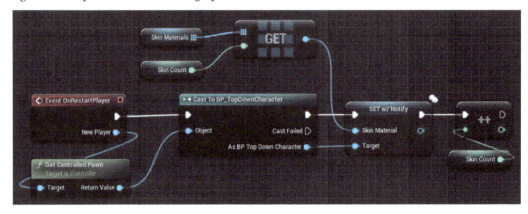

Figure 3.23 – The Game Mode graph

Now that the prototype has been created, it's time to test (and play) it!

Testing the game

Run the game as a listen server – each character should have its colorized skin synchronized across the network and the points gained for each player should be correctly displayed on the character itself. *Figure 3.24* shows the game prototype in action:

Figure 3.24 – Testing the game prototype

So, you've finally tested your multiplayer game prototype: players can run around and get the falling pickups, ready to gain points. As funny as it seems, this is just the beginning of multiplayer game development!

Summary

In this chapter, you created a prototype of your first multiplayer game and gained knowledge about synchronizing Actors and variables across the network. Moreover, you started testing the prototype through the UE system, which emulates multiple connections concurrently, and achieved all this through the use of Blueprints.

However, moving forward, you will transition to using the C++ programming language, which may seem a little daunting, but I assure you that I will strive to make this shift as effortless as possible!

It's time to leave your prototype to its destiny... we have more important things to do! In the next chapter, you'll start creating a game from scratch. You will develop it in C++ with all the advantages that come with this kind of development.

Part 2: Networking and Multiplayer Games in Unreal Engine

In the second part of this book, you will lay the foundation for a complete multiplayer project using Unreal Engine. From there, you will delve into the essential features of the Unreal Engine Gameplay Framework, as well as how they are implemented within a multiplayer context.

This part includes the following chapters:

- *Chapter 4, Setting Up Your First Multiplayer Environment*
- *Chapter 5, Managing Actors in a Multiplayer Environment*
- *Chapter 6, Replicating Properties Over the Network*
- *Chapter 7, Using Remote Procedure Calls (RPCs)*

4

Setting Up Your First Multiplayer Environment

Setting up a full networked game in UE5 can be an intimidating task. It requires knowledge of networking, coding, and the engine itself, all of which can be overwhelming for even experienced developers. But with the right guidance and some elbow grease, it is possible to create an engaging multiplayer experience in no time (well, sort of...)!

To prevent multiple issues with rethinking and modifications, the first step should be gaining a clear understanding of the project's topic. This avoids confusion from the onset and enables a smoother workflow. After that, you will need to create an Unreal project and get things set up properly. This includes creating your **Gameplay Framework (GF)** classes so that you have access to all the necessary features needed for development, as well as configuring your project settings to use such classes.

By the end of this chapter, you will have a solid understanding of programming in UE with C++ and will have laid the foundation for your multiplayer game.

Through the next sections, I will present you with the following topics:

- Introducing Unreal Shadows – Legacy of the Lichlord
- Understanding C++ in Unreal Engine
- Starting your Unreal multiplayer project
- Adding the player classes

Technical requirements

To follow along with this chapter, you should have set up Visual Studio (or JetBrains Rider) with all Unreal dependencies, as explained in *Chapter 1, Getting Started with Multiplayer Game Development*.

You'll be using some starter content available in this book's companion repository located at `https://github.com/PacktPublishing/Multiplayer-Game-Development-with-Unreal-Engine-5`.

Through this link, locate the section for this chapter and download the following `.zip` file: `Unreal Shadows - Starter Content`. If you somehow get lost during the progress of this chapter, in the repository, you will also find the up-to-date project files here: `Unreal Shadows - Chapter 04 End`.

Also, to fully understand this chapter, it is necessary to have some basic knowledge about C++ programming while I guide you through the key characteristics of the main peculiarities of the UE framework.

Introducing Unreal Shadows – Legacy of the Lichlord

Consider the following passage from a (never published) fantasy book called *Unreal Shadows – Legacy of the Lichlord*:

"The air was thick with the stench of decay as the three thieves made their way into the Lichlord's dungeon. Their mission was clear: infiltrate the fortress, find the king's knight, and bring him back alive. Anything they could find lying around was theirs to take home.

As they crept through the shadowy corridors, they all knew that they were not alone: dozens of undead minions lurked around every corner, their greenish eyes staring blankly.

The guild had faced their fair share of dangerous foes before, but never had they encountered such a formidable army of the undead. Quietly, they slipped past the corridors, careful not to attract any attention. The last thing they needed was to draw the entire horde down upon them."

Congratulations – you have just been hired to create the video game adaptation of this best-selling book! And what's more, it will be a multiplayer game!

Explaining the project brief

The game you'll be developing will be a **third-person shooter** that will use the **hide and seek** gameplay twist, as introduced in *Chapter 1, Getting Started with Multiplayer Game Development*. This means that this will be a stealth game where players will survive only by moving quietly and carefully.

In this multiplayer game, each participant will play the role of a member of the Guild of Thieves, a secret organization of rogues and thieves, infiltrating the realm of an undead wizard. The main aim will be to rescue non-player characters that are kept (hopefully alive!) in the dungeon prisons. Additionally, players will collect treasures and equipment from past and less lucky adventurers.

Each character will have the ability to do the following:

- Move around by walking or running

- Handle a weapon

- Get power-ups

- Equip new weapons

- Increase skills by means of experience points

The primary focus of this game will be on stealthy movement, as the undead army will prove too strong for the character to engage in direct combat. As a result, movement (especially running) and wielding weapons will create noise, making the previously unaware enemies instantly alert to the player's presence.

Enemies will be represented by the Lichlord minions, a horde of undead skeletons that will wander around the level unaware of the player characters.

Excessive noise from the characters or falling into traps will alert nearby enemies, making it nearly impossible to complete the game. Regrettably for the player characters, gaining experience points will only be made possible by defeating enemies, adding further engagement to the overall experience!

> **Note**
>
> As this book is about multiplayer game programming rather than game design, balancing game mechanics will not be a primary focus of gameplay; instead, the focus will be on making things function effectively.

Starting the project

We want the game to be visually appealing, but I'm guessing that most of you might not have a 3D modeling background (I don't have one!). That's why we will be using some amazing assets by Kay Lousberg (https://kaylousberg.com/) that are freely available for personal and commercial purposes.

Figure 4.1 shows one of the packs we will be using:

Figure 4.1 – The KayKit Dungeon Pack

You will start by creating a brand-new project starting from the **Blank** template available in UE5 and then you will add some assets from the aforementioned kits; however, to avoid the tedious task of importing them correctly, I have already packaged them for you.

The project files, along with the code for each chapter, can be found on this book's companion project page located here: `https://github.com/PacktPublishing/Multiplayer-Game-Development-with-Unreal-Engine-5`.

Having established what you will be working on, it is now time to gain an understanding of how C++ is used within UE5. The following section will provide a brief introduction to the primary features offered by the engine framework.

Understanding C++ in Unreal Engine

If you share my love for game development and programming, you'll likely find that writing C++ code in UE5 is quite fun and actually not too hard to get started with. Epic Games made a great job of adding features that make C++ easy to use for (almost) everyone.

Although it is possible to write standard C++ code in UE5, to achieve better performance with your games, it is advisable to use the engine's most common features such as the built-in Reflection System and memory management.

Blueprints and C++

As you may already know, UE provides two methods for programming your game logic: Blueprint Visual Scripting and C++.

Blueprints Visual Scripting makes it easier for developers who don't have extensive coding experience to create complex game mechanics without writing any code. On the other hand, **C++** is an **object-oriented programming** (**OOP**) language that requires more technical knowledge but offers much greater control over the game engine than Blueprints does.

It should be noted that C++ and Blueprints are strictly connected, as Blueprints provide a visual representation of the underlying C++ code and adhere to its principles, including inheritance and polymorphism. While Blueprints do not demand advanced coding skills, they do follow the same principles as the programming language in terms of data types, pointers, references, and other rules.

Both languages can be used together in UE5 projects and most of the time, what you can achieve with C++ can equally be done in Blueprints; however, C++ excels in customizing core features of UE or creating plugins that extend its functionality even further beyond what's available out of the box.

Although both Blueprint Visual Scripting and C++ offer powerful toolsets when working with UE projects, C++ provides lower-level access by way of object-oriented coding techniques – that's why it is very important to have a strong knowledge of it once you start developing multiplayer games.

Understanding C++ classes

An Unreal Engine C++ class is, well, a regular C++ class!

If you have already a good knowledge of OOP in C++, you will feel at home here: the process of creating a new UE C++ class begins by first defining what type of object it will represent, such as an Actor or a Component. Once the type has been defined, variables and methods are declared in the header file (.h) and code logic is implemented in the source file (.cpp).

While the source file behaves like a regular C++ file of its kind, the header file will let you declare additional information for variables and functions that will be used by Blueprints inheriting from your class. Additionally, it will ease the pain of managing memory at runtime (I will get back to this in a while).

With the release of UE5, Epic Games introduced an amazing inspection tool called **C++ Header Preview** that lets you inspect your Blueprint Classes as if they were written in C++. To activate it, simply select from the main menu **Tools | C++ Header Preview** and select your desired class. *Figure 4.2* shows the header file of the BP_BasePickup created during the last chapter.

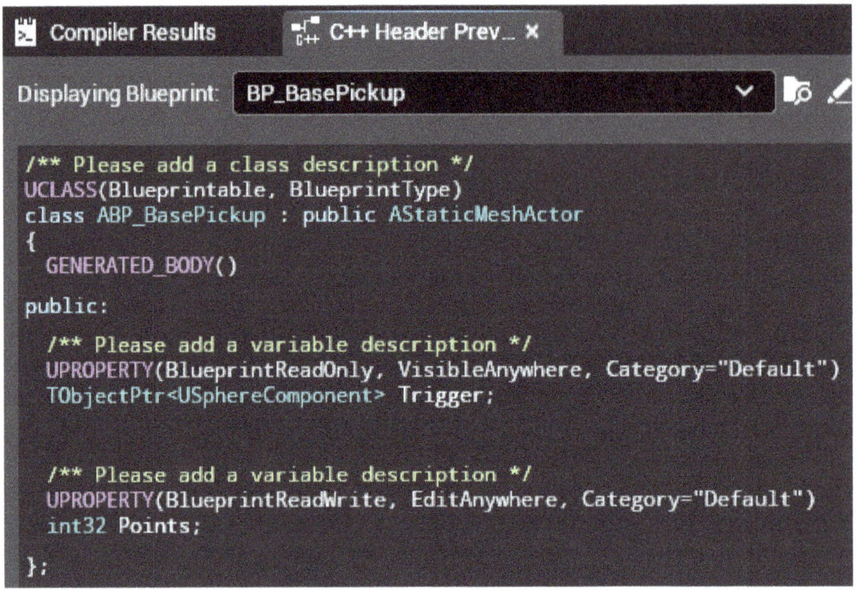

Figure 4.2 – The C++ Header Preview tool in action

In UE, there are three main class types that you'll be deriving from during development:

- A **UObject** is the base class of UE and provides most of the main features available in UE, such as **garbage collection** (**GC**) (yes, UE provides it!), networking support, reflection of properties and methods, and so on. An **AActor** is a UObject that can be added to a game level either from the Editor or at runtime: in this second case, we say that the Actor has been *spawned*. In a multiplayer environment, an AActor is the base type that can be replicated during networking and it will provide information for any Component that will need synchronization.

- A **UActorComponent** is the basic class for defining Components that will be attached to an Actor or to another Component belonging to the Actor itself.

Additionally, you'll be using these entities:

- A **UStruct** is used to create plain data structures and does not extend from any particular class

- A **UEnum** is used to represent enumerations of elements

As a final note, throughout this book, you will notice that class names start with some letters that will not be visible once the class is used in the Editor. UE makes use of prefixes to point out the class type. The main prefixes used are as follows:

- **U** is used for generic objects deriving from UObject (for instance, components)

- **A** is used for objects deriving from an Actor (i.e., AActor) and that can be added to a level

- **F** is used for generic classes and structures such as the `FColor` structure

- **T** is used for templates such as `TArray` or `TMap`

- **I** is used for interfaces

- **E** is used for enums

- **B** is used for `bool` or `uint8` (which may be used instead of `bool`)

> **Note**
>
> Please keep in mind that most of these prefixes are mandatory; if you try to name a class deriving from Actor without the A prefix, you will get an error. UE will hide the prefix once in the Editor. This rule applies only to C++ classes; Blueprints can be named without such prefixes.

Now that you are familiar with the main types available in UE, it's time to explore the main features of a class header in order to understand its core functionalities.

Anatomy of a UE C++ header

The C++ header of an Actor in UE5 will look like the following piece of code:

```
#include "Engine/StaticMEshActor.h"
#include "APickup.generated.h"

UCLASS(Blueprintable, BlueprintType)
class APickup : public AStaticMeshActor
{
  GENERATED_BODY()
public:
  APickup();

  UPROPERTY(BlueprintReadOnly, VisibleAnywhere, Category="Default")
  TObjectPtr<class USphereComponent> Trigger;

  UPROPERTY(BlueprintReadWrite, EditAnywhere, Category="Default")
  int32 Points;

  UFUNCTION(BlueprintCallable)
  void Reactivate();
};
```

As you can see, there are a lot of things going on here.

First of all, you will notice a `#include "APickup.generated.h"` declaration. This mandatory line of code is autogenerated by the **Unreal Header Tool** (**UHT**) and includes all the macros your code will need to properly work in the engine. This file needs to be the last `include` file declared in your header or the compiler will throw an error.

> **Note**
>
> The UHT is a custom parsing and code generation tool that supports the UObject system in Unreal Engine. The UHT is used to parse C++ headers for Unreal and generate the boilerplate code required for the engine to work with the user-created classes.

The class constructor (in this case, `APickup()`) is used to set default values for properties as you may do with a regular C++ class; what's more, you will be using it to create and add Components to the Actor itself.

Next, you will find some declarations, such as `UCLASS()`, `GENERATED_BODY()`, `UPROPERTY()`, and `UFUNCTION()`, that are used by UE and each has a precise function. If you are wondering about the meaning of the attributes called `BlueprintReadOnly`, `VisibleAnywhere`, and similar, don't be afraid! I'll be explaining their meaning in *Chapter 5*, *Managing Actors in a Multiplayer Environment*.

In the next subsection, I'll show you the exact meaning of each of them.

The Unreal Engine Reflection System

The term **Reflection** specifies the capability that allows a program to inspect its own structure at runtime. This feature is immensely valuable and serves as one of the core technologies employed by UE, supporting a variety of systems such as detail panels in the Editor, serialization, garbage collection, network replication, and communication between Blueprint and C++.

As there is no native support for Reflection in C++, Epic Games has developed its own system for gathering, examining, and altering data related to C++ classes, structs, and so on in UE.

In order to use Reflection, you will need to annotate any type or property that you want to make visible to the system by marking them with annotations such as `UCLASS()`, `UFUNCTION()`, or `UPROPERTIES()`.

To enable such annotations, you'll be using the `#include "APickup.generated.h"` declaration I introduced in the last subsection (this declaration is autogenerated when you create a class with the Unreal Class Wizard, so you won't have to worry about it).

The following list provides the fundamental markup elements accessible within the Reflection System:

- `UCLASS()`: Used to generate reflection data for a class that needs to derive from `UObject`
- `USTRUCT()`: Used to generate reflection data for a struct

- `GENERATED_BODY()`: This markup will be replaced with all the needed boilerplate code for the type

- `UPROPERTY()`: Used to tell the engine that the associated member variable will have some additional features, such as Blueprint accessibility or replication across the network (and this will mean a lot to you later on!)

- `UFUNCTION()`: Allows, among other things, to call this function from an extending Blueprint Class or override the function from the Blueprint itself

The Reflection System is also used by the garbage collector so you don't have to worry about memory management, as you will see in the next subsection.

Memory management and garbage collection

With thousands (sometimes tens of thousands!) of active objects in a game level, GC is an essential part of programming. It's like the janitor of your running code – it helps keep everything tidy and organized by automatically collecting and disposing of objects that are no longer needed. It's a great way to make sure your program runs smoothly without any memory leaks or performance issues, so you can focus on creating awesome features instead.

C++ does not natively implement GC, so UE implements its own system: you will just need to ensure that valid references to the objects are maintained. In order to enable GC for your classes, you need to assure that they inherit from `UObject`; then the system will keep a list of objects (also called **root**) that should not be garbage-collected. As long as an object is listed in the root, it will be preserved from deletion; once it is removed from this list, it will be deleted from memory the next time the garbage collector is called (i.e., at certain intervals).

> **Note**
> Actors are only destroyed at the level's shutdown unless you call the `Destroy()` method on them: in this case, they will be immediately removed from the game and deleted by the garbage collector when activated.

In this section, I have introduced you to the main features that distinguish an Unreal Engine project from a regular C++ one. In the next section, you will begin to apply this knowledge by creating an empty project and extending the main Unreal GF classes.

Starting your Unreal multiplayer project

In this section, you are finally going to start developing the multiplayer project (I know you are eager to begin it!). You'll be creating an Unreal C++ blank project and adding the already packaged assets I will provide you. Then, you'll be creating the GF classes needed to manage a multiplayer session. So, let's get started.

Creating your project file

Let's start by creating a blank project:

1. Open the Epic Games Launcher and launch the Unreal Editor.

2. From the **Games** section, select the **Blank** template.

3. In **Project Defaults**, select **C++** as the project type.

4. Make sure the **Starter Content** field is unselected as you won't be using it.

5. Give the project a meaningful name (for example, UnrealShadows_LOTL).

6. Click the **Create** button.

7. Once the UE project has been created, get the UnrealShadows-StarterContent.zip file you downloaded at the beginning of this chapter and unzip it in your computer.

8. Navigate to your project Content folder located at [Your Project Path] | UnrealShadows_LOTL | Content.

9. Copy the content of the unzipped file (_ExternalActors_, Blueprints, KayKit, and Maps folders) into the Content folder to add all the needed assets to your project.

Once you have copied the files, they should appear in the UE Editor and be available in your project. If the files do not pop up in the Content Browser, simply close the Editor and open it again to let UE update the Content folder.

You will notice that I have already added two levels (**Level_01** and **Level_Boss**) to the Maps folder: these levels will be used during the book and have been created for ease of development. You are free to create your own maps or add additional assets. which can be located at **Content | KayKit | Dungeon Elements**.

Just to check that everything went as expected, open the Level_01 map and you should see the level shown in *Figure 4.3*:

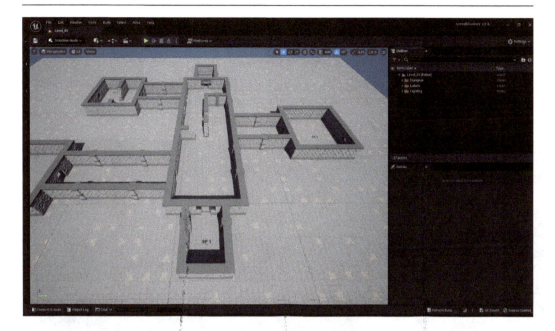

Figure 4.3 – The Level 01 map

It's time to add some of the main classes used in any UE5 project, the ones that extend the GF elements.

Creating the project game instance

As you probably already know, in UE5, a **GameInstance** is a class responsible for managing high-level data that needs to persist across level changes or game sessions. It is essentially a globally accessible UObject that can store any data you want to keep across the entire game, such as the player score, and other information that needs to be shared across different levels or game sessions.

A class extending a GameInstance can be created as a Blueprint Class or in C++ and is instantiated when the game is started and is only destroyed when the game is shut down.

> **Important note**
>
> As with most C++ Unreal Engine projects, you will be working with a mix of C++ classes and Blueprints. C++ classes are located in the **All | C++ classes | UnrealShadows_LOTL** folder and can only be added there (or in a subfolder). If you can't find this folder, you have probably created a Blueprint-only project. Don't despair, once the first C++ has been created (more on this in a minute), the Unreal Engine Editor will take care of it, transforming your Blueprint-only project into a C++ one and everything will be in place!

To create your project GameInstance, follow these steps:

1. On the main menu, select **Tools | New C++ Class…**.

2. The **Add C++ Class** wizard will open, showing the **CHOOSE PARENT CLASS** section. Select the **All Classes** tab and, in the search field, type game instance.

3. Select the **GameInstance** class, as shown in *Figure 4.4*:

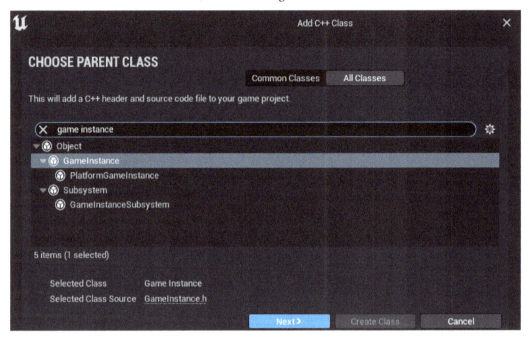

Figure 4.4 – The class creation wizard

4. Click **Next** to access the **NAME YOUR NEW GAME INSTANCE** panel.

5. In the **Name** field, insert US_GameInstance. You can leave the other fields as they are so that the panel looks like *Figure 4.5*:

Figure 4.5 – Naming your class

6. Click the **Create Class** button to generate your class files.

> **Note**
>
> I'll be using the US_ prefix for most of the classes in the project extending the main GF elements: this is just a shorthand for UnrealShadows and will let us see that these files are from our project.

Once the creation process has ended, you will get two new files: US_GameInstance.h and US_GameInstance.cpp. Congratulations – you have just created your first Unreal C++ class!

Opening the header file, you will see the following code:

```
// Fill out your copyright notice in the Description page of Project
Settings.

#pragma once

#include "CoreMinimal.h"
#include "Engine/GameInstance.h"
#include "US_GameInstance.generated.h"

/**
 *
 */
UCLASS()
class UNREALSHADOWS_LOTL_API UUSGameInstance : public UGameInstance
```

```
{
  GENERATED_BODY()

};
```

The source file will be empty, apart from the header `#include` declaration:

```
// Fill out your copyright notice in the Description page of Project
Settings.


#include "US_GameInstance.h"
```

As you can see, this class extends the base `GameInstance` class (i.e., `UGameInstance`) and it currently does nothing apart from the macro declarations that were introduced in the previous section. However, as the project progresses, new features such as data collection or online services management will be added to it.

> **Note**
>
> If you named your project with a name other than mine (i.e., `UnrealShadows_LOTL`), you will get a different API export name in your class declaration; as you can see from the previous code, mine is `UNREALSHADOWS_LOTL_API`. Please keep this in mind throughout the book, as my code will reference this name and you may get a compilation error. To fix this, you should change the `UNREALSHADOWS_LOTL_API` text with `YOUR_PROJECT_NAME` (in all caps), with the `_API` suffix.

This game instance needs to be added to the project settings so it will be the one instantiated at runtime. To do so, follow these steps:

1. From the main menu, open **Project Settings**. Then click on the **Project | Maps & Modes** section.

2. In the **Game Instance Class** drop-down menu, select **UG_GameInstance**, as depicted in *Figure 4.6*:

Figure 4.6 – The game instance assigned to the project

Now that we have a game instance assigned to the project, it's time to create a Game Mode for the menu and lobby levels.

Creating the Game Mode and the Game State

In UE, a **Game Mode** is a class that controls the game rules, such as how a player joins the game, how to transition between levels, and other game-specific settings. The Game Mode is typically paired with a **Game State** class, which manages the current state of the game, such as the score, time remaining, and other important information. Together, the Game Mode and Game State classes allow developers to create complex and customized game mechanics in UE.

If you check your `C++ Classes` folder, you will notice that there is already a Game Mode named `UnrealShadowsLOTLGameModeBase` (the name may differ slightly if you named your project differently from mine). This is an autogenerated class extending `AGameModeBase` from the GF.

You won't be using this because you need to create a class from `AGameMode`; this class extends `AGameModeBase` by adding some features that will enhance the multiplayer system, such as game rules and win/lose conditions. To extend the Game Mode with your own settings, follow these steps:

1. Create a new C++ class just like you did for the game instance in the previous sections.

2. From the **All Classes** section, select **GameMode** and click **Next**.

3. Name your class US_GameMode and click the **CreateClass** button.

4. Once the class has been created, it's time to set it as the default Game Mode for all your levels. To do this, open **Project Settings** and select the **Maps & Modes** section.

5. Then, click on the **Default GameMode** drop-down menu and select **US_GameMode**, as shown in *Figure 4.7*:

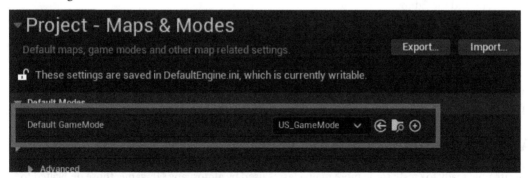

Figure 4.7 – The default game mode

6. Close the **Project Settings** window.

Now that the Game Mode has been defined, it's time to create a Game State:

1. Create another C++ class that will extend from GameState (from the **All Classes** section).

2. After clicking **Next**, name your class US_GameState and click the **CreateClass** button.

3. Now, declare **Game State** inside the **Game Mode**, so that they are interconnected and fully functional in the level. To do this, open the US_GameMode files by double-clicking on the corresponding icon in the C++ Classes folder of the Unreal Editor. This will open the header and source files inside your IDE.

4. Declare a constructor inside US_GameMode.h by adding these two lines of code:

    ```
    public:
        AUS_GameMode();
    ```

5. Implement the constructor inside US_GameMode.cpp by adding this piece of code:

    ```
    #include "US_GameState.h"

    AUS_GameMode::AUS_GameMode()
    {
        GameStateClass = AUS_GameState::StaticClass();
    }
    ```

    The previous code essentially declares the Game State class for US_GameMode to be the previously created US_GameState. Keep in mind that this declaration can be performed also in child Blueprints; this will enable class switching through a drop-down menu in the Editor. Ultimately, this is a matter of personal taste as you may be more code-oriented and prefer the code solution or you may want to take advantage of the impressive interplay between native code and the Editor.

In this section, you have created the main classes that will be used by the system to handle a multiplayer session. At the moment, these are just empty containers waiting for some game logic to be added; be patient, we still have so many chapters to fill this void!

In the next section, you'll be creating the classes needed to handle the character input and presence in the game.

Adding the player classes

You are now ready to create some more main classes used by almost any UE game: those dedicated to managing the input from the player and showing the character in-game, along with its state.

The **Player Controller** is responsible for managing input from the player's input devices (such as keyboard and mouse), and for sending commands to the player's character so it will perform the corresponding actions. The Player Controller class is typically used to control a **Pawn** class or a **Character** class that represents the player in a game.

Finally, the **Player State** is a class that holds information about a player's game state, such as experience points, score, and other relevant data. It exists on both the server and clients to ensure that all players have access to the same information.

Let's create these three classes:

1. Create a C++ class extending `PlayerController` and name it `US_PlayerController`.
2. Create another C++ class extending `Character` and name it `US_Character`.
3. Finally, create a C++ class extending `PlayerState` and call it `US_PlayerState`.

These three classes should be added to the Game Mode, the same way the Game State was added, but to get a bit more flexibility to our `Character` class, you'll be creating a Blueprint from it. To get a Blueprint out of a newly created C++ class, you need to compile the project.

You are now going to compile your source code for the first time to check that everything has been properly set.

Compiling your source code

Compiling in an Unreal Engine project refers to the process of converting human-readable code written in C++ and Blueprint into executable code that the computer can understand and run – this is an essential step in the development process. UE provides tools to streamline the compiling process and improve the development experience.

In Unreal Engine, you can leverage **Live Coding**, a feature that enables your application's C++ code to be rebuilt and its binaries patched while the UE engine is running.

With Live Coding, you can modify C++ classes, compile them, and observe the changes taking effect while the Editor is running – all without interrupting the play-testing sessions or work in progress. This feature boasts enormous advantages for iterative development, especially when using C++ runtime logic such as gameplay code or frontend user interactions.

Live coding is enabled by default, and you can initiate a Live Coding build by pressing *Ctrl +Alt + F11* on your keyboard when utilizing your IDE or Unreal Engine.

Alternatively, to start the compilation process with Live Coding disabled, you can click the **Compile** button at the bottom right of the Unreal Engine Editor, as depicted in *Figure 4.8*:

Figure 4.8 – The Compile button

Once the source code has been compiled, you should get a success message. Otherwise, you will get the usual errors or warnings from a failed compilation; in this case, it is essential to ensure that your code is written correctly and free from errors.

Once your project has been successfully compiled, it's time to create a Blueprint out of your `Character` class.

Creating the Character Blueprint Class

As you'll be working on some customization for your character later on, it's essential to have the extra flexibility provided by a Blueprint Class.

As you have successfully compiled your code, you may expect that the classes you created will now be ready to be available in the Blueprint creation wizard. This is a correct assumption and you are going to test it right now. Let's do so:

1. Navigate to the `Content | Blueprints` folder.
2. Create a Blueprint Class that will inherit from `US_Character` and name it `BP_Character`.
3. Save and close the Blueprint: you are not going to do anything yet on it.

This new Blueprint should be added to the Game Mode as the default Pawn to be used during a game session. Unfortunately, a Blueprint Class cannot be directly referenced in a C++ class. This means you'll have to find it through a method called `FClassFinder` available in the `ConstructorHelpers` utility class.

Adding the Player classes to the Game Mode

You are now going to declare the newly created classes to the Game Mode. Let's open again the `US_GameMode.cpp` file and add some code logic. In the `declarations` section, add the following block of code:

```
#include "US_PlayerController.h"
#include "US_PlayerState.h"
#include "US_Character.h"
#include "UObject/ConstructorHelpers.h"
```

This will declare all the GF classes you will be declaring, and the `ConstructorHelpers` utility class.

Then, before the closing bracket of the constructor, add the following block of code:

```
PlayerStateClass = AUS_PlayerState::StaticClass();
PlayerControllerClass = AUS_PlayerController::StaticClass();

static ConstructorHelpers::FClassFinder<APawn>
PlayerPawnBPClass(TEXT("/Game/Blueprints/BP_Character"));
if (PlayerPawnBPClass.Class != nullptr)
{
    DefaultPawnClass = PlayerPawnBPClass.Class;
}
```

As you can see, the first two lines of code declare `PlayerStateClass` and `PlayerControllerClass` in a similar way as you did in the previous section for `GameStateClass`.

Meanwhile, retrieving a Blueprint reference (i.e., `PlayerPawnBPClass`) from a C++ class works differently from how it works for a regular C++ class: you need to hardcode a path to your project. This may be not an ideal solution because files can be moved around or deleted but, well... it works!

Just keep in mind that my file path (i.e., `"/Game/Blueprints/BP_Character"`) may be slightly different from yours, depending on your folder organization.

Now that the Game Mode class has been modified, click the **Compile** button in the Unreal Editor.

Once you get a successful result, it's time to look at the Game Mode instance to check that everything is correct. To do this, follow these steps:

1. Open the **Project Settings | Maps & Modes** section.
2. Locate the **Selected GameMode** field and expand it by clicking the small arrow next to it.
3. Check that the GF classes we have created are all correctly allocated, as shown in *Figure 4.9*:

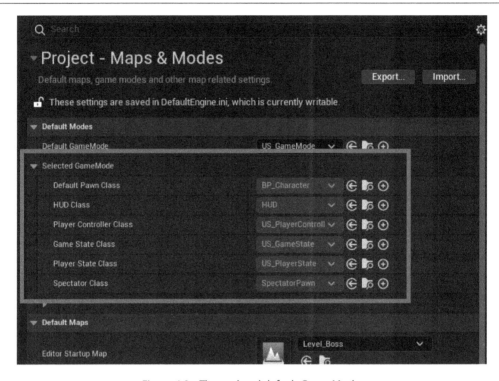

Figure 4.9 – The updated default Game Mode

In this last section, you have completed the Game Mode setup by adding all the GF classes you'll be expanding in the next chapters.

Summary

In this chapter, you were briefed about the project you'll be developing through the rest of the book: a multiplayer stealth game involving thieves, secret treasures, and a ton of undead minions. The road is still long, but the Lichlord must be stopped!

After that, you were introduced to the main topics of the Unreal Engine C++ "dialect." There are a lot of additional features involved and many more will be discovered throughout the rest of the book. One of the most exciting things is that, if things are set up properly, you won't have to worry about memory management: Unreal Engine flawlessly handles it. What's more, by adding decorations to your classes, variables, and functions, you can expose them to the Blueprint system, letting your project be more flexible and accessible to non-code-oriented developers.

Lastly, you created the main classes that will be used by your game and that extend those offered by the GF. Starting from the persistent GameInstance, you went to the Game Mode, and then to all the player-oriented elements. You now have a solid base to start developing your multiplayer project.

In the next chapter, I will guide you through the creation of the player character by presenting how to manage it in a multiplayer environment.

5

Managing Actors in a Multiplayer Environment

To properly set up a multiplayer environment in UE5, it's important that you understand how an Actor's connection is managed, as well as how its attributes are relevant during a game session.

In this chapter, you will begin enhancing the player character (which currently is just an empty shell) to gain a comprehensive understanding of the previously mentioned concepts. To do this, you'll add more components to the Character class (a camera is something you will absolutely need!) and implement the player input logic.

Additionally, you will learn why it is important to know who owns an Actor in a multiplayer environment and how it behaves depending on how it is relevant in the level.

By the end of the chapter, you will have solid knowledge of how to manage an Actor within an Unreal multiplayer game, allowing you to create more robust and efficient multiplayer experiences.

So, in this chapter, I will present you with the following topics:

- Setting up the character
- Controlling the connection of an Actor
- Understanding Actor relevancy
- Introducing authority

Technical requirements

To follow the topics presented in this chapter, you should have completed the previous chapter and understood its content.

Additionally, if you would prefer to begin with the code from the companion repository for this book, you can download the `.zip` project files at `https://github.com/PacktPublishing/Multiplayer-Game-Development-with-Unreal-Engine-5`.

You can download the files that are up to date with the end of the last chapter by clicking the `Unreal Shadows - Chapter 04 End` link.

Setting up the character

Before I start writing about topics such as connections, authority, and roles, I need you to properly set up the player character – at the moment, our poor hero is just represented by an empty class!

So, in this section, you will add a camera and some user input and set up the main functionalities that will allow the thief character to move around the level in search of treasures and gold!

Adding basic settings to the character

In the next few steps, you'll add the components that will make up the third-person camera behavior and implement their logic. After that, you'll set some default values for the components that are already available in the Character class: the Arrow, Capsule, and SkeletalMesh components.

Adding a Camera component to the character

To get started, open the `US_Character.h` header class. You will be adding a Camera component and a Spring component that will connect the camera to the Capsule component available in the Character class. To do this, add these two component declarations after the `GENERATED_BODY()` macro:

```
UPROPERTY(VisibleAnywhere, BlueprintReadOnly, Category = Camera, meta
= (AllowPrivateAccess = "true"))
TObjectPtr<class USpringArmComponent> CameraBoom;

UPROPERTY(VisibleAnywhere, BlueprintReadOnly, Category = Camera, meta
= (AllowPrivateAccess = "true"))
TObjectPtr<class UCameraComponent> FollowCamera;
```

In the previous code block, we are declaring a Camera component and a Spring component that will create the camera system. First, you will notice the `UPROPERTY()` declaration on both variables with some property specifiers. Let me explain them:

- The `VisibleAnywhere` property indicates that this property is visible in all related windows of the Unreal Engine Editor but cannot be edited

- The `BlueprintReadOnly` property indicates that this property can be read by Blueprints but not modified

- The `Category` property specifies the category of the property when displayed in the **Blueprint Details** panel

You will also notice a meta declaration that lets you control how the property interacts with various aspects of Unreal Engine and the Editor: in this case, AllowPrivateAccess indicates that a private member should be accessible from a Blueprint. We need this as these properties' accessibility is not explicitly declared, and so they default to private.

> **Note**
>
> For an exhaustive list of property specifiers, please check the official Epic Games documentation, which can be found here: https://docs.unrealengine.com/5.1/en-US/unreal-engine-uproperty-specifiers/.

Next, look at the class keyword before the type – this is a C++ **class forward declaration**. If you are unfamiliar with this, it is a way to declare the class name and its members without providing the full class definition. This can be useful in situations where you want to use a class in a header file but do not want to include the entire class definition, which can make compilation slower and create unnecessary dependencies.

Lastly, you will notice the TObjectPtr<T> template – this is a new addition in UE5 and has been introduced to replace raw pointers (for example, USpringComponent*) in header files with UProperties. The TObjectPtr<T> template is intended only for member properties declared in the headers of your code. For functions and short-lived scope within your C++ code in .cpp files, using TObjectPtr<T> provides no additional advantages over using raw pointers.

As the Camera and Spring components are private, you need to add two getter methods for them. Inside the public declaration of the header, locate this line of code:

```
virtual void SetupPlayerInputComponent(UInputComponent*
PlayerInputComponent) override;
```

Then, below this line, add the following:

```
FORCEINLINE USpringArmComponent* GetCameraBoom() const { return
CameraBoom; }
FORCEINLINE UCameraComponent* GetFollowCamera() const { return
FollowCamera; }
```

These two methods will let you access the pointer components, and the FORCEINLINE macro forces the code to be inlined; this is going to give your code some performance benefits as you will avoid a function call when using this method.

Implementing the camera behavior

Now that your properties have been added, it's time to add some code logic to handle them. Open the .cpp file and add the following includes at its top:

```
#include "Camera/CameraComponent.h"
#include "Components/CapsuleComponent.h"
#include "GameFramework/CharacterMovementComponent.h"
#include "GameFramework/SpringArmComponent.h"
```

Then, inside the constructor (i.e., AUS_Character::AUS_Character()), add this code:

```
CameraBoom =
CreateDefaultSubobject<USpringArmComponent>(TEXT("CameraBoom"));
CameraBoom->SetupAttachment(RootComponent);
CameraBoom->TargetArmLength = 800.0f;
CameraBoom->bUsePawnControlRotation = true;
```

Here, CreateDefaultSubobject()<T> is a function that is used to create a new subobject of a class that will be owned by another object. A **Subobject** is essentially a component or a member variable of an object, and the method is typically called within an object's constructor to initialize its subobjects (in this case, the components).

The SetupAttachment() method will reparent a component to another one. In this case, you are attaching the Camera component to RootComponent, which is actually the Capsule component.

Let's give the camera a similar treatment. Add this code block just after the previous lines of code:

```
FollowCamera =
CreateDefaultSubobject<UCameraComponent>(TEXT("FollowCamera"));
FollowCamera->SetupAttachment(CameraBoom,
USpringArmComponent::SocketName);
FollowCamera->bUsePawnControlRotation = false;
```

The only real difference here is that you are reparenting the camera to the Spring component instead of the root one.

You have just created some sort of "chain of command" where the camera is connected to the Spring component that is connected to the root of the Actor – this will let the camera follow the character with a "springy" behavior whenever the camera hits an obstacle and provide a better feel for the player.

Setting up the default component properties

As a last step, you'll be modifying some properties to create a default setup for your Character class. In the constructor, add these lines of code:

```
bUseControllerRotationPitch = false;
bUseControllerRotationYaw = false;
bUseControllerRotationRoll = false;

GetCapsuleComponent()->InitCapsuleSize(60.f, 96.0f);

GetMesh()->SetRelativeLocation(FVector(0.f, 0.f, -91.f));
static ConstructorHelpers::FObjectFinder<USkeletalMesh>
SkeletalMeshAsset(TEXT("/Game/KayKit/Characters/rogue"));
if (SkeletalMeshAsset.Succeeded())
{
    GetMesh()->SetSkeletalMesh(SkeletalMeshAsset.Object);
}

GetCharacterMovement()->bOrientRotationToMovement = true;
GetCharacterMovement()->RotationRate = FRotator(0.0f, 500.0f, 0.0f);
GetCharacterMovement()->MaxWalkSpeed = 500.f;
GetCharacterMovement()->MinAnalogWalkSpeed = 20.f;
GetCharacterMovement()->BrakingDecelerationWalking = 2000.f;
```

Here, you are just changing some of the default values of the character Actor and its components. The only thing to note is that you are getting the character model and assigning it to SkeletalMeshComponent by means of the FObjectFinder() utility method available in the ConstructorHelpers class you've used before.

Updating the Character Blueprint

Now it's time to compile your project, just to check that you don't have any syntax errors and that the character has been properly set up. To do this, save your files, go back to the Unreal Editor, and click the **Compile** button.

Once the compilation phase has finished, open the **BP_Character** Blueprint, and you should notice that your changes didn't show up. This happens because the Blueprint has not been updated. To fix this, select **File | Refresh All nodes**. You should now see the **Camera Boom** and **Follow Camera** elements added to the hierarchy in the **Components** panel, as depicted in *Figure 5.1*:

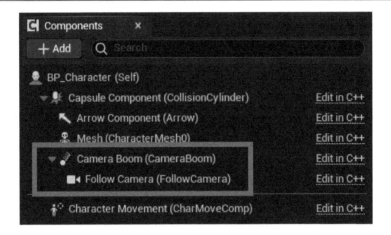

Figure 5.1 – The newly added character components

You probably still won't see the updated mesh in the SkeletalMesh component. To fix this, take the following steps:

1. Select the **Mesh** elements in the **Components** panel and look for the **Skeletal Mesh Asset** field in the **Details** panel.

2. If **Skeletal Mesh Asset** shows a value of **None**, click on the **Reset Property** arrow next to it, as shown in *Figure 5.2*:

Figure 5.2 – The Reset Property button

3. Double-check the **Use Controller Rotation Yaw Y** property, as it may also need a reset.

Now you should be able to see the viewport updated with the selected mesh added to it, as shown in *Figure 5.3*:

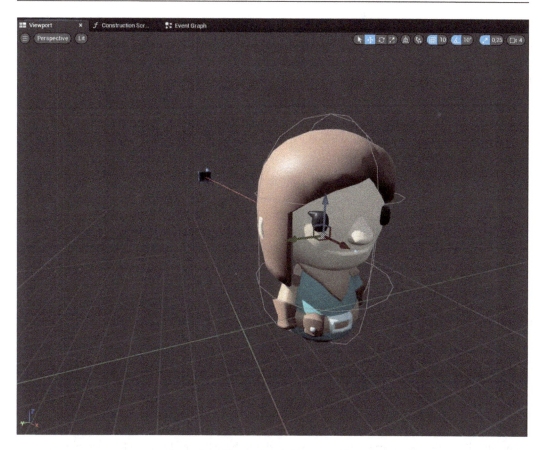

Figure 5.3 – The updated character Blueprint

With your character set up, it's time to make it move by adding some user interaction.

Adding interaction to the character

Now we will add input settings for the character. To do this, we will be using the new **Enhanced Input System** that has been introduced in UE5. This new system provides developers with more advanced features than the previous one (known simply as the Input System), such as complex input handling and runtime control remapping. As the old system is being deprecated, it will probably be removed from Unreal Engine sooner or later, so it is best to stay updated on the changes.

The most important thing to know about the Enhanced Input System is how it communicates with your code: this is achieved through **Input Actions** that represent what the character can do during play (i.e., walk, jump, or attack). A group of Input Actions can be collected inside an **Input Mapping Context** that represents a set of rules for what will trigger the included actions.

At runtime, UE5 will check a list of **Input Triggers** to determine how user input activated an Input Action, validating patterns such as long presses, release events, or double-clicks. Before triggering inputs, the system can pre-process the raw input through a list of **Input Modifiers** that will alter the data, such as setting a custom dead zone for the thumbstick or getting a negative value from the input itself.

In this section, you'll create some basic interaction for your character, which needs to move, sprint, and interact with objects (we'll leave the attack actions to later chapters). The sprint and interact actions will be activated by pressing a button, while the move action will be controlled by a keyboard/mouse combo or by the controller thumbsticks.

> **Note**
>
> If you want to explore the full range of possibilities offered by the Enhanced Input System, you can check the official documentation by visiting this web page: `https://docs.unrealengine.com/5.1/en-US/enhanced-input-in-unreal-engine/`.

Creating Input Actions

To start creating Input Actions, take the following steps:

1. Open your **Content Browser** and add a folder named `Input`.

2. Inside the folder, right-click and select **Input | Input Action** to create an Input Action asset.

3. Name it `IA_Interact`.

4. Create three other Input Actions and name them `IA_Look`, `IA_Move`, and `IA_Sprint`.

Let's begin editing the **IA_Interact** action – we need it to be activated by a single press of a button (or key), and this action should be dispatched the moment the button has been pressed. To do so, double-click on the asset to open it and do the following:

1. Click on the + button next to the **Triggers** field to add a trigger.

2. Click the dropdown that should have been created and select **Pressed** – this option will avoid dispatching multiple events if the player holds the button.

3. Leave the rest as it is – just check that **Value Type** has been set to the default value of **Digital (bool)**.

The final result of the interact action asset is shown in *Figure 5.4*:

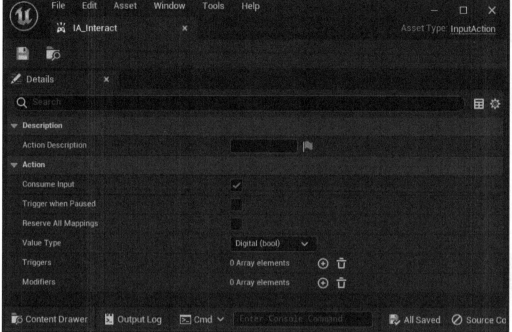

Figure 5.4 – The interact action settings

The **IA_Sprint** action is pretty similar to the interact one but needs to trigger a press event when the character starts sprinting and trigger a release event when the character stops sprinting.

Double-click on the **IA_Sprint** asset to open it and change the settings as described here:

1. Add two triggers by clicking the + button next to the **Triggers** field twice.
2. Click the first dropdown that should have been created and select **Pressed**.
3. Click the second dropdown and select **Released**.
4. Leave the rest as it is, checking that **Value Type** has been set to the default value of **Digital (bool)**.

The final result of the sprint action asset is shown in *Figure 5.5*:

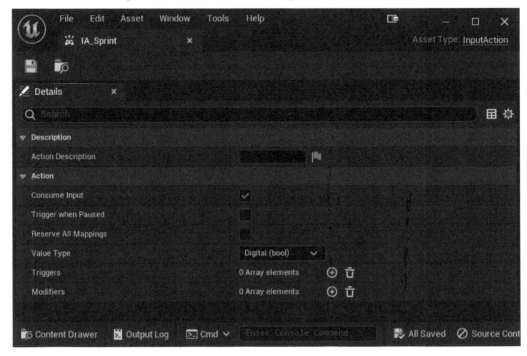

Figure 5.5 – The sprint action settings

It's time to set up the **IA_Move** asset, so open it and simply change **Value Type** to **Axis2D (Vector2D)** as shown in *Figure 5.6*:

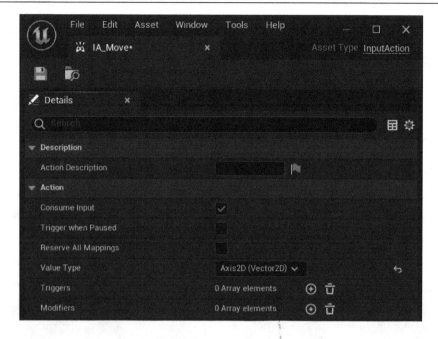

Figure 5.6 – The move action settings

As a last step, open the **AI_Look** asset and change **Value Type** to **Axis2D (Vector2D)**, as shown in *Figure 5.7*:

Figure 5.7 – The look action settings

Now that the basic actions have been defined, it's time to create the Mapping Context and set its properties.

Setting up the Input Mapping Context

As explained already, a Mapping Context refers to a set of Input Actions that identifies a specific situation in which the player may find themselves. The "context" you need to create here is the base actions a character can do (move, look around, and interact), so it's time to open the **Content Browser** and create this asset:

1. Right-click on the `Input` folder and select **Input | Input Mapping Context**.

2. Name the newly created asset `IMC_Default` and double-click on it to start editing.

3. Click the + button next to the **Mappings** field. In the drop-down menu, select **IA_Interact**.

4. Repeat this step three more times to add **IA_Sprint**, **IA_Move**, and **IA_Look**.

By the end of these steps, you should have something similar to *Figure 5.8*:

Figure 5.8 – The Input Mapping Context panel

Now that the context has been created, it's time to map the input the player will be using. As I have stated before, we'll let them use a controller or a mix of keyboard and mouse interaction. At the moment, all mappings should be set to **None**; this means that no input will pass through this context.

Let's solve this by starting with the **IA_Interact** mapping:

1. Click on the keyboard icon below **IA_Interact** and press the *I* (for Interact) key on your keyboard.

2. Then click on the + button to the right of the **IA_Interact** field to add another mapping.

3. From the drop-down menu, select **Gamepad | Gamepad Face Button Bottom**. Alternatively, if you have a game controller connected to your PC, you can simply click on the keyboard icon and then press the corresponding button (for instance, the *A* button for an Xbox controller).

   Now we are going to set the mapping for **IA_Sprint**:

4. Set **Left Shift** for if the player is using the keyboard.

5. Set **Gamepad | Gamepad Left Thumbstick Button** for if the player is using the controller (this second option will allow the player to press the thumbstick to sprint).

Next, **IA_Move** will let the player use the left thumbstick controller or the usual WASD keys – this means you will add five interactions: one for the thumbstick and then four for the up, down, left, and right directions. Let's add them to the Mapping Context, starting with the thumbstick settings:

1. Add **Gamepad | Gamepad Left Thumbstick 2D-Axis** to the mappings. Additionally, add a modifier from the **Modifiers** list with the value **Dead Zone**.

2. Moving on to the directions, for the right direction (mapped on your keyboard as *D*), add a **Keyboard | D** mapping with no modifiers.

3. For the left direction (mapped on your keyboard as *A*), add a **Keyboard | A** mapping. Then add a modifier with the value **Negate**. This will grant negative values from this interaction (i.e., movements to the right are positive, while movements to the left are negative).

4. For the forward direction (mapped on your keyboard as *W*), add a **Keyboard | W** mapping. Then, add a modifier with the value **Swizzle Input Axis Values**, which will convert *x* values into *y* (and vice versa), so you'll get a "forward" value for your character.

5. Lastly, for the backward direction (mapped on your keyboard as *S*), add a **Keyboard | S** mapping. Then, add a modifier with the value **Swizzle Input Axis Values** and an additional one with the value **Negate**. This will grant negative values from this interaction in a similar way to the left movement explained for the *A* key.

Finally, the **IA_Look** mapping is going to be controlled by the right thumbstick of the controller or by the movement of the mouse. To add such settings, take these steps:

1. From the drop-down menu, select **Gamepad | Gamepad Right Thumbstick 2D-Axis** for the controller. Additionally, add a modifier from the **Modifiers** list with a value of **Dead Zone**, so the thumbstick won't send data when in the rest position.

2. Select a **Mouse | Mouse XY 2D-Axis** interaction for the mouse. Then add a modifier from the **Modifiers** list with the value **Negate** and uncheck the **X** and **Z** checkboxes, leaving just the **Y** value selected. This will grant negative values for the mouse interaction – for instance, moving it forward will let the character move the camera down, and moving it backward will move the camera up.

You should now have a Mapping Context similar to the one shown in *Figure 5.9*:

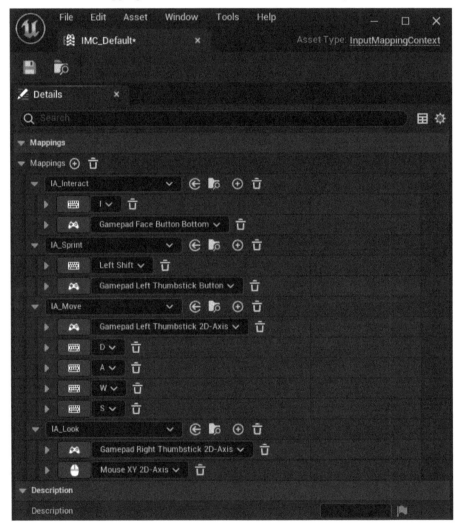

Figure 5.9 – The complete Mapping Context

Now that the Mapping Context has been defined, it's time to set up the character so that it can receive input from the player.

Importing the Enhanced Input Module

Let's get back to the IDE, as you are now ready to add some components and code logic to your character. As we are using the Enhanced Input System, the first thing you will need to do is to add it to the module declaration in the `Build.cs` file.

To do so, open `UnrealShadows_LOTL.Build.cs` in the `Source` folder of your C++ project (the name may vary slightly if your project was named in a different way). Then locate the following line of code:

```
PublicDependencyModuleNames.AddRange(new string[] { "Core",
"CoreUObject", "Engine", "InputCore" });
```

Change it by adding the Enhanced Input module:

```
PublicDependencyModuleNames.AddRange(new string[] { "Core",
"CoreUObject", "Engine", "InputCore", "EnhancedInput" });
```

This will make the Enhanced Input module available to your project, and you'll be ready to start implementing the user interaction, something that you'll do right now.

Adding user interaction to the character

To add user interaction to the character, you will need to declare the Enhanced Input assets you created just a few moments ago.

In the next steps, you will declare the Mapping Context and action references to your code, along with the corresponding methods. After that, you'll implement the code logic needed to handle all actions. Finally, you'll declare these actions inside the character Blueprint.

Declaring input properties and functions

The first thing to do is to add the needed asset references for the Mapping Context and the actions that should be added to the `US_Character.h` header file. Open the header file, which should already include the following lines of code (if not, add it as a public declaration):

```
virtual void SetupPlayerInputComponent(UInputComponent*
PlayerInputComponent) override;
```

Next, declare a pointer to the Input Mapping Context and a pointer for each Input Action. To do this, add the following code in the class implicit `private` section (i.e., just after the GENERATED_BODY() macro), just after the components declarations:

```
UPROPERTY(EditAnywhere, BlueprintReadOnly, Category = "Input", meta =
(AllowPrivateAccess = "true"))
TObjectPtr<class UInputMappingContext> DefaultMappingContext;
```

```
UPROPERTY(EditAnywhere, BlueprintReadOnly, Category = "Input", meta =
(AllowPrivateAccess = "true"))
TObjectPtr<class UInputAction> MoveAction;
UPROPERTY(EditAnywhere, BlueprintReadOnly, Category = "Input", meta =
(AllowPrivateAccess = "true"))
TObjectPtr<UInputAction> LookAction;
UPROPERTY(EditAnywhere, BlueprintReadOnly, Category = "Input", meta =
(AllowPrivateAccess = "true"))
TObjectPtr<UInputAction> SprintAction;
UPROPERTY(EditAnywhere, BlueprintReadOnly, Category = "Input", meta =
(AllowPrivateAccess = "true"))
TObjectPtr<UInputAction> InteractAction;
```

As a last step for the header declarations, add the following methods in the `protected` section, just after the `BeginPlay()` method declaration:

```
void Move(const struct FInputActionValue& Value);
void Look(const FInputActionValue& Value);
void SprintStart(const FInputActionValue& Value);
void SprintEnd(const FInputActionValue& Value);
void Interact(const FInputActionValue& Value);
```

As you can see, you added a method for each of the interactions you defined before. Just remember that in the **IA_Sprint** asset, you declared a **Pressed** and a **Released** trigger, so you will need to handle them with two corresponding methods (i.e., `SprintStart()` and `SprintEnd()`).

Implementing the Mapping Context for the character

In the next steps, you'll implement the Mapping Context by initializing it and binding each input action to the corresponding methods.

Open `US_Character.ccp` and add the following block of code, which includes all the classes you'll be using in the next steps:

```
#include "Components/InputComponent.h"

#include "GameFramework/Controller.h"

#include "EnhancedInputComponent.h"
#include "EnhancedInputSubsystems.h"
```

Then, look for the `BeginPlay()` method and, after the `Super` declaration, add this block of code:

```
if (APlayerController* PlayerController =
Cast<APlayerController>(Controller))
{
```

```
    if (UEnhancedInputLocalPlayerSubsystem* Subsystem = ULocalPlayer
::GetSubsystem<UEnhancedInputLocalPlayerSubsystem>(PlayerController-
>GetLocalPlayer()))
    {
        Subsystem->AddMappingContext(DefaultMappingContext, 0);
    }
}
```

The first line of code checks that the Controller is a `PlayerController` by means of a `Cast<T>` template.

> **Note**
>
> When working in Unreal Engine, it is common to perform casts to specific classes frequently (as you already did in the previous chapters with Blueprints). You may already be used to casts in pure C++, but you should be aware that Unreal has slightly different behavior, as it is possible to safely cast to types that may not be valid. If you are used to regular C++ crashes in such cases, you'll be happy to know that Unreal will simply return a safer `nullptr`.

Then, the code will try to get an Enhanced Input Subsystem from the player and, if successful, will add a Mapping Context to it. From this point on, all the actions declared inside the context will be "tracked" by the input system.

Of course, you will need to bind these actions to a corresponding method implementation (i.e., move, sprint, interact, etc.). To do this, look for the `SetupPlayerInputComponent()` method and, after the `Super()` declaration, add this block of code:

```
if (UEnhancedInputComponent* EnhancedInputComponent =
Cast<UEnhancedInputComponent>(PlayerInputComponent))
{
    EnhancedInputComponent->BindAction(MoveAction,
ETriggerEvent::Triggered, this, &AUS_Character::Move);
    EnhancedInputComponent->BindAction(LookAction,
ETriggerEvent::Triggered, this, &AUS_Character::Look);
    EnhancedInputComponent->BindAction(InteractAction,
ETriggerEvent::Started, this, &AUS_Character::Interact);
    EnhancedInputComponent->BindAction(SprintAction,
ETriggerEvent::Started, this, &AUS_Character::SprintStart);
    EnhancedInputComponent->BindAction(SprintAction,
ETriggerEvent::Completed, this, &AUS_Character::SprintEnd);
}
```

As you can see, we are calling the `BindAction()` method on the input component pointer to bind each action to the corresponding method.

Implementing the actions

Now you are ready to implement the methods for each action. Let's start with the Move method. Add the following block of code:

```
void AUS_Character::Move(const FInputActionValue& Value)
{
    const auto MovementVector = Value.Get<FVector2D>();
    GEngine->AddOnScreenDebugMessage(0, 5.f, FColor::Yellow,
FString::Printf(TEXT("MovementVector: %s"), *MovementVector.
ToString()));

    if (Controller != nullptr)
    {
        const auto Rotation = Controller->GetControlRotation();
        const FRotator YawRotation(0, Rotation.Yaw, 0);

        const auto ForwardDirection = FRotationMatrix(YawRotation).
GetUnitAxis(EAxis::X);
        const auto RightDirection = FRotationMatrix(YawRotation).
GetUnitAxis(EAxis::Y);

        AddMovementInput(ForwardDirection, MovementVector.Y);
        AddMovementInput(RightDirection, MovementVector.X);
    }
}
```

As you can see, the first thing that this code does is to get the 2D vector from the Value parameter. This vector contains the *x* and *y* directions for the left thumbstick (or the keyboard) and indicates the direction in which the character should move. I have added an onscreen message to keep track of this value.

Next, if there is a Controller possessing this Actor, we compute the forward and right directions of the Character and move it in the corresponding direction (this is something you should already be familiar with if you've ever tried the Unreal Third Person template).

The next method you'll be implementing is the Look() one, so add these lines just after the Move() function:

```
void AUS_Character::Look(const FInputActionValue& Value)
{
    const auto LookAxisVector = Value.Get<FVector2D>();
    GEngine->AddOnScreenDebugMessage(1, 5.f, FColor::Green,
FString::Printf(TEXT("LookAxisVector: %s"), *LookAxisVector.
ToString()));
```

```
    if (Controller != nullptr)
    {
        AddControllerYawInput(LookAxisVector.X);
        AddControllerPitchInput(LookAxisVector.Y);
    }
}
```

As you can see, we are getting the 2D vector from the Value parameter that, this time, will come from the right thumbstick or the mouse. After that, we add a yaw/pitch to the Controller; this will cause the Spring component and, consequently, the Camera component, to rotate around the character.

For the sprint action, the character has two methods available – one for starting the sprint and one for ending it. Add this code block after the previous function:

```
void AUS_Character::SprintStart(const FInputActionValue& Value)
{
    GEngine->AddOnScreenDebugMessage(2, 5.f, FColor::Blue,
TEXT("SprintStart"));
    GetCharacterMovement()->MaxWalkSpeed = 3000.f;
}

void AUS_Character::SprintEnd(const FInputActionValue& Value)
{
    GEngine->AddOnScreenDebugMessage(2, 5.f, FColor::Blue,
TEXT("SprintEnd"));
    GetCharacterMovement()->MaxWalkSpeed = 500.f;
}
```

This code simply increases the maximum speed of the character when it is sprinting.

> **Note**
>
> The walk and sprint values are hardcoded; we will need to get these values from a dataset later on as we progress through the book.

The last method you need to implement is the Interact() one but, at the moment, we don't have anything to interact with! So, you'll just add an onscreen message inside the function:

```
void AUS_Character::Interact(const FInputActionValue& Value)
{
    GEngine->AddOnScreenDebugMessage(3, 5.f, FColor::Red,
TEXT("Interact"));
}
```

The last thing you need to do to make the character fully functional is to add the input assets to the Blueprint.

Updating the character Blueprint

To update the Blueprint, take the following steps:

1. Save all the files you have modified and get back to the Unreal Editor.
2. Click the **Compile** button and wait for the success message.
3. Open your **BP_Character** Blueprint and select the **Class Defaults** section.
4. Search for the **Input** category in the **Details** panel. You should get the **Default Mapping Context** property along with the four actions that have been created.
5. Click the drop-down button for **Default Mapping Context** and select the corresponding asset (there should be only one to choose).
6. For each action property, select the corresponding action asset from the drop-down menu.

The result of the previous steps is depicted in *Figure 5.10*:

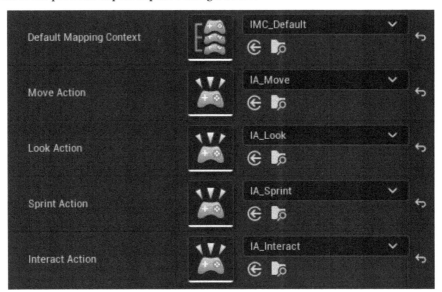

Figure 5.10 – The Blueprint input settings

The character is finally complete! It's been hard, but you are now ready to test it.

Testing the character's movement

Now that the base user interaction has been implemented, it's time to start testing it on a playable level. Open the **Level_01** map and do the following:

1. Look for the **SP 1** (for *SpawnPoint 1*) label in the level and add a **Player Start** Actor near it.
2. Set **Net Mode** to **Listen Server** with **3** players.
3. Hit the **Play** button to test the game.

You should be able to move the characters and make them sprint and look around.

You may be wondering how it is possible that you are already playing a networked game even though you did not add any multiplayer code logic. The answer is in the Character class, which is already set to be replicated – just open the **BP_Character** Blueprint and look for the **Replication** category. You will find out that **Replicate Movement** has been set by default and also that the **Replicates** property is set to true.

You may also have noticed that while the character on the server window moves and sprints smoothly, on the client's window, movements seem a bit jumpy when you are running. This is happening because you are trying to execute the sprint action on the client, but the server is the one who is actually in command – as a result, the client will make the character move faster, but the server will bring it back to its move position. Basically, at the moment, we are trying to "cheat" on the client, but the server, which is authoritative, will forbid you from doing this. Obviously, this is a bug in our code, but we still have to understand the full meaning of replication and how to execute functions from the server.

To fix this bug, you will need to know more about replication. Just be patient – I will give you more detailed information about this topic in *Chapter 6, Replicating Properties Over the Network*, and *Chapter 7, Using Remote Procedure Calls (RPCs)*.

Now that you have created your own hero character from scratch, it's time to get some knowledge on how an Actor connection is controlled: I will introduce this topic in the next section.

Controlling the connection of an Actor

Now that you have created a fully working character, it's time to understand how a connection is handled inside Unreal Engine (to quickly refresh your understanding of how connections work, you can refer back to *Chapter 2, Understanding Networking Basics*).

Each connection has its own PlayerController that has been created expressly for it; in this case, we say that the PlayerController is "owned" by that connection.

In Unreal Engine, Actors can have an **Owner**: if the outermost Owner of an Actor is a PlayerController, then the PlayerController becomes the Owner of that Actor. This means that the first Actor is also owned by the same connection that owns the PlayerController.

The concept of ownership is used during Actor replication to determine which connections receive updates for each Actor: for instance, an Actor may be flagged so that only the connection that owns that Actor will be sent property updates for it.

As an example, let's imagine that your thief character (which is basically an Actor) is possessed by a `PlayerController` – this `PlayerController` will be the Owner of the character. During gameplay, the thief gets a pickup that grants a magical dagger: once equipped, this weapon will be owned by the Character. This means that the `PlayerController` will also own the dagger. In the end, both the thief Actor and the dagger will be owned by the `PlayerController` connection. As soon as the thief Actor is no longer possessed by the Player Controller, it will cease to be owned by the connection, and so will the weapon.

If you have developed standalone games, you may be used to retrieving the Player Controller or the character by using nodes such as Get Player Controller or Get Player Character (or their corresponding C++ versions, `UGameplayStatics::GetPlayerController()` and `UGameplayStatics::GetPlayerCharacter()`). Using these functions in a networked environment may be the cause of many issues if you don't know what you are doing, as you will get different results depending on the context.

As an example, calling the Get Player Controller function with Player Index equal to 0 will give you the following results:

- The listen server's `PlayerController` if you are calling it from a listen server
- The first client's `PlayerController` if you are calling it from a dedicated server
- The client's `PlayerController` if you are calling it from a client

If things seem confusing, they will become even more so, considering that the index will not be consistent across the server and different clients.

That's why, when developing multiplayer games in Unreal Engine, you will most probably use some of the following functions (or their corresponding nodes):

- `AActor::GetOwner()`, which returns the Owner of an Actor instance
- `APawn::GetController()`, which returns the Controller for the Pawn or Character instance
- `AController::GetPawn()`, which returns the Pawn possessed by the Controller
- `APlayerState::GetPlayerController()`, which will return the Player Controller that created the Player State instance (remote clients will return a null value)

Regarding components, you should be aware that they have their own way of determining their owning connection – they will start by following the component's outer chain until they find the Actor that owns them. From there, the system will proceed, as explained previously, to determine the owning connection of that Actor. To get the Owner of the component, you'll use the `UActorComponent::GetOwner()` method.

In this section, we have just "scratched the surface" of what an Owner is and how to get info about it, but you should be aware that connection ownership is so important that it will be pervasive throughout the rest of the book: in other words, the idea of owning a connection is deemed crucial enough to be addressed throughout the multiplayer project we are developing.

In the next section, I'm going to introduce a topic that is deeply connected with connection ownership: relevancy.

Understanding Actor relevancy

Relevancy is the process of determining which objects in a scene should be visible or updated based on their importance to the player. This is an important concept in Unreal Engine, and by understanding how it works, you can make sure your game runs efficiently. In this section, we will explore this topic and show an example of how it works depending on its settings.

Understanding relevancy

In Unreal Engine, the term **relevancy** refers to how the Engine determines which Actors in the game world should be replicated to which clients, based on their current locations, and which Actors are relevant to the player's current view or area.

A game level can have a size varying from very small to really huge. This may pose a problem in updating everything on the network and for every client connected to the server. As the playing character may not need to know every single thing that's happening in the level, most of the time, it's just enough to let it know what is near.

As a consequence, the Engine uses several factors to let the player know if something has changed on an Actor: these factors span from the distance to the Actor itself, its visibility, and whether the Actor is currently active in the game world. An Actor that is deemed irrelevant will not be replicated to the player's client, and this will reduce network traffic and improve game performance.

Unreal uses a virtual function named `AActor::IsNetRelevantFor()` to test the relevancy of an Actor. This test evaluates a set of properties that is intended to provide a reliable estimate of the Actors that can actually influence a client. The tests can be summarized as follows:

- **First Check**: The Actor is relevant if the following applies:

  - Its `bAlwaysRelevant` flag is set to `true`

  - Or, it is owned by the `Pawn` or `PlayerController`

  - Or, it is the `Pawn` object

  - Or, the `Pawn` object is the instigator of an action such as noise or damage

- **Second Check**: If the Actor's bNetUseOwnerRelevancy property is true and the Actor itself has an Owner, the owner's relevancy will be used.

- **Third Check**: If the Actor has the bOnlyRelevantToOwner property set to true and does not pass the first check, then it is not relevant.

- **Fourth Check**: If the Actor is attached to another Actor's skeleton, then its relevancy is determined by the relevancy of its parent.

- **Fifth Check**: If the Actor's bHidden property is set to true and the root component is not colliding with the checking Actor, then the Actor is not relevant.

- **Sixth Check**: if AGameNetworkManager is set to use distance-based relevancy, the Actor is relevant if it is closer than the net cull distance.

> Note
>
> The Pawn/Character and PlayerController classes have slightly different relevancy checks as they need to consider additional information, such as the movement component.

It should be noted that this system is not perfect, as the distance check may give a false negative when dealing with large Actors. Additionally, the system does not take into account sound occlusion or other complexities related to ambient sounds. Nevertheless, the approximation is precise enough to get good results during gameplay.

After presenting all this theory, it is time to shift our focus back to the project and begin implementing a tangible example. In the following subsection, you will see relevancy in action by testing your character.

Testing relevancy

To test the effect of relevancy during gameplay, you'll create a simple pickup and play around with its settings.

Creating the Pickup Actor

Start by creating a new C++ class inheriting from **AActor** and call it US_BasePickup. Then, open the generated header file and add these two component declarations in the private section:

```
UPROPERTY(VisibleAnywhere, BlueprintReadOnly,
Category="Components",  meta = (AllowPrivateAccess = "true"))
TObjectPtr<class USphereComponent> SphereCollision;

UPROPERTY(VisibleAnywhere, BlueprintReadOnly, Category="Components",
meta = (AllowPrivateAccess = "true"))
TObjectPtr<class UStaticMeshComponent> Mesh;
```

You should be familiar with the previous code – we are just declaring the Collision component for triggering the pickup and the Mesh component for its visual aspect.

Next, in the `protected` section, just after the `BeginPlay()` declaration, add a declaration that will handle the character overlap with the Actor:

```
UFUNCTION()
void OnBeginOverlap(UPrimitiveComponent* OverlappedComponent, AActor*
OtherActor, UPrimitiveComponent* OtherComp, int32 OtherBodyIndex, bool
bFromSweep, const FHitResult& SweepResult);
```

Immediately after that, add the declaration for the pickup action:

```
UFUNCTION(BlueprintCallable, BlueprintNativeEvent, Category =
"Pickup", meta=(DisplayName="Pickup"))
void Pickup(class AUS_Character* OwningCharacter);
```

We need this function to be callable inside a Blueprint, so we use the `BlueprintCallable` specifier.

Then, the `BlueprintNativeEvent` specifier states that the function can be overwritten by a Blueprint, but it also has a default native C++ implementation that will be called if the Blueprint does not implement anything.

To natively implement the method, in the `US_BasePickup.cpp` file, we will need to implement a C++ function with the same name as the primary function but with `_Implementation` added to the end.

Finally, to the `public` section – and after the corresponding properties, in order to avoid forward declarations – add two getters for the components we declared previously:

```
FORCEINLINE USphereComponent* GetSphereCollision() const { return
SphereCollision; }


FORCEINLINE UStaticMeshComponent* GetMesh() const { return Mesh; }
```

Now that the header has been fully declared, open the `US_BasePickup.cpp` file to start adding code logic to your Actor. First of all, add the necessary includes at the top of the file:

```
#include "US_Character.h"
#include "Components/SphereComponent.h"
```

Then, inside the constructor, add the following block of code, which creates the two components and attaches them to the Actor:

```
SphereCollision =
CreateDefaultSubobject<USphereComponent>("Collision");
```

```
RootComponent = SphereCollision;
SphereCollision->SetGenerateOverlapEvents(true);
SphereCollision->SetSphereRadius(200.0f);

Mesh = CreateDefaultSubobject<UStaticMeshComponent>("Mesh");
Mesh->SetupAttachment(SphereCollision);
Mesh->SetCollisionEnabled(ECollisionEnabled::NoCollision);
```

Immediately after that, set bReplicates to true (as Actors do not replicate by default):

```
bReplicates = true;
```

Inside the BeginPlay() function, add a dynamic multi-cast delegate for the overlap event:

```
SphereCollision->OnComponentBeginOverlap.AddDynamic(this, &AUS_
BasePickup::OnBeginOverlap);
```

> **Note**
>
> To give proper attention and focus to replication, I have designated *Chapter 6, Replicating Properties Over the Network*, for an in-depth exploration of this topic.

Now add the overlap handler just after the closing bracket of the BeginPlay() function:

```
void AUS_BasePickup::OnBeginOverlap(UPrimitiveComponent*
OverlappedComponent, AActor* OtherActor,
                                    UPrimitiveComponent* OtherComp,
int32 OtherBodyIndex, bool bFromSweep, const FHitResult& SweepResult)
{
    if (const auto Character = Cast<AUS_Character>(OtherActor))
    {
        Pickup(Character);
    }
}
```

The previous block of code is quite straightforward: after having checked that the overlapping Actor is AUS_Character (i.e., our multiplayer hero), we simply call the Pickup() method.

To complete the pickup logic, you will now add the Pickup() C++ implementation:

```
void AUS_BasePickup::Pickup_Implementation(AUS_Character *
OwningCharacter)
{
    SetOwner(OwningCharacter);
}
```

The code logic of this method can be implemented inside the inheriting Blueprints, but for the sake of demonstration, we are just setting the Owner of this Actor to the overlapping one: this is an important step in making things work in the next relevancy tests.

It's now time to get back to the Unreal Engine Editor and do some "magic" – after all, this is a book about creating a fantasy game!

Creating a pickup Blueprint class

To test the effects of relevancy in action, you'll create a Blueprint pickup… Well, sort of. Upon first examination, relevancy can exhibit some peculiar tendencies. This is precisely why we'll be conjuring up a marvelously mystical tome that hovers in mid-air!

Open the Unreal Engine Editor and take the following steps:

1. Compile your project to add the pickup to the available classes of your Blueprints.

2. In your `Blueprints` folder, create a new **Blueprint Class** inheriting from **AUS_BasePickup** and name it `BP_SpellBook`.

3. In the **Blueprint Details** panel, select a mesh for the **Static Mesh** property – I opted for the **spellBook** model.

   To make the book float, we are going to move the mesh up and down by using a **Timeline** node. To do so, follow these steps:

4. Open the Blueprint Event Graph, right-click on the canvas, and add a **Timeline** node – give it a name such as `Float`.

5. Double-click on the node to open the corresponding editor.

6. Click the **+ Track** button to add a new **Float** track and name it `Alpha`. The button is shown in *Figure 5.11*:

Figure 5.11 – The Track button

7. Click on the **Loop** button to enable the loop mode. The button is shown in *Figure 5.12*:

Figure 5.12 – The Loop button

8. Right-click on the curve panel and select the **Add key to...** option. Then, set **Time** to **0** and **Value** to **0**.

9. Create another key, but this time set **Time** to **2.5** and **Value** to **0.5**.

10. Create one last key, this time with **Time** equal to **5** and **Value** equal to **0**.

11. Right-click on each of the keys and set the **Key Interpolation** value to **Auto**.

The final result of the **Timeline** node is shown in *Figure 5.13*:

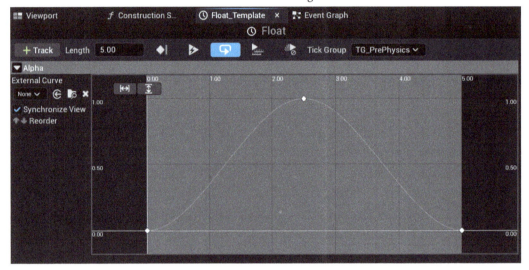

Figure 5.13 – The Timeline node settings

You have just created a sinusoidal value that will indefinitely loop between 0 and 1 values; you'll use this floating value to move the book up and down. To implement this floating movement, return to the Event Graph and do the following:

12. Connect the **Event Begin Play** node to the **Timeline** node.

13. Drag the **Mesh** component from the **Components** panel onto the Event Graph canvas. Click and drag from its outgoing pin to add a **Set Relative Location** node.

14. Connect the **Set Relative Location** incoming execution pin to the **Update** execution pin of the **Timeline** node.

15. Connect the **Timeline** node **Alpha** pin to a **Multiply** node and set the second parameter of this last node to **100**.

16. Right-click on the **New Location** pin of the **Set Relative Location** node and select **Split Struct Pin** to expose the X, Y, and Z values.

17. Connect the **Result** pin of the **Multiply** node to **New Location Z** of the **Set Relative Location** node.

The complete graph is shown in *Figure 5.14*:

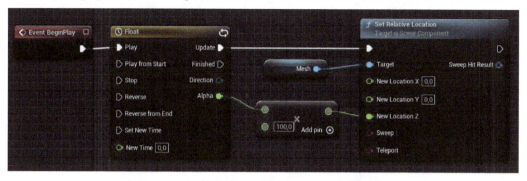

Figure 5.14 – The floating book graph

Please note that this floating animation is purely a visual effect, so we just won't worry about whether it is synchronized over the network.

Now that the Blueprint item has been created, it's time to add it to the level and test its pickup functionality – something we are going to do in the next subsection.

Testing the relevancy settings

It's now time to test how the spell book behaves in a multiplayer environment when relevancy settings are changed.

First of all, drag an instance of the **BP_SpellBook** Blueprint into the level, near the PlayerStart Actor, so that the player will be in the line of sight once it has been spawned.

Open the **PB_SpeelBook** Blueprint and, with the **Class Defaults** panel selected, look for the **Replication** category. The default settings should be similar to the ones shown in *Figure 5.15*:

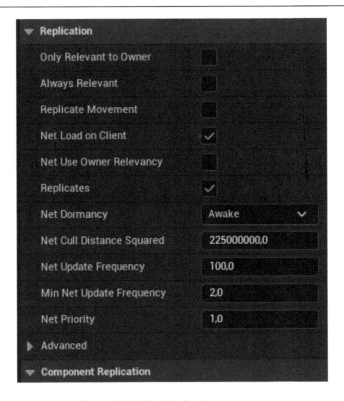

Figure 5.15 – The Replication category

Try playing the game as a listen server with three players, and every player should see the book as expected. Things are going to get a bit trickier in a moment...

Stop the application from playing and get back to the **BP_SpellBook** Blueprint. Look for the **Net Load on Client** property and uncheck it. As this property will load the Actor during map loading, we need to disable it, so the Actor will be loaded only when it becomes relevant for the client.

You are now ready to test different situations, depending on the properties you change in the next steps.

Setting the net cull distance

The first situation you will be testing is about distance culling – at the moment, your object is set to be relevant at a very far distance. To check this, run the game again, and you should see no difference since your last gameplay. But what happens if you lower **Net Cull Distance Squared** to a very low number, for instance, **500**? You will get really "weird" behavior: the server window will show the book, while the two clients will not!

With one of the client windows active, try walking near the zone where the book should be, and it will immediately pop up! Didn't I already warn you that this book was nothing short of magical?

The property you just changed sets the square of the distance that will be used to make the Actor relevant to the client. This means that the spell book will "magically" appear as soon as the character is within the square root of this distance. As the server is authoritative (i.e., knows everything), it will always show the Actor.

Let's now test a way to set the Actor as always relevant and, as such, always visible.

Setting the Actor as always relevant

Return to the spell book Blueprint and set the **Always Relevant** property to **True**, leaving the rest as it was in the previous example. When you play the game, you will notice that every client will be able to see the book from the start. This happens because the book has now been marked as something that should be relevant no matter where the character is in the level; as a consequence, it will be immediately loaded by the client and visible to the players.

This is obviously not a desirable situation – getting a continuous update for every Actor in the level is something we don't want to happen, considering that there could be a multitude of moving elements in our game. But you probably already imagined that, didn't you?

Let's avoid this issue by setting relevancy based on the Owner of the Actor.

Setting the relevancy for the Owner

You may remember that the C++ code for the `Pickup()` function assigns the Owner of the pickup to the character overlapping it. Instead, in this Blueprint, we'll see what happens if the Actor is relevant only to the Owner:

1. Set the **Only Relevant to Owner** property to **True**.
2. Set the **Always Relevant** property to **False**.
3. Set **Net Cull Distance Squared** to a really low number, say **10**.

With the last step, we are setting the spell book so that it won't be relevant to any client unless it is directly on the object; this will let us test who is the Owner of the Actor.

The clients won't be able to see the book unless they enter its collision zone, which is when the character becomes the Owner of the pickup. Once another character enters the pickup zone, it will become the new Owner and the book will become relevant. After a few moments, the first client will see the book disappear as the character is no longer the Owner of the pickup, and so it is no longer relevant to it!

As a final note, there is one last property you should be aware of: **Net Use Owner Relevancy** will return the relevancy of an Actor depending on its owner relevancy. This will come in handy once you assign a weapon to a character or to an enemy!

In this section, you have now unlocked the mystical secrets of relevancy and witnessed it in action. This concept will prove invaluable as you begin optimizing your game, but it's always best to lay a strong foundation and set the right course from the very beginning. The following section will introduce another significant concept, namely authority.

Introducing authority

As we mentioned in *Chapter 2, Understanding Networking Basics*, the term **authority** refers to which instance of the game has the final say over certain aspects of the game state. In an Unreal Engine multiplayer environment, the server is authoritative over the game state: this means that the server makes the final decisions about things such as player movement, damage calculation, and other game mechanics.

When a client requests to perform an action that affects the game state, it sends a message to the server requesting permission to perform that action. The server then determines whether the action is valid and, if so, updates the game state accordingly. Once the server has updated the game state, it sends a message to all clients to inform them of the updated state.

In Unreal Engine, Actors can be either locally or remotely controlled, and the concept of authority is important in determining which controls are valid. Actors that are locally controlled have authority over their own actions, while those that are remotely controlled receive commands from the server and follow those commands.

Overall, the concept of authority ensures that all players see a consistent game state and that no one player has an unfair advantage.

Controlling authority with the Role and Remote Role properties of an Actor

In Unreal Engine, there are two properties that return important information about Actor replication: **Role** and **Remote Role**. These two properties provide information about who has authority over the Actor, whether the Actor is replicated or not, and the method of replication.

In Unreal Engine, an Actor can have one of four possible roles during network play:

- ROLE_Authority: The running instance has authoritative control over the Actor
- ROLE_AutonomousProxy: The running instance is an autonomous proxy of the Actor
- ROLE_SimulatedProxy: The running instance is a locally simulated proxy of the Actor
- ROLE_None: In this case, the role is not relevant

Overall, the `Role` and `RemoteRole` properties are used to control how an Actor behaves during network play in Unreal Engine, and their values can differ depending on the Actor's ownership and replication settings. In particular, the `Role` property specifies the Actor's role on the local machine, while the `RemoteRole` property specifies the Actor's role on the remote machine.

As an example, if `Role` is set to `ROLE_Authority` and `RemoteRole` is set to either `ROLE_SimulatedProxy` or `ROLE_AutonomousProxy`, then the current instance of the game is responsible for replicating this Actor to remote connections.

It should be noted that only the server replicates Actors to connected clients as clients will never replicate Actors to the server. This means that only the server will have `Role` set to `ROLE_Authority` and `RemoteRole` set to `ROLE_SimulatedProxy` or `ROLE_AutonomousProxy`.

Autonomous and simulated proxy

While testing the spell book pickup (well, it was not strictly a "pickup," but you get the point), you may have noticed that once the Actor's Owner changed, the book did seem to stay relevant to both the old and the new Owner for a moment. To avoid using excessive amounts of CPU resources and bandwidth, the server does not replicate Actors during every update but at a frequency that is determined by the `AActor::NetUpdateFrequency` property.

The same thing will happen when updating any Actor during movement, and the client will receive data at predefined intervals; as a consequence, the player may get seemingly erratic updates on an Actor. To avoid these kinds of issues, the Engine will try to extrapolate movement based on the latest data available.

The default behavior relies on predicting the movement and is governed by a **Simulated Proxy** by setting the role to the value of `ROLE_SimulatedProxy`. In this mode, the client continuously updates the location of the Actor based on the latest velocity received from the server.

When an Actor is controlled by a `PlayerController` object, you may use an **Autonomous Proxy** by setting the role to a value of `ROLE_AutonomousProxy`. In this case, the system will receive additional information directly from the human player, making the process of predicting future actions smoother.

In this section, you've gained some insight into the realms of authority and Actor roles. These notions shall undoubtedly come in handy in future chapters, especially as you delve into the complexities of topics such as character weaponry and enemy AI.

Summary

In this chapter, you made further progress in developing your multiplayer project by updating your character with the required movement and interaction features – this was achieved with the help of the Enhanced Input System provided by Unreal Engine.

Next, you gained some clarity on who's pulling the strings of an Actor in a multiplayer environment by understanding what an Owner is.

After that, you started to see the light on the all-important role of relevancy in gaming. As you discovered for yourself, it's crucial to know how properties are set, or things will start to take a big turn for the weird.

Lastly, you gained some valuable insights into the different roles that make up an Unreal Engine multiplayer game and why they play a crucial role in replicating an Actor's behavior across multiple clients.

This brings us to a final question: what does "replicating" an object mean exactly? Well, I guess it's time to take a stroll or indulge in a cup of coffee to recharge your batteries. You will need to summon all your energy and focus, for I will unveil (almost) all the secrets of replication in the next chapter!

6

Replicating Properties Over the Network

Replication is an important concept when it comes to creating multiplayer games with Unreal Engine. In particular, **property replication** allows for the synchronization of objects between multiple players, letting them interact in a shared environment. This feature also handles things such as character movement and physics calculations, ensuring everyone has a consistent experience and view of the game world, regardless of the platform type, and that no one has an advantage due to cheating or latency issues.

In this chapter, you'll start working on replication, mainly focusing on property replication of your character skills. Next, starting from the base pickup you created in the last chapter, you'll implement a coin pickup that will grant the character experience points that will give the character a level-up during gameplay. Finally, you'll apply replication by updating a simple user interface that will show the character experience points and level.

At the end of this chapter, you will have a good grasp of how an Actor replicates in a multiplayer setting and the properties that come with it. Essentially, you'll understand how Actors behave and operate in a multi-player environment.

In the next sections, I will present the following topics:

- Adding character stats
- Understanding property replication
- Handling characters level-ups
- Adding a HUD to the game

Technical requirements

To follow the topics presented in this chapter, you should have completed the previous ones and understood their content.

Additionally, if you would prefer to begin with code from the companion repository for this book, you can download the .zip project files provided in this book's companion project repository:

https://github.com/PacktPublishing/Multiplayer-Game-Development-with-Unreal-Engine-5.

You can download the files that are up to date with the end of the last chapter by clicking the Unreal Shadows – Chapter 05 End link.

Adding character stats

Before introducing property replication and implementing it in the project, our thief hero needs to be ready for such a big step: that's why I'll guide you through the creation of a set of statistics that will be plugged into the Character class.

The first thing to do is to define your character stats. In particular, you will need the following data:

- A walk and a sprint speed, to handle the different paces of your character during gameplay
- A damage multiplier to manage more powerful hits whenever the character levels up
- A level-up value to check whenever the character has reached the next level
- A stealth multiplier that will handle how much noise the character makes when walking or sprinting

You may have noticed that your character has no health – that is because this is a stealth game and players will have to move carefully through the dungeon. Once they are discovered, they won't have the option of facing a swarm of undead lackeys in this particular game! As a consequence, gameplay will be more focused on defeating enemies from a distance or slipping silently away from them.

With the previous information, you'll create a data structure containing all the data points for initializing the character, and then you'll create a data table that will let you manage the experience your thief will gain during gameplay. So, let's get started.

Creating the stats structure

To begin, you need to create a structure that will include all the aforementioned statistics. As this is not a class, you won't need to create it from Unreal Engine Editor but from the IDE instead.

> **Note**
>
> Non-class entities cannot be made directly from within Unreal Editor.

Open your IDE and create a file in your UnrealShadows_LOTL | Source | UnrealShadows_
LOTL folder called US_CharacterStats.h (as this is a data structure, you won't need a .cpp
file). Then, open the file and insert the following code:

```cpp
#pragma once

#include "CoreMinimal.h"
#include "Engine/DataTable.h"
#include "US_CharacterStats.generated.h"

USTRUCT(BlueprintType)
struct UNREALSHADOWS_LOTL_API FUS_CharacterStats : public
FTableRowBase
{
  GENERATED_BODY()

  UPROPERTY(BlueprintReadWrite, EditAnywhere)
  float WalkSpeed = 200.0f;

  UPROPERTY(BlueprintReadWrite, EditAnywhere)
  float SprintSpeed = 400.0f;

  UPROPERTY(BlueprintReadWrite, EditAnywhere)
  float DamageMultiplier = 1.0f;

  UPROPERTY(BlueprintReadWrite, EditAnywhere)
  int32 NextLevelXp = 10.0f;

  UPROPERTY(BlueprintReadWrite, EditAnywhere)
  float StealthMultiplier = 1.0f;

};
```

The include section is self-explanatory – after that, along with the standard C++ struct keyword
to declare a structure, you will notice an USTRUCT() declaration instead of UCLASS() and an F
prefix on the structure name (i.e., FUS_CharacterStats). This is the standard method to declare
a structure in Unreal Engine. Then, in order to let Unreal Editor create data tables from this structure
(more on this in a few moments), the FTableRowBase type is extended.

Inside the structure declaration, we are just adding a list of properties – all of them are marked `BlueprintReadWrite` to let Blueprints access and modify the data, and `EditAnywhere` to let you edit the values inside the data table you are going to create in the next steps.

Creating a stats data table

Now you have created a data structure for your character and are ready to create the actual data from it. In Unreal Engine, we will use a **DataTable** object, a tabular structure that organizes interconnected data in a coherent and practical manner. The data fields can include any valid `UObject` property – including asset references from the projects, such as materials or textures.

To create your character data table, see the following steps:

1. Open your `Blueprints` folder in the Content Browser.

2. Compile your project in order to make the C++ structure available in the Editor.

3. Right-click in the Content Browser and select **Miscellaneous | Data Table**.

4. In the **Pick Row Structure** pop-up window, select **US_CharacterStats** from the drop-down menu, as depicted in *Figure 6.1*:

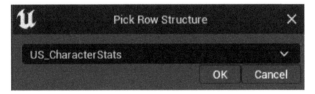

Figure 6.1 – The data table creation panel

5. Click the **OK** button to generate the data table and name it `US_CharacterStats`.

6. Double-click on the newly created asset to open it. You will get an empty dataset as shown in *Figure 6.2*:

Figure 6.2 – The empty data table

> **Note**
>
> A data table can also be generated by importing a .csv or .json file into your project. Additionally, Unreal Engine will let you easily export your project tables in .csv and .json formats. For more information about the importing and exporting processes, check the official documentation linked here: https://docs.unrealengine.com/5.1/en-US/data-driven-gameplay-elements-in-unreal-engine/.

With your table open, it's time to add some data rows organized by character levels – you do want to let your character grow when they gain enough experience, don't you?

Let's start by adding a single row for your character base level:

1. Click on the **Add** button in the **Table** panel.

2. The **Row Name** field will be named **NewRow**; however, right-click on it and select **Rename**. Change the name of this field to level_01.

3. You are now ready to set some stats for the first experience level of your character. Look for the **Row Editor** section in the data table and insert the following values:

    - **Walk Speed** = 250,0

    - **Sprint Speed** = 800,0

    - **Damage Multiplier** = 1,0

    - **Next Level Xp** = 10

    - **Stealth Multiplier** = 1,0

The final result should be the same as the settings shown in *Figure 6.3*:

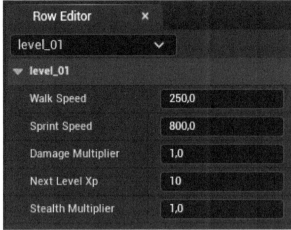

Figure 6.3 – Settings for the level_01 character

We are going to add a couple more levels to handle the experience growth of the character during gameplay. Repeat the same steps as before, but call the two new rows `level_02` and `level_03` respectively. Then use the following values for the **level_02** row:

- **Walk Speed** = 275,0
- **Sprint Speed** = 850,0
- **Damage Multiplier** = 1,1
- **Next Level Xp** = 25
- **Stealth Multiplier** = 1,5

And add the following values for the **level_03** row:

- **Walk Speed** = 300,0
- **Sprint Speed** = 900,0
- **Damage Multiplier** = 1,0
- **Next Level Xp** = 50
- **Stealth Multiplier** = 2

These are purely indicative values – you are free to tweak them to suit your own needs and add as many additional levels as you wish.

Now that you have added a dataset for your character's experience, you are ready to read the info included directly from your code. That's why I need you to go back to the `US_Character.h` header file to add the data table declaration.

Reading the data table from the character

In this section, you are going to add the data table to the character in order to read its values depending on the experience level. The first thing to do is to add a reference to the `US_Character.h` header file. So, in the `private` section of the header file, after all the existing declarations, add this code:

```
UPROPERTY(EditAnywhere, BlueprintReadOnly, Category = "Character
Data", meta = (AllowPrivateAccess = "true"))
class UDataTable* CharacterDataTable;


struct FUS_CharacterStats* CharacterStats;
```

The first declaration will let you reference the data table directly from the child Blueprint Classes, while the structure declaration will let you reference a single row from the data table and use it as the character statistics.

After that, you will need to create a function that will allow the system to update the current level of the character. In the `public` section, add the following method declaration:

```
void UpdateCharacterStats(int32 CharacterLevel);
```

The last thing you need to add to the class header is a getter function for the stats structure. Still in the `public` section, just before the last closing bracket, add the following line of code:

```
FORCEINLINE FUS_CharacterStats* GetCharacterStats() const { return
CharacterStats; }
```

You can now save this file and open `US_Character.cpp` to handle the data retrieval. At the top of the file, add the `include` declarations for the classes you'll be using in a moment:

```
#include "US_CharacterStats.h"
#include "Engine/DataTable.h"
```

Next, implement the `UpdateCharacterStats()` method by adding the following code at the end of the file:

```
void AUS_Character::UpdateCharacterStats(int32 CharacterLevel)
{
 if(CharacterDataTable)
 {
  TArray<FUS_CharacterStats*> CharacterStatsRows;
  CharacterDataTable->GetAllRows<FUS_CharacterStats>(TEXT("US_
```

```
Character"), CharacterStatsRows);

  if(CharacterStatsRows.Num() > 0)
  {
    const auto NewCharacterLevel = FMath::Clamp(CharacterLevel, 1,
CharacterStatsRows.Num());
    CharacterStats = CharacterStatsRows[NewCharacterLevel - 1];

    GetCharacterMovement()->MaxWalkSpeed = GetCharacterStats()-
>WalkSpeed;
  }
 }
}
```

As you can see, first we check that the data table is referenced (you'll add it later, from the character Blueprint) and then use the `GetAllRows<T>()` method to fetch all the table rows into a local array (i.e., the `CharacterStatsRows` variable). If there is at least one row in the data table, we get the one corresponding to the level of the character minus 1 (i.e., for a level 1 character, we will get the row number 0). Notice, as well, the `FMath::Clamp()` method, which guarantees we are not trying to get a level value that's higher than the available rows in the dataset.

After that, we retrieve the `WalkSpeed` column from the row and assign its value to the `MaxWalkSpeed` property of the character movement component – this means that, if there is a data table assigned, your character will start the game with a value from the dataset and not from the constructor.

You are now ready to update your character stats to level 1 – something you are about to do in the `BeginPlay()` function. To do so, inside the `BeginPlay()` function, and just before the closing bracket, add this code:

```
UpdateCharacterStats(1);
```

The last thing you need to do is to update the two sprint methods that, at the moment, are using hardcoded values but need to use the data table stats. To do so, search for the `SprintStart()` method and find the following line:

```
GetCharacterMovement()->MaxWalkSpeed = 3000.f;
```

Then, change it to the following code:

```
if (GetCharacterStats())
{
 GetCharacterMovement()->MaxWalkSpeed = GetCharacterStats()-
>SprintSpeed;
}
```

Let's do the same with the `SprintEnd()` method, which should be positioned just after the previous one. Find the following line:

```
GetCharacterMovement()->MaxWalkSpeed = 500.f;
```

Then change it using the following code block:

```
if(GetCharacterStats())
{
  GetCharacterMovement()->MaxWalkSpeed = GetCharacterStats()-
>WalkSpeed;
}
```

In both cases, the code is self-explanatory – we just check that there is valid data referenced in the character stats and assign the sprint or walk speed to the character movement component.

Now save your file and compile the project, just to be sure that everything is fine and ready for the next step.

Your character is now ready to accept the data table we created at the beginning of this chapter.

Adding the data table to the character

To add the data table asset to the character, switch back to Unreal Editor and follow these steps:

1. Open the **BP_Character** Blueprint.
2. Select the **Class Defaults** tab and, in the **Details** panel, look for the **Character Data** category.
3. In the **Character Data Table** attribute, click on the drop-down menu and select **DT_CharacterStats**.

Your character is now ready to use the statistics from the dataset – even though the poor thief is locked into a level 1 experience level, later on, you will set them free in the dungeon and see how they fare!

Test the game to check that everything works properly. Just remember what I said in the previous chapter: movement is still buggy as the client and the server are trying to force the character to conform to different speed values, but you are nearing the solution.

So, in this section, you have improved the character by adding some statistics retrieved from a data table and using them to initialize some properties. At the moment, you have just used the movement ones, but don't be afraid! Once the character is completed, everything will fall into place.

In the upcoming section, we'll dive into the topic of property replication in Unreal – something that will come in handy when it's time to level up your character and something you'll be doing by the end of this chapter.

Understanding property replication

As stated before, property replication allows for the synchronization of objects in an Unreal multiplayer environment. It should be noted that, as the server is authoritative, updates will never be sent by the client. Obviously, the client may (politely) ask the server to change a property value, and the server will behave accordingly. Additionally, property replication acts as a reliable service: consequently, the Actor on the client will have the same value as the server sooner or later.

This means that if you're trying to modify, from the client, a property that is replicated, any changes you make to that property will only be temporary. You should be already familiar with this topic as the character's movement logic, at the moment, is a bit buggy – we are trying to make the character run from the client, but the server is blocking our commands as soon as the network is updated.

This is happening because, as soon as the server sends an update to the client with a new value for that property, any changes that you made locally on the client will be overwritten and replaced with the new, correct value from the server. Consequently, if the server does not update frequently, it may take a while for the client to be notified about the new, correct value.

Fixing that nasty bug is something we will be doing in *Chapter 7, Using Remote Procedure Calls (RPCs)*, where you'll need to learn how to call a function from the client to the server. The main focus of this chapter, however, is to understand how to replicate properties. So, without further ado, let's check how things work under the hood!

Enabling property replication

In order for a property to be replicated, you need to set up a few things. First of all, in the Actor constructor that will contain the property, you will need to set the bReplicates flag to true.

> **Note**
>
> A class or Blueprint extending from APawn or ACharacter will have the bReplicates property set to true by default, while a regular Actor won't.

Then, the property that should be replicated will need to have the Replicated specifier added to the UPROPERTY() macro. As an example, you can replicate the score for your character with the following code:

```
UPROPERTY(Replicated)
int32 Score;
```

If you are in need of a callback function to be executed when a property is updated, you can use `ReplicatedUsing=[FunctionName]` instead – this attribute will let you specify a function that will be executed when an update is sent to the client. For example, if you want to execute a method called `OnRep_Score()` whenever your character score is replicated, you will write something similar to the following code:

```
UPROPERTY(ReplicatedUsing="OnRep_Score")
int32 Score;
```

You will then need to implement the `OnRep_Score()` method in the same class; this function must declare the `UFUNCTION()` macro.

Once all the replication properties are properly decorated by the previous attributes, they need to be declared inside the `AActor::GetLifetimeReplicatedProps()` function by using the `DOREPLIFETIME()` macro. Using the previous score example, you will need to declare the `Score` property by using the following code:

```
DOREPLIFETIME(AMyActor, Score);
```

After a property is registered for replication, it cannot be unregistered, as Unreal Engine will optimize data storage to reduce the computation time: this means that, by default, you will not have much control over how a property replicates.

Luckily, you can use the `DOREPLIFETIME_CONDITION()` macro instead, which will let you add an additional condition for more precise control over replication. Values for these conditions are predefined – one example is `COND_OwnerOnly`, which will only send data to the Actor's owner (we will use this value later in the chapter). As another example, if you need even more fine-grained control in property replication, you can use the `DOREPLIFETIME_ACTIVE_OVERRIDE()` macro, which will let you use your own conditions defined inside the Actor.

The major downside of using additional conditions for replication is performance, as the engine will need to do additional checks before replicating a property – this means that it is advisable to use the `DOREPLIFETIME()` macro in situations where no pressing requirements dictate the use of an alternative option.

Now that you understand how an object can be replicated, it's time for me to introduce how objects are referenced across the network.

Referencing Actors and components over the network

Sooner or later, you will need to reference an Actor or a component from your code – this means that, in a multiplayer game, you will need to know whether the reference can be replicated or not. Simply put, an Actor or a component can be referenced over the network only if it is supported for networking.

There are some simple rules that will help you determine whether your object can be referenced over the network:

- If an Actor is replicated, it can also be replicated as a reference

- If a component is replicated, it can also be replicated as a reference

- Non-replicated Actors and components need to be stably named in order to be replicated as references

> **Note**
>
> An object that is **stably named** means that an entity that will be present in both the server and the client that has the same name. For instance, an Actor is stably named if it was not spawned during gameplay but was loaded directly in the level from a package.

This section has provided you with an introduction to the fundamental concepts of network replication in Unreal Engine, explaining how it interacts with Actors and components. If you feel a bit lost about too much theory, don't be afraid! You'll be taking all that theory and transforming it into a tangible, working example by creating a level-up system for your character.

Handling character level-ups

As I previously mentioned, in this section, you are going to level up your hero's experience and skills. As usual, you'll be dabbling in code magic to make it happen! After all, you are programming a fantasy game.

I know it might seem like a good idea to write your code inside the Character class but trust me when I say that there's actually a much better spot for it. That is the `PlayerState` class, which we incidentally have already set for this occasion – a while ago, I asked you to create the `US_PlayerState` class and now is the time to add some valuable code in it.

As introduced in *Chapter 4, Setting Up Your First Multiplayer Environment*, `PlayerState` is a class that holds information about a player's game state and exists on both the server and clients. As we need to synchronize experience points and levels for the character, this is the ideal location to place everything.

What we need to do here is to keep track of experience points and, as soon as the character reaches a new level, broadcast the information across the network and update the character statistics.

But first, the most important thing is to have a clear idea of what we are going to do.

Planning ahead

As the `PlayerState` class will keep important information about the character, it's mandatory to think ahead about what you want to achieve and how to get to that point – this means we have to plan exactly what we will be adding to this class.

Here are some of the main features this gameplay framework class will implement:

- Keeping track of the character's current level and experience points
- Synchronizing the aforementioned properties over the network
- Updating the Character class whenever the player levels up
- Broadcasting events whenever the character gets some experience points or levels up

As a starting point, in the next subsection, we'll start by declaring the required properties and functions.

Declaring PlayerState properties and functions

In the following steps, we are going to define the main properties that will let the character level up whenever they have enough experience – this means we will need to track the thief's experience points and level. Additionally, whenever values change, we will replicate these properties over the network and notify this event to each registered Actor in the game.

So, let's start by opening the `US_PlayerState.h` file and adding the following code in the `protected` section:

```
UPROPERTY(EditDefaultsOnly, BlueprintReadOnly, ReplicatedUsing="OnRep_
Xp", Category = "Experience")
int Xp = 0;

UPROPERTY(EditDefaultsOnly, BlueprintReadOnly, ReplicatedUsing="OnRep_
CharacterLevelUp", Category = "Experience")
int CharacterLevel = 1;

UFUNCTION()
void OnRep_Xp(int32 OldValue) const;

UFUNCTION()
void OnRep_CharacterLevelUp(int32 OldValue) const;
```

As you can see, the first thing we have done is declare the two properties `Xp` (short for experience points) and `CharacterLevel`; both can be modified in Unreal's **Details** panel for playtesting purposes thanks to the `EditDefaultsOnly` attribute, but `BlueprintsReadOnly` makes them non-modifiable in a Blueprint, to keep all the level-up logic inside the C++ source code.

As an additional attribute, we use the `ReplicatedUsing` attribute, which I introduced in the previous section. This will let us execute a function whenever a property is updated – in this case, we have set `OnRep_Xp` for the Xp property and `OnRep_CharacterLevelUp` for `CharacterLevel`.

Next, create a `public` section in your header file and add this code:

```
UFUNCTION(BlueprintCallable, Category="Experience")
void AddXp(int32 Value);
```

This function will let us assign new experience points to the `PlayerState`. We need to make it `BlueprintCallable` in order to use this function from our Blueprints – for instance, from a pickup.

Just after that, add this declaration:

```
virtual void GetLifetimeReplicatedProps(TArray<FLifetimeProperty>&
OutLifetimeProps) const override;
```

As explained in the previous section, we need to override this method in order to declare the properties that will be replicated (more on this in a moment).

All the necessary setup for implementing replication in our two properties has been completed, but a few additional elements still need to be incorporated to ensure everything works properly. We need to broadcast some information whenever these properties change – this will come in handy when you implement a user interface later in this chapter.

To implement such functionality, you'll be using **delegates**. You may be already familiar with this topic in C++, but you should be aware that, in Unreal Engine, a delegate provides a way to call member functions on C++ objects in a generic, type-safe manner through dedicated macros.

> **Note**
>
> If you want more information about the types of delegates supported by Unreal Engine and how they can be used in your project, check out the official documentation, which can be found here: `https://docs.unrealengine.com/5.1/en-US/delegates-and-lamba-functions-in-unreal-engine/`.

As we want broadcast events for the two properties, we will be declaring two delegates – one for each property. At the beginning of the header file, just before the `UCLASS()` declaration, add the following code:

```
DECLARE_DYNAMIC_MULTICAST_DELEGATE_OneParam(FOnXpChanged, int32,
NewXp);
DECLARE_DYNAMIC_MULTICAST_DELEGATE_OneParam(FOnCharacterLevelUp,
int32, NewLevelXp);
```

These two lines are pretty similar – they both declare a **dynamic multi-cast delegate** with a single parameter. Being dynamic, the delegate can be serialized, and so, used in a Blueprint, while the multi-cast declaration will allow you to attach multiple function delegates and use the `Broadcast()` method to notify every listener of changes in your system. We will use these features in our Blueprint classes to bind events and react accordingly.

Let's declare our `delegate` function. Create a `protected` section, and add the following two lines of code, which will be used to broadcast the events:

```
UPROPERTY(BlueprintAssignable, Category = "Events")
FOnXpChanged OnXpChanged;


UPROPERTY(BlueprintAssignable, Category = "Events")
FOnCharacterLevelUp OnCharacterLevelUp;
```

As their purpose is self-explanatory, I guess it's time stop talking and start writing down the implementation!

Implementing the PlayerState logic

Now that all the properties and methods have been declared, you are going to implement the PlayerState logic – whenever the character gains some experience, you should check whether it has reached enough points to level up. Experience points gained and level-ups should be broadcast to the system, in order to keep everything synchronized.

Start by opening the `US_PlayerState.cpp` file and adding the required `include` declarations:

```
#include "US_Character.h"
#include "US_CharacterStats.h"
#include "Net/UnrealNetwork.h"
```

Next, add the implementation for the `GetLifetimeReplicatedProps()` method:

```
void AUS_
PlayerState::GetLifetimeReplicatedProps(TArray<FLifetimeProperty>&
OutLifetimeProps) const
{
  Super::GetLifetimeReplicatedProps(OutLifetimeProps);

  DOREPLIFETIME_CONDITION(AUS_PlayerState, Xp, COND_OwnerOnly);
  DOREPLIFETIME_CONDITION(AUS_PlayerState, CharacterLevel, COND_
OwnerOnly);
}
```

As you can see, we are using the DOREPLIFETIME_CONDITION() macro, introduced in the previous section, to declare that the Xp and CharacterLevel properties should be replicated – in this case, we just want the property to be replicated on the owning player of the character (i.e., in the player's client), and we do so by using the COND_OwnerOnly flag.

Next, add the implementation for the AddXp() method using the following code:

```
void AUS_PlayerState::AddXp(const int32 Value)
{
 Xp += Value;
 OnXpChanged.Broadcast(Xp);

 GEngine->AddOnScreenDebugMessage(0, 5.f, FColor::Yellow,
FString::Printf(TEXT("Total Xp: %d"), Value));

 if (const auto Character = Cast<AUS_Character>(GetPawn()))
 {
  if(Character->GetCharacterStats()->NextLevelXp < Xp)
  {
    GEngine->AddOnScreenDebugMessage(3, 5.f, FColor::Red, TEXT("Level
Up!"));

    CharacterLevel++;
    Character->UpdateCharacterStats(CharacterLevel);
    OnCharacterLevelUp.Broadcast(CharacterLevel);
  }
 }
}
```

Here, whenever we receive an experience point update, we simply add the value to the character pool (i.e., the Xp property). Next, we ascertain that the character is an AUS_Character type through a cast and, if the cast is successful, we retrieve its statistics to check whether it should level up. If the check is successful, we simply increase the character level and call the UpdateCharacterStats() method to make the thief update the skill row. As we change the values for the properties, we then broadcast the new value to all listeners. A couple of (temporary) debug messages complete the code.

The PlayerState is now almost finished – we just need to broadcast the values to the clients whenever values are updated from the server side. To do so, add this last block of code to the file:

```
void AUS_PlayerState::OnRep_Xp(int32 OldValue) const
{
 OnXpChanged.Broadcast(Xp);
}
```

```
void AUS_PlayerState::OnRep_CharacterLevelUp(int32 OldValue) const
{
  OnCharacterLevelUp.Broadcast(CharacterLevel);
}
```

The broadcast call is self-explanatory – every registered Actor will receive the notification, along with the new value for the Xp and CharacterLevel properties.

So, in the preceding steps, you have successfully developed a fully operational replication system that effectively manages the character experience gained and skill development. I'm aware that the task at hand may feel daunting and even sometimes counter-intuitive, but with time and practice, you can rest assured that everything will become easier and more manageable!

There's still something missing in our game: actual experience points. Let's not waste any time and work on adding an item that our character can use to gain experience points. In the next steps, you'll be creating some coins, starting with the previously created US_BasePickup class, to grant your thief the much-desired experience.

Adding coin pickups to the level

So, we are ready to create some coins that will be used in the game to add experience points to the character – this will be a simple Blueprint that will be spawned whenever enemies are killed or that will be available in the level.

To do this, go back to Unreal Editor and compile the project, in order to update it with all your improvements. Then, navigate to the Blueprints folder and complete the following steps:

1. Right-click in the Content Browser and select **Blueprint Class | US_BasePickup** to create a new Blueprint from it.

2. Name the Blueprint BP_GoldCoinPickup and double-click on it to open it.

3. In the **Components** panel, select the **Mesh** component and assign to the **Static Mesh** attribute the **coin** static mesh. Change its scale to **2**, in order to make it more visible in the game.

Your Blueprint should now be similar to the one shown in *Figure 6.4*:

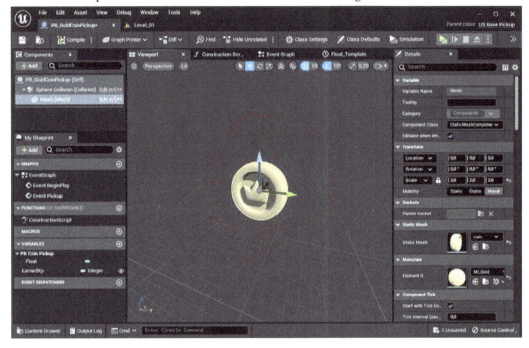

Figure 6.4 – The gold coin Blueprint

Now that the pickup has a base shape, it's time to add some code logic to make things fully functional. Open the **Event Graph** tab and take the following steps:

4. Create a variable of type **Integer** and call it **EarnedXp**, giving it a default value of **5**.

5. Right-click in the canvas and look for **Event Pickup**, adding it to the graph.

6. Add a **Cast To US_PlayerState** node and connect its incoming execution pin to the outgoing execution pin of the event.

7. Click and drag from the **Owning Character** pin of the **Event** node and, after releasing the button, add a **Get PlayerState** node from the options that appear.

8. Connect the **PlayerState** outgoing pin to the **Object** pin of the **Cast** node.

9. Click and drag from the outgoing **As Us PlayerState** pin to create an **Add Xp** node.

10. Connect the success execution pin of the cast node to the incoming execution pin of the **Add Xp** node.

11. Drag a **Get Earned Xp** node from the **Variables** section into the canvas and connect its pin to the **Value** pin of the **Add Xp** node.

12. Finally, add a **Destroy Actor** node and connect it to the outgoing execution pin of the **Add Xp** node.

The final result of the graph is shown in *Figure 6.5*:

Figure 6.5 – The Coin Event graph

As you can see, the visual scripting code is quite straightforward – whenever a character picks up a coin, its PlayerState will be updated with the experience points granted by it.

To test the game, just drag a bunch of coins inside your level and play the game. Every time a character picks up a coin, you should see a display message, and when the character has enough experience, you should get another message, the level-up one.

It should be noted that, in the previous code, the pickup event will be called both on the client and on the server – this is something that should not be done as it may provoke issues in your game. Luckily, in this case, the PlayerState will correctly handle the data, so we don't have to worry about it. You will learn how to handle trickier situations in *Chapter 6, Replicating Properties Over the Network*.

As an extra exercise, you can add a floating animation to the coin, just like you did for the spell book in *Chapter 5, Managing Actors in a Multiplayer Environment*.

Adding coin subclasses

As an optional step, you can create different coin pickups with different values for experience points. Here's how to do so:

1. Right-click on **PB_GoldCoinPickup** and select **Create Child Blueprint Class**, naming the asset BP_SilverCoinPickup.

2. Assign a value of **3** to **Earned Xp** and **MI_Metal** as the mesh material.

To provide your character with various items to search for, repeat this step as many times as you desire. This will grant your character a diverse set of treasures to seek out.

In this section, you have created a level-up system for your thief hero. With the help of replication, a character will get the correct level-up notification upon reaching enough experience points. At the moment, this can be achieved by collecting coin pickups around the level – later on, you'll spawn treasure upon defeating those nasty Lichlord minions!

In the next section, I will guide you through the creation of a simple UI that will show the character level and the experience points that have been gained; you'll perform this task by listening to PlayerState notifications and reacting accordingly.

Adding a HUD to the game

In this section, you will create a **Heads Up Display** (**HUD**) for the game that will assist in monitoring the player character's progress during the game. As you may already know, the best way to create such information is through the **Unreal Motion Graphics** (**UMG**) system – a GUI-based editor that allows developers to create user interface elements for their game, such as menus, HUDs, and other display screens. You'll be using this system to create the HUD widget with the relative info.

What we need to show at the moment is quite simple – one set of text showing the character's experience points and another set showing the level.

Let's start by creating the Blueprint and the visual elements.

Creating the Widget Blueprint

To create the Widget Blueprint, within Unreal Editor, take the following steps:

1. Open your `Blueprints` folder, right-click on the Content Browser, and select **User Interface | Widget Blueprint** to create a **User Widget** Blueprint. Name the newly created asset `WB_HUD` and double-click on the asset to open it.

2. Drag a **Canvas** element from the **Palette** tab into the **Designer** view. This canvas will act as the main container for your visual elements.

3. Drag a **Text** element into the previously added **Canvas** and call it **XpLabel**. Make sure that the **Is Variable** field in the **Details** panel is checked to expose this element in the graph you'll be using later.

4. Position the label somewhere on the canvas that suits your needs; in my case, I opted for the top-left corner of the screen.

5. Drag another **Text** element into the **Canvas** instance and call it **CharacterLevelLabel**. Again, make sure that the **Is Variable** field in the **Details** panel is checked to expose this element in the graph you'll be using later.

6. Position the label somewhere on the canvas that suits your needs; in my case, I opted for the top-right corner of the screen.

The final result of your HUD should be similar to *Figure 6.6*:

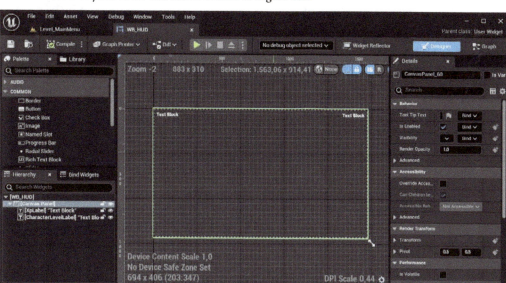

Figure 6.6 – The HUD designer panel

Now that you have created the widget, it's time to add some Visual Scripting code to make it fully functional.

Adding code logic to the Widget Blueprint

In the following steps, you'll add some code logic to the Blueprint, in order to listen to events from the PlayerState and react accordingly.

Creating a custom event for the experience points label

Let's start by creating a custom event that will update the experience points label. To do this, open the **Graph** panel of your widget and take the following steps:

1. Create a custom event and call it OnXpChanged_Event.

2. Select it and, in the **Details** panel, add an input of type **Integer**. Name it NewXp.

3. From the **MyBlueprint** panel, drag a getter node for **XpLabel**.

4. From the **XpLabel** outgoing pin, click and drag, adding a **SetText (Text)** node.

5. Connect the **OnXpChanged_Event** execution pin to the incoming **SetText (Text)** execution pin.

6. Connect the **New Xp** pin of the **Event** node to the **In Text** pin of the **SetText (Text)** node. This operation will automatically add a **To Text (Integer)** node converter.

The final result of this piece of code is shown in *Figure 6.7*:

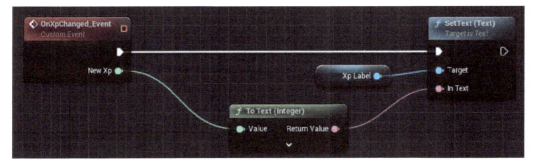

Figure 6.7 – The Xp custom event

As an additional, optional step, you may want to add an **Append** node – this is usually used to prefix some descriptive text to be shown in the text label, such as `Experience Points` (for example, `Experience Points: 150`).

Now that you have a custom event to handle the experience points label, it's time to do the same for the character level.

Creating a custom event for the character level label

Let's now create a custom event that will update the character level label:

1. Create a custom event and call it `OnCharacterLevelUp_Event`.

2. Select it and, in the **Details** panel, add an input of type **Integer**. Name it `NewLevel`.

3. From the **MyBlueprint** panel, drag a getter node for **CharacterLevelLabel**.

4. From the **CharacterLevelLabel** outgoing pin, click and drag and, after releasing the mouse button, select a **SetText (Text)** node from the options that appear.

5. Connect the **OnLevelLabelChanged_Event** execution pin to the incoming **SetText (Text)** execution pin.

6. Connect the **New Level** pin of the **Event** node to the **In Text** pin of the **SetText (Text)** node. This operation will automatically add a **To Text (Integer)** node converter.

The final result of this piece of code is shown in *Figure 6.8*:

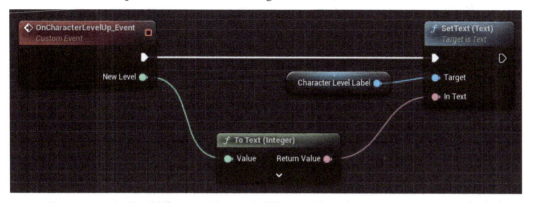

Figure 6.8 – The character level custom event

Just like the previous label, you may want to use the **Append** node to prefix the character level label with descriptive text such as `Level:` (for example, `Level: 1`).

Now that you have a custom event to handle the character level label, it's time to bind these events to the notifications broadcast by the PlayerState.

Binding to PlayerState events

In this final step of the Widget Blueprint, you will bind the previously created events to the PlayerState, in order to update the HUD every time an update notification is dispatched:

1. Add an **Event on Initialized** node to the graph. This node is executed only once during the game (i.e., when the object has been initialized) and is the best place to add bindings.

2. Connect the event to a **Delay** node with **Duration** equal to **0,2**. As the PlayerState won't be available at initialization time, waiting until it is available is a quick solution to solve the issue.

3. Add a **Branch** node and connect its incoming execution pin to the **Completed** execution pin of the **Delay** node. Connect the **False** execution pin of the **Branch** node to the incoming execution pin of the **Delay** node; this will create a loop that will go on until the PlayerState has been properly initialized.

    Now we are going to recover the PlayerState from the player owning this widget.

4. Add a **Get Owning Player** node to the graph. This node returns the player that is controlling (i.e., owns) the HUD.

5. From the **Return Value** pin of this node, click and drag to create a **Get PlayerState** node.

6. From the **PlayerState** outgoing pin of the newly created node, click and drag to create a **Cast To US_PlayerState** node. Right-click on this node and, from the options, select **Convert to Pure Cast**. As the game is based on the US_PlayerState class, we are pretty sure that we are going to recover that type of PlayerState, so we don't need to worry about validation.

7. Connect the **Success** pin of the **Cast To US_PlayerState** node to the **Condition** pin of the **Branch** node.

8. From the outgoing **As US PlayerState** pin, click and drag to create a new variable by selecting **Promote to variable**. You will automatically get a **Set PlayerState** node in the graph – name the variable PlayerState.

9. Connect the **True** execution pin of the **Branch** node to the incoming **Set PlayerState** execution pin.

The visual scripting code created so far is shown in *Figure 6.9*:

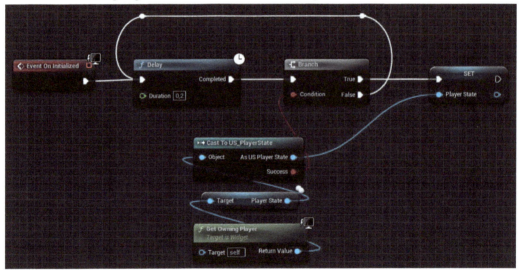

Figure 6.9 – The first part of the PlayerState binding

Now that you have a reference to the PlayerState, it's time to bind the custom events to the delegate you created in the previous sections.

10. From the outgoing pin of the **Set PlayerState** node, click and drag to create a **Bind Event to On Xp Changed** event; this event is available thanks to the delegate declaration included in the US_PlayerState class.

11. Connect the outgoing execution pin of **Set PlayerState** to the incoming execution pin of the **Bind Event to On Xp Changed** node.

12. From the **Event** pin of the bind node, click and drag to add a **Create Event** node. This node has a drop-down menu – here, select **OnXpChanged_Event (NewXp)**, which will execute the **OnXpChanged_Event** custom event whenever the system receives the corresponding notification from the PlayerState.

13. Connect the outgoing execution pin of the **Bind Event to On Xp Changed** node to an **On Xp Changed Event** node; this will call the event upon initialization, to update the HUD.

14. From the **Variables** section, drag a **Get PlayerState** node and from it, create a **Get Xp** node. Connect the outgoing pin of the **Get Xp** node to the **New Xp** pin of the **On Xp Changed Event** node.

This portion of the Visual Scripting code is shown in *Figure 6.10*:

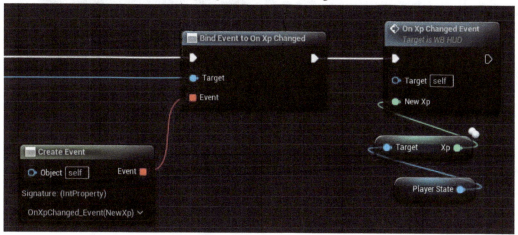

Figure 6.10 – The second part of the PlayerState binding

The last part of the binding phase is almost identical to the steps you have just taken, with the exception that we are creating a binding for the player level.

15. From the outgoing pin of the **On Xp Changed Event** node, click and drag to create a **Bind Event to On Character Level Up** node.

16. Drag a **Get PlayerState** node from the **Variables** section and connect it to the **Target** pin of the **Bind Event to On Character Level Up** node.

17. From the **Event** pin of the **Bind Event to On Character Level Up** node, click and drag to add a **Create Event** node. From the drop-down menu, select **OnCharacterLevelUp_Event (NewLevel)**. This selection will execute the **OnCharacterLevelUp_Event** custom event whenever the system receives the corresponding notification from the PlayerState.

18. Connect the outgoing execution pin of the **Bind** node to an **On Character Level Up Event** node; this will call the event upon initialization, to update the HUD.

19. From the **Variables** section, drag a **Get PlayerState** node to create a **Get Character Level** node. Connect the outgoing pin of the **Get Character Level** node to the **New Level** pin of the **On Character Level Up Event** node.

This final part of the graph is shown in *Figure 6.11*:

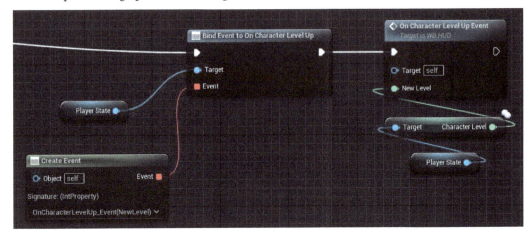

Figure 6.11 – The final part of the PlayerState binding

You have finally created all the bindings to listen to any PlayerState notifications and update the HUD accordingly. It's now time to add the final step – showing the HUD in-game.

Adding the HUD to the character

Now you will add the HUD to the player viewport. If you are already familiar with Unreal Engine user interfaces in standalone games, you may already know how things work.

However, you should be aware that, in a multiplayer environment, a user interface widget should be attached to the game viewport only if the character is controlled locally (i.e., is the owning client). If you don't check whether the character creating the widget is controlled locally, you will create a widget for each character spawned in the level – including those controlled by other players and replicated in the client. Having a cluttered mess of superimposed HUDs is obviously something you don't want to have in your game!

To add the HUD to the character, follow these steps:

1. Start by finding the **BP_Character** Blueprint and opening it.

2. In the Event Graph, find the **Begin Play** event. Then, add a **Branch** node to the execution pin of the event.

3. Connect the **Condition** pin of the **Branch** node to an **Is Locally Controlled** node – this will guarantee we are attaching the HUD only to the character controlled by the client.

4. From the **True** execution pin of the **Branch** node, create a **Create Widget** node. From the **Class** drop-down menu, choose **WB_HUD** to select our HUD.

5. Connect the outgoing execution pin of the **Create Widget** node to an **Add to Viewport** node. Connect the **Return Value** pin to the **Target** pin.

The final result of the graph can be seen in *Figure 6.12*:

Figure 6.12 – Adding the HUD to the viewport

The previous Visual Scripting code is pretty easy to understand, but it is important to mention that the viewport is only added to the character controlled by the client, as having multiple HUDs overlaying each other would not be desirable!

Now that everything has been properly set, you are going to test your game to see how it works!

Testing the game

To test the game, start playing it as a listen server and check that everything works fine. In particular, you should see the following behaviors:

- At the start of the game, the HUD should show 0 experience points and the character level equal to 1

- Every time a character picks a coin up, the HUD should update the total experience points

- If the target experience points are reached, the player should level up and the HUD will show the new level

The final result should be pretty similar to the one shown in *Figure 6.13*:

Figure 6.13 – The Final HUD

If everything goes according to plan, you're all set to embark on the next exciting chapter of the Lichlord multiplayer epic: client-server communication!

Summary

In this chapter, I have introduced you to one of the most important topics in the Unreal Engine multiplayer framework: replication.

As a first step, you created some statistics for the player, in order to make your gameplay more flexible. You did this through structures and data tables – a topic that will come in handy even if you are developing a standalone game.

Next, I explained the topic of property replication and how to apply it to your project. Once the main concepts were defined, you started using them on the PlayerState, in order to keep track of the character's progress during gameplay.

As a last step, you created a HUD to show this progress to the player. Replication is mostly important here as each client should get its own updates and show them to the player.

In the next chapter, you'll dive deeper into the mystical realm of replication, flexing your skills in the delicate art of calling methods from client to server and back again like it's nobody's business.

Get ready to take things to the next level – we're about to climb the staircase of multiplayer development, two steps at a time!

7

Using Remote Procedure Calls (RPCs)

Now that you have a strong grip on the world of property replication, it's time to introduce you to the way in which functions can be called across the network. In Unreal, this is achieved through **Remote Procedure Calls (RPCs)** – one of the most powerful features of the engine networking system.

In this chapter, you will learn how to execute functions through RPCs and understand how to run them on the server, on a client, or on all clients that have an instance of a particular object.

Additionally, you will learn about the common requirements for properly calling these types of functions – in particular, I will explain the difference between a reliable and an unreliable function.

Finally, you will obviously apply this newfound, precious knowledge to the project you have developed so far.

So, in the next sections, I will present the following topics:

- Understanding what an RPC is
- Executing RPCs over the network
- Implementing a door system

Technical requirements

To follow the topics presented in this chapter, you should have completed the previous ones and understood their content.

Additionally, if you would prefer to begin with code from the companion repository for this book, you can download the .zip project files provided in this book's companion project repository:

https://github.com/PacktPublishing/Multiplayer-Game-Development-with-Unreal-Engine-5

You can download the files that are up to date with the end of the last chapter by clicking the `Unreal Shadows - Chapter 06 End` link.

Understanding what an RPC is

An **RPC** is a function that can be called locally but is executed on a different machine – for instance, a server computer may call a function on a client computer that will command it to spawn a visual effect or a sound somewhere in the level. Another useful application of an RPC is the ability to send messages bi-directionally between a server and a client over a network connection.

There are three types of RPCs available in Unreal Engine:

- **Server**: The function will be called by an object on the client PC but executed only on the server version of that same object. The client must own the object calling the method (if you need to, please check *Chapter 5*, *Managing Actors in a Multiplayer Environment*, for a refresher about owning an Actor).

- **Client**: The function will be called on the server by an object but executed only on the client version that owns the object calling it.

- **NetMulticast**: The function can be called on the server by an object and executed on the server and all client versions of the object calling it. It can also be called by a client but, in this case, it will only be executed locally (i.e., on the client calling it).

In order for a function to be properly executed as an RPC, it must be called by an Actor and the Actor must be replicated. Additionally, the function needs to be decorated with the `UFUNCTION()` macro.

A function that will run just on the owning client will be declared in the `.h` file as in the following piece of code:

```
UFUNCTION(Client)
void DoSomething_Client();
```

In the corresponding `.cpp` file of the previous header, you will need to implement this function with the `_Implementation` suffix. The autogenerated code for this class – located in the `.generated.h` file – will automatically include a call to the `_Implementation` method when necessary. For a refresher on the `.generated.h` file, please check *Chapter 4*, *Setting Up Your First Multiplayer Environment*.

Looking at an example, let's say your `.h` header file has a method declaration similar to the following piece of code:

```
UFUNCTION(Server)
void DoSomething_Server();
```

You will need to implement the following function in your `.cpp` file:

```
void DoSomething_Server_Implementation()
{ /* Your code here */ }
```

A method is not always guaranteed to be received by the recipient due to performance reasons; however, this behavior can be adjusted, as demonstrated in the following subsection.

Reliability of an RPC

RPCs are unreliable by default – this means there is no guarantee that the function call will reach its destination. This is usually acceptable if the executed code is not so important, such as a visual effect spawned on a client or a random noise played near the character; if the message is not received, the effect will simply not spawn or the sound won't be heard, but gameplay will not be affected.

There are, however, some cases where you want to enforce reliability and guarantee that a message will securely arrive at its destination – as an example, in this chapter, you will execute the sprint action from the server side (you don't really want to lose that very important interaction with the player). To make sure that an RPC call is executed on the remote machine, you can utilize the `Reliable` keyword.

To illustrate this point, a function that should be executed reliably on a client will be declared with the following code:

```
UFUNCTION(Client, Reliable)
void DoSomethingReliably_Client();
```

This will guarantee that the method call will be received by the client and properly executed, without any risk of data loss over the network because of unreliability.

> **Note**
>
> Avoid using reliable RPCs during the `Tick()` event and exercise caution when binding them to player input. This is because players can repeatedly press buttons very quickly, leading to an overflow of the queue for reliable RPCs.

In addition to reliability, you may want a method to be validated in order to be executed – this is something I'm going to show you right now!

Validating RPCs

Unreal Engine offers an additional feature that adds the ability to check that functions will execute without bad data or input – this is what **validation** is all about.

To declare that a method should be validated for an RPC call, you need to add the `WithValidation` specifier to the `UFUNCTION()` declaration statement and implement an additional function that will return a `bool` type and be named as the validated function, but with the `_Validate` suffix.

As an example, a method marked with validation will have a declaration in the `.h` file, similar to the following code:

```
UFUNCTION(Server, WithValidation)
void DoSomethingWithValidation();
```

Then, in the `.cpp` file, you will need to implement two methods. The first one will be the regular function, and will look like the following code:

```
void DoSomethingWithValidation_Implementation()
{ /* Your code here */ }
```

The second one will be the actual validation function, and will look like the following code:

```
bool DoSomethingWithValidation_Validate()
{ /* Your code here */ }
```

The `_Validate` function will return `true` if the code is validated, or `false` otherwise. If validation succeeds, the corresponding method will be executed; otherwise, it won't.

In this section, I have introduced RPCs and how Unreal Engine copes with them. Bear with me – if you're working in the networked games industry, mastering RPCs is key to keeping your job and growing your career!

Now that you have a solid understanding of how an RPC should be implemented, it's time to write some code – and we are going to start by hunting down that pesky little bug that is stopping our thief hero from sprinting freely (and correctly!) around the dungeon.

Executing RPCs over the network

In this section, you'll do some practice with RPCs by fixing the issue we are experiencing with making the character sprint correctly. As you may remember, when the character is sprinting on the client, you will get "jumpy" behavior – the character seems to start running but it is immediately brought back to a walking speed.

This happens because the sprint action is being executed on the player client, but it is not being executed on the server, which is the one that is in command; hence, the override from the server slows the character to its move speed on every update. This means that you are trying to move your character at a sprint speed but, as soon as the server replicates the movement on the client, it will bring the character back to moving speed.

We don't even want the client to control this kind of important interaction – remember that it is the server who is in command – so, get back to the project and start typing some code to fix this problem!

Calling a function on the server

To make our character run, we simply have to execute the movement speed change on the server, instead of on the client. This will guarantee total control over the behavior and correct replication on all clients.

Let's start by opening the US_Character.h file and do some code declarations. In the protected section, add these two methods:

```
UFUNCTION(Server, Reliable)
void SprintStart_Server();

UFUNCTION(Server, Reliable)
void SprintEnd_Server();
```

These functions have the Server attribute, which, as explained in the previous section, will execute them on the server. We have also added the Reliable attribute because we don't want to lose this RPC due to the default unreliability of the system. The _Server suffix is not mandatory and is written just for clarity (some people use a prefix, so it is up to your personal taste!).

Now open the US_Character.cpp file and implement the two functions by adding the following code:

```
void AUS_Character::SprintStart_Server_Implementation()
{
  if (GetCharacterStats())
  {
   GetCharacterMovement()->MaxWalkSpeed = GetCharacterStats()-
>SprintSpeed;
  }
}

void AUS_Character::SprintEnd_Server_Implementation()
{
  if (GetCharacterStats())
  {
   GetCharacterMovement()->MaxWalkSpeed = GetCharacterStats()-
>WalkSpeed;
  }
}
```

The code is pretty straightforward as we are just executing the speed change inside these two new functions and, in just a moment, we are going to remove them from their previous positions (i.e., from the client calls).

Here, just notice the `_Implementation` suffix – this is mandatory as the `SprintStart_Server()` and `SprintEnd_Server()` functions will be auto-generated by Unreal in the `.generated.h` class file and will be responsible for calling the actual implementations.

We now need to change the `SprintStart()` and `SprintEnd()` functions, in order to call the corresponding server fuctions (i.e., `SprintStart_Server()` and `SprintEnd_Server()`). Find those two functions and remove all their content (i.e., the changes to `MaxWalkSpeed`) and then, in the `SprintStart()` function, add this simple line of code:

```
SprintStart_Server();
```

In the `SprintEnd()` function, add this line of code:

```
SprintEnd_Server();
```

To make the sprint action fully operational, we need to take one final step. At the moment, if the character is running and levels up, the movement will revert to walking speed. This happens because, in the `UpdateCharacterStats()` function, we set the `MaxWalkSpeed` property to the new walk speed, even if the character is sprinting.

Let's fix this by finding the `UpdateCharacterStats()` method and adding, at its very beginning, the following code:

```
auto IsSprinting = false;
if(GetCharacterStats())
{
  IsSprinting = GetCharacterMovement()->MaxWalkSpeed ==
GetCharacterStats()->SprintSpeed;
}
```

This block of code just checks whether the character is sprinting and stores the result in a local variable.

Then, find this line of code:

```
GetCharacterMovement()->MaxWalkSpeed = GetCharacterStats()->WalkSpeed;
```

Add the following command just after it:

```
if(IsSprinting)
{
  SprintStart_Server();
}
```

As easy as it is, if the character was sprinting, we would just call the corresponding method on the server to update everything properly.

We're almost done with the movement management, but there are still a few small things we need to work on. Don't worry though, we're working hard to get everything done by the end of *Chapter 10, Enhancing the Player Experience*. So sit tight and stay tuned!

In this section, you have started implementing a simple RPC in your Character class. In particular, you have sent a command from the client that owns the character to the server, in order to properly update the movement speed.

In the next section, you'll add some more fancy RPCs for your game. Specifically, you'll develop a nifty door-opening system. Get ready to flex those programming skills!

Implementing a door system

In this section, you'll repeat some of the previously explained topics about RPCs but with a small tweak – you'll be developing some Actor-to-Actor communication over the network. What's more, it will be between a C++ class – your character – and a Blueprint Class, a door that should be opened.

To accomplish this behavior, you will use a feature that you previously created in *Chapter 4, Setting Up Your First Multiplayer Environment* – the interact action. It may have slipped your mind with all the stuff you have developed so far, but fear not – it's time to dust it off and put it to work once again.

Creating the Interactable interface

To create communication between your character and the door, you'll use an **interface**. As you may already know, interfaces in C++ are a powerful tool for creating abstractions between different classes. They allow you to define a contract that all implementing classes must adhere to, thereby allowing you to create code that is more maintainable, extensible, and reusable.

In Unreal Engine, interfaces differ from traditional programming interfaces in that it is not mandatory to implement all functions. Instead, it is optional to implement them. What's more, you can declare an interface in C++ and implement it in a Blueprint – and that's exactly what you'll be doing here.

Let's start by opening your development IDE and creating a file named `US_Interactable.h`. Then, add the following code to the file:

```
#pragma once

#include "CoreMinimal.h"
#include "UObject/Interface.h"
#include "US_Interactable.generated.h"

UINTERFACE(MinimalAPI, Blueprintable)
```

```
class UUS_Interactable : public UInterface
{
 GENERATED_BODY()
};


class UNREALSHADOWS_LOTL_API IUS_Interactable
{
 GENERATED_BODY()

public:
 UFUNCTION(BlueprintCallable, BlueprintNativeEvent, Category =
"Interaction", meta=(DisplayName="Interact"))
 void Interact(class AUS_Character* CharacterInstigator);

 UFUNCTION(BlueprintCallable, BlueprintNativeEvent, Category =
"Interaction", meta=(DisplayName="Can Interact"))
 bool CanInteract( AUS_Character * CharacterInstigator) const;
};
```

You may notice something weird in the code you just added – there are two classes. In order to properly declare an Unreal Engine interface, you need to declare two classes:

- A class with a U prefix and extending UInterface: This is not the actual interface but an empty class whose sole aim is to make the class visible in the Unreal Engine system

- A class with an I prefix: This is the actual interface and will contain all the interface method definitions

As you can see, the U-prefixed class is decorated with the UINTERFACE() macro and the Blueprintable attribute will let you implement this interface from a Blueprint. Isn't it cool?

Finally, we declare a couple of functions called Interact() and CanInteract(), respectively. The two of them can be called and implemented in a Blueprint (thanks to the BlueprintCallable and BlueprintNativeEvent attributes).

Even though we will not be implementing the second function (i.e., CanInteract()) in our door Blueprint, it is nice to have such a feature – for instance, to check whether the character can open a door with a key that can be found somewhere in the dungeon. As I told you before, interfaces in Unreal Engine do not force implementation for all method declarations.

So, you have created an interface to allow the character to... well, interact with something. It's time to let the thief character perform this heroic action – something you are going to implement in the next subsection.

Implementing the interact action

You are now ready to get back to the US_Character.h header class and add some code logic for the interact action. As we have already done for the character movement, we will need to execute this interaction from the server.

To do so, open the header file and look for this declaration in the protected section:

```
void Interact(const FInputActionValue& Value);
```

Add the corresponding server call just after it:

```
UFUNCTION(Server, Reliable)
void Interact_Server();
```

As for the sprint action, this call must be Reliable as we need to make sure that it will be executed properly, and no information will be lost.

As a last step, add the following line of code to the private section:

```
UPROPERTY()
AActor* InteractableActor;
```

You will be using this property as a reference to the object that should be interacted with.

Now that the header has been properly updated, open US_Character.cpp and add the following includes at the start of the file:

```
#include "US_Interactable.h"
#include "Kismet/KismetSystemLibrary.h"
```

Then, look for the Interact() method that, up to now, has just been an empty shell. Inside the method, add the following:

```
Interact_Server();
```

This code performs a simple RPC to the corresponding server interaction implementation. As you obviously need to implement the server call, add it to your code, just after the Interact() function:

```
void AUS_Character::Interact_Server_Implementation()
{
  if(InteractableActor)
  {
    IUS_Interactable::Execute_Interact(InteractableActor, this);
  }
}
```

The call is executed only if a reference to the `InteractableActor` is found.

If you come from an OOP background and are not familiar with the way interfaces work in Unreal, this call may seem pretty weird – we are performing the call to an Actor reference without any type checking! This is the way interfaces work in Unreal Engine; they are just messages that are sent to an object reference. If the object does not implement that interface, the call will simply be lost.

Obviously, we want the call to be executed to something that can be interacted with (i.e., that implements the `US_Interactable` interface). To achieve this, we are going to continuously check whether the character is pointing at anything that implements the interface and, if something is found, we will reference it in the `InteractableActor` property.

Look for the `Tick()` method in your `.cpp` class and start adding the following piece of code:

```
if(GetLocalRole() != ROLE_Authority) return;
FHitResult HitResult;
FCollisionQueryParams QueryParams;
QueryParams.bTraceComplex = true;
QueryParams.AddIgnoredActor(this);

auto SphereRadius = 50.f;
auto StartLocation = GetActorLocation() + GetActorForwardVector() *
150.f;
auto EndLocation = StartLocation + GetActorForwardVector() * 500.f;

auto IsHit = UKismetSystemLibrary::SphereTraceSingle(
 GetWorld(),
 StartLocation,
 EndLocation,
 SphereRadius,
 UEngineTypes::ConvertToTraceType(ECC_WorldStatic),
 false,
 TArray<AActor*>(),
 EDrawDebugTrace::ForOneFrame,
 HitResult,
 true
);
```

The first thing we do here is to check whether the instance that is executing the trace has the authority to do so – this means only the server will perform the traces for all the characters, and it's obviously done to avoid cheating from the client side.

Then, we perform a regular sphere trace to check whether the character is pointing at something. If you are not familiar with an Unreal Engine **trace**, it is a tool used to detect collisions and overlapping between objects. It is used for things such as line of sight, weapon fire, and even AI pathfinding. Traces can be configured using parameters such as collision channels, object type filtering, shapes, start/end points, and so on, which allows you to specify exactly what kind of collision should be detected and how it should interact with the environment.

> **Note**
>
> For more information about the inner workings of traces in Unreal Engine, you can check the official documentation, which can be found here: https://docs.unrealengine.com/5.1/en-US/traces-with-raycasts-in-unreal-engine/.

After the trace, the result is stored in the HitResult variable, which we are going to use to check whether we have found an interactable Actor. To do so, add the next code just after the code you have just written:

```
if (IsHit && HitResult.GetActor()->GetClass()-
>ImplementsInterface(UUS_Interactable::StaticClass())))
{
  DrawDebugSphere(GetWorld(), HitResult.ImpactPoint, SphereRadius, 12,
FColor::Magenta, false, 1.f);
  InteractableActor = HitResult.GetActor();
}
else
{
  InteractableActor = nullptr;
}
```

The previous check is the core of our interaction control – if the object that has been traced implements the US_Interactable interface, we store the reference and draw a magenta-colored debug sphere for testing purposes. If nothing is found, we just clean up the InteractableActor property from any previous reference.

To check that everything works as expected, you can open Unreal Engine Editor and, after compiling, you can play the game. The server should now draw a red sphere trace for each character and turn green when hitting something. We still don't have anything to interact with, so you will not see the debug sphere.

In the next subsection, you will implement a door Blueprint that will react to the character interaction.

Creating the door Blueprint

It's now time to create something that can be interacted with, and we will do this by adding some doors to the dungeon. So, let's open the Blueprints folder and complete the following steps:

1. Create a new Blueprint Class derived from **Actor**, name it **BP_WoodenDoor**, and open it.

2. In the **Details** panel, check the **Replicates** attribute to enable replication for this Actor.

3. Add a **StaticMesh** component and assign the door mesh to the **Static Mesh** property.

4. In the **Components** panel, select the **StaticMesh** component and, in the **Details** panel, check **Component Replicates** to enable replication.

The final result should be similar to the one depicted in *Figure 7.1*:

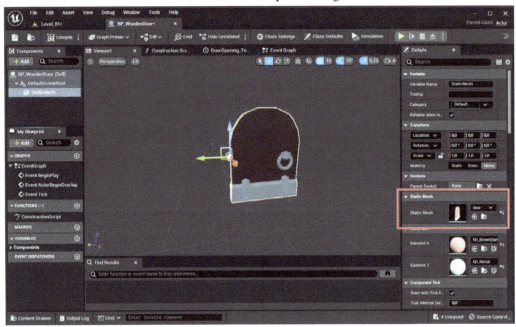

Figure 7.1 – The wooden door Blueprint

Now, open the Event Graph and do the following:

5. Create a variable of type **Boolean** and call it DoorOpen. In its **Details** panel, set the **Replication** property to **Replicated**.

6. Select the **Class Settings** tab and, in the **Interfaces** category, add the **US_Interactable** interface. This will add the **Interfaces** section into the **My Blueprint** window.

7. In the **Interfaces** section of the **My Blueprint** tab, open the **Interaction** category, right-click on the **Interact** method, and select **Implement Event**. This will add an **Event Interact** node on the Event Graph.

8. From the outgoing pin of the event, add a **Branch** node and, in the **Condition** pin, add a getter node of the **DoorOpen** variable from the **Variables** section.

9. Connect the **False** pin of the **Branch** node to a **Setter** node for the **Door Open** variable and check this last node's incoming value pin to set it to **True**.

The Event Graph created so far is shown in *Figure 7.2*:

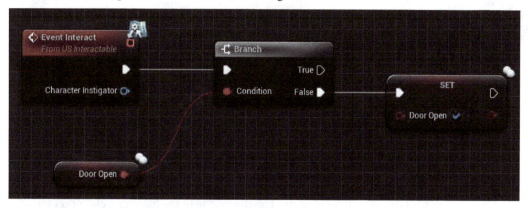

Figure 7.2 – Door check

The graph at the moment is quite simple; it's just checking whether the door has already been opened and, if it is closed, marks it as open. You are going to complete the Blueprint by making the door mesh rotate in an opening animation.

10. Connect the outgoing pin of the **Set Door Open** node to a **Timeline** node. Call this node **DoorOpening** and double-click on it to open its corresponding graph.

11. Add a **Float Track** and call it **RotationZ**. Add two keys to the track with the values **(0, 0)** and **(1, -90)** respectively.

The timeline window is shown in *Figure 7.3*:

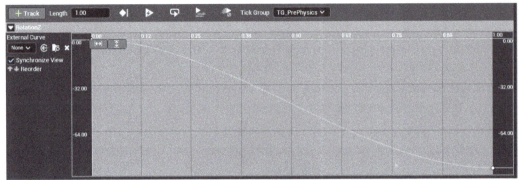

Figure 7.3 – The door timeline window

12. Return to the main Event Graph and drag a reference of the **StaticMesh** component from the **Components** panel into the graph itself.

13. Connect the outgoing pin of this reference to a **Set Relative Rotation** node.

14. Right-click on the **New Rotation** pin and select **Split Struct Pin** to expose the **New Rotation Z** value.

15. Connect the **Update** execution pin of the **Timeline** node to the incoming execution pin of the **Set Relative Rotation** node. Connect the **Rotation Z** pin with the **New Rotation Z** to complete the graph.

This final part of the graph is depicted in *Figure 7.3*:

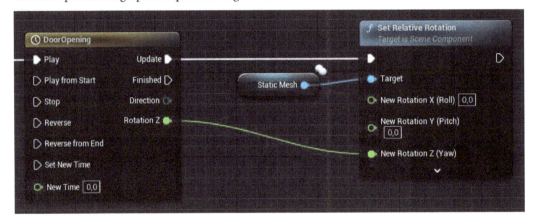

Figure 7.4 – The second part of the graph

This part of the graph will just start a rotation animation on the *z* axis of the mesh, making it open when interacted with.

Let's now give the thief hero a moment to shine and roam the dungeon, eagerly opening doors to seek out prisoners to liberate and treasures to unearth!

Testing the interact action

Open your game level and drag an instance or two of the door Blueprint to start testing the game. Whenever the server-controlled sphere trace hits a door, you should be able to see a magenta-colored sphere, indicating that the object can be interacted with. Hitting the *I* key on the client will open the door and show the hidden treasures (or perils!) behind.

The final result of the interaction check, along with the debug sphere, is displayed in *Figure 7.4*:

Figure 7.5 – The interaction check in action

So, the door system has finally been created and you are now free to put as many doors as you want inside the dungeon. As an additional exercise, you can create a Blueprint child class from **BP_WoodenDoor** and use the **door_gate** mesh to add some kind of variation to your level.

In this final section, you have implemented a Blueprint that allows the character to interact with other Actors in the game. Specifically, you have created a door system that can be opened through player interaction and will be synchronized over the network. This means that every connected player will see the correct updates.

Summary

In this chapter, you were introduced to one of the most important and useful features of the Unreal Engine multiplayer environment, remote procedure calls, or RPCs. As you have seen, they allow you to execute functions from a server to a client and vice versa.

In this chapter, you called requests from the client to the server, by improving the character sprint system and by adding interaction logic between the character and other Actors in the game (i.e., the dungeon doors). Rest assured that, by the end of the book, you will also have seen other use cases for RPCs as they are quite ubiquitous in multiplayer games.

This chapter ends the second part of this book – starting from the next chapter, you'll be working on implementing some AI logic over the network. Let's spice things up by rounding up those pesky Lichlord minions and giving our character a challenge to step up to!

Part 3:
Improving Your Game

In this part of the book, you will discover how to enhance your game's appeal to players. This process begins with the creation of captivating opponents. Afterward, you will augment the capabilities of the player characters and add some non-player characters to interact with. Additionally, you will learn how to troubleshoot and debug networked systems within Unreal Engine.

This part includes the following chapters:

- *Chapter 8, Introducing AI into a Multiplayer Environment*
- *Chapter 9, Extending AI Behaviors*
- *Chapter 10, Enhancing the Player Experience*
- *Chapter 11, Debugging a Multiplayer Game*

8

Introducing AI into a Multiplayer Environment

Artificial Intelligence (**AI**) systems offer an exciting and unique gaming experience for players by providing dynamic challenges that are unpredictable and engaging. This allows developers to create immersive worlds with realistic behavior from **non-player characters** (**NPCs**).

In this chapter, I will introduce you to the basics of AI in Unreal Engine but, as this is a book about multiplayer games, I will not go deep into the details of the system – instead, you will take the first steps in the creation of opponents, which will make your game fully playable from a networked point of view.

By the end of the chapter, you will have created an enemy Actor that wanders around the level and actively pursues the player's character once it is detected. This will serve as a starting point for creating more diverse and compelling enemies in your game.

So, in this chapter, I will present you with the following topics:

- Setting up the AI system

- Creating an AI opponent

- Adding opponents to the level

Technical requirements

To follow the topics presented in this chapter, you should have completed the previous ones and understood their content.

Additionally, if you would prefer to begin with code from the companion repository for this book, you can download the .zip project files provided in this book's accompanying project repository:

https://github.com/PacktPublishing/Multiplayer-Game-Development-with-Unreal-Engine-5

You can download the files that are up to date with the end of the last chapter by clicking the `Unreal Shadows - Chapter 07 End` link.

Setting up the AI system

Crafting an AI opponent in Unreal Engine can be quite a hard task. Luckily, this book is focused on boosting your multiplayer prowess, rather than getting bogged down in all the details of AI, so I will not go deep into the Unreal Engine AI system. However, if you want to make your game enjoyable, it definitely helps to have some know-how on creating a worthy AI opponent.

In order to make the AI character move around the level, you will need to define which areas are allowed and which are not (as an example, you will most definitely need to give the character a safe place that the opponents won't dare to step into). Once we've done that, in the next steps, we will create these areas so that the AI system can manage the minions' walking paths. Once we've done that, we'll be well on our way to creating awesome, mindless, walking undead.

To make everything work properly, first of all, we need to give our minion opponents something to walk on. As you may already know, Unreal Engine uses a **Navigation System** to let AI Actors navigate a level using pathfinding algorithms.

The Navigation System takes the collision geometry in your level and generates a **Navigation Mesh**, which is then split into portions (i.e., polygon geometries) that are used to create a graph. This graph is what **agents** (such as AI characters) use to navigate to their destination. Each portion is given a cost, which agents then use to calculate the most efficient path (the one with the lowest overall cost). It's like a smart GPS for your game characters!

> **Note**
>
> If you want more information about the Unreal Engine Navigation System and its inner workings, you can visit the official Epic Games documentation at this link: `https://docs.unrealengine.com/5.1/en-US/navigation-system-in-unreal-engine/`.

To add a Navigation Mesh to the level, you will need to take the following steps:

1. Open the game level you've been working on so far and, from the **Quickly add to the project** button, select **NavMeshBoundsVolume**. This will add the **NavMeshBoundsVolume** component to the level and a **RecastNavMesh** Actor.

2. In the **Outliner**, select **NavMeshBoundsVolume** and, with the **Scale** tool enabled, resize it so that it covers your desired portion of the level – avoid the spawn region for your player characters, as you want to give them a safe place to rest or escape to if needed.

3. Hit the *P* key on your keyboard to show the newly created Navigation Mesh, which should look similar to the one depicted in *Figure 8.1*:

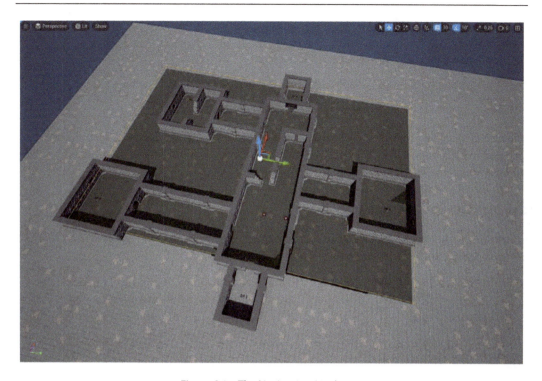

Figure 8.1 – The Navigation Mesh area

The green-colored area (i.e., the Navigation Mesh) represents the places where the AI character can walk. You will notice that walls and doors will create "holes" in this mesh, so the AI will be forbidden to step into it. Don't worry about the portions outside of your dungeon – there are no open doors to connect them, so the minions won't be able to reach them.

In this section, you were briefly introduced to the Unreal Engine Navigation System and you have set up a navigable area for the soon-to-be-created AI opponents. As I see you're eager to start coding, let's fire up your programming IDE and start writing some code together! It's time to summon some undead minions and let them walk around the dungeon.

Creating an AI opponent

In this section, you'll start by creating a class for your hero's foes, complete with the basic ability to patrol and attack. Sure, they might not be the sharpest guys around, but hey, they're the Lichlord's undead minions – not exactly known for their intelligence, are they?

We'll be starting by extending the Character class, which, as you may already know, can be controlled by an `AIController`, allowing independent actions during gameplay.

At this point, we want the minion to have the following features:

- A random patrolling movement around the level

- A perception system that will allow it to see and hear the player's character

- The ability to seek out the player once it has been detected

In the next chapters, we'll extend the Character class further by adding some more features such as health and spawnable goodies (when the AI has been defeated) but for now, we'll just focus on the movement and perception system.

Adding the navigation module

The first thing to do in order to have an agent that can navigate through a Navigation Mesh is to add the corresponding module to your project.

To do this, get back to your programming IDE and open your project build file – the one named UnrealShadows_LOTL.Build.cs (or similar, if you opted for a different project name). Locate the following line of code:

```
PublicDependencyModuleNames.AddRange(new string[] { "Core",
"CoreUObject", "Engine", "InputCore", "EnhancedInput" });
```

Change it by adding the NavigationSystem declaration, like this:

```
PublicDependencyModuleNames.AddRange(new string[] { "Core",
"CoreUObject", "Engine", "InputCore", "EnhancedInput",
"NavigationSystem" });
```

With the project settings updated, we can start working on the minion AI, by creating a dedicated class.

Creating the minion class

It's time to create the AI minion class, so create a new class derived from Character and name it US_Minion. Once the class has been created, open the US_Minion.h header file and, in the private section, add the following code:

```
UPROPERTY(VisibleAnywhere, BlueprintReadOnly, Category = "Minion
Perception", meta = (AllowPrivateAccess = "true"))
TObjectPtr<class UPawnSensingComponent> PawnSense;

UPROPERTY(VisibleAnywhere, BlueprintReadOnly, Category = "Minion
Perception", meta = (AllowPrivateAccess = "true"))
TObjectPtr<class USphereComponent> Collision;
```

```
UPROPERTY()
FVector PatrolLocation;
```

The `Collision` property will be used as a trigger for the AI to grab the character, while `PatrolLocation` will be used to tell the AI where to go if not chasing the character.

The `PawnSense` property is the declaration for `PawnSensingComponent`, a component that can be used by the AI character to see and hear pawns around the level (i.e., the player characters). This component is quite straightforward to use and is easily configurable, letting you make the opponent more or less "dumb" during gameplay. You'll get mere info on this in a minute or two when you'll be initializing it.

Now it's time to add some properties to the `public` section. Just add the following code:

```
UPROPERTY(EditDefaultsOnly, BlueprintReadOnly, Category="Minion AI")
float PatrolSpeed = 150.0f;

UPROPERTY(EditDefaultsOnly, BlueprintReadOnly, Category="Minion AI")
float ChaseSpeed = 350.0f;

UPROPERTY(EditDefaultsOnly, BlueprintReadOnly, Category="Minion AI")
float PatrolRadius = 50000.0f;
```

We have defined two movement speed properties: `PatrolSpeed` will be used when the minion is walking around aimlessly, while `ChaseSpeed` will be used whenever the minion is seeking the character, in order to make it a new pawn for the Lichlord's army! The `PatrolRadius` property will be used to find a new location in the level for the minion to inspect.

After the properties, you will be declaring the public methods needed for the correct behavior of the AI opponent. Still in the `public` section, add this block of code to declare them:

```
UFUNCTION(BlueprintCallable, Category="Minion AI")
void SetNextPatrolLocation();

UFUNCTION(BlueprintCallable, Category="Minion AI")
void Chase(APawn* Pawn);

virtual void PostInitializeComponents() override;

FORCEINLINE UPawnSensingComponent* GetPawnSense() const { return
PawnSense; }

FORCEINLINE USphereComponent* GetCollision() const { return Collision;
}
```

The `SetNextPatrolLocation()` and `Chase()` methods will be used to let the AI character move around the scene, looking for a new spot or seeking the player character. The `PostInitializeComponent()` override will be used to register the character events. Lastly, we are declaring the usual getters for the character components that have been added.

The last step in the header declaration is to add the event handlers for this character:

```
UFUNCTION()
void OnPawnDetected(APawn* Pawn);

UFUNCTION()
void OnBeginOverlap(AActor* OverlappedActor, AActor* OtherActor);
```

The first one will manage the minion logic once it has detected a pawn with its senses, while the second one will be used to check whether a player character has been captured.

The header has finally been declared – please note that, at the moment, we are not taking into consideration the hearing capabilities of the minion; this is something we are going to implement in the next chapter when our thief hero starts to make some noise!

Implementing the minions' behaviors

You've declared all your functions and properties, so now it's time to put them to good use by implementing some behaviors for your AI minions. Let's make sure everything is running smoothly and get this project rolling!

Open the `US_Minion.cpp` file and add the following `include` statements at the top:

```
#include "AIController.h"
#include "NavigationSystem.h"
#include "US_Character.h"
#include "Components/CapsuleComponent.h"
#include "GameFramework/CharacterMovementComponent.h"
#include "Perception/PawnSensingComponent.h"
#include "Blueprint/AIBlueprintHelperLibrary.h"
#include "Components/SphereComponent.h"
```

As usual, these lines of code will declare the classes we will use from now on. After you have done that, it's time to implement the constructor by adding the needed components and initializing all the properties.

Declaring the constructor

Once the `include` statements have been properly declared, you can start by locating the AUS_ Minion() constructor and inserting the character initialization. Inside the brackets, just after the PrimaryActorTick.bCanEverTick declaration, add the following code:

```
bUseControllerRotationPitch = false;
bUseControllerRotationYaw = false;
bUseControllerRotationRoll = false;

AutoPossessAI = EAutoPossessAI::PlacedInWorldOrSpawned;
AIControllerClass = AAIController::StaticClass();

PawnSense =
CreateDefaultSubobject<UPawnSensingComponent>(TEXT("PawnSense"));
PawnSense->SensingInterval = .8f;
PawnSense->SetPeripheralVisionAngle(45.f);
PawnSense->SightRadius = 1500.f;
PawnSense->HearingThreshold = 400.f;
PawnSense->LOSHearingThreshold = 800.f;

Collision =
CreateDefaultSubobject<USphereComponent>(TEXT("Collision"));
Collision->SetSphereRadius(100);
Collision->SetupAttachment(RootComponent);

GetCapsuleComponent()->InitCapsuleSize(60.f, 96.0f);
GetCapsuleComponent()->SetGenerateOverlapEvents(true);

GetMesh()->SetRelativeLocation(FVector(0.f, 0.f, -91.f));
static ConstructorHelpers::FObjectFinder<USkeletalMesh>
SkeletalMeshAsset(TEXT("/Game/KayKit/Skeletons/skeleton_minion"));
if (SkeletalMeshAsset.Succeeded())
{
  GetMesh()->SetSkeletalMesh(SkeletalMeshAsset.Object);
}

GetCharacterMovement()->bOrientRotationToMovement = true;
GetCharacterMovement()->RotationRate = FRotator(0.0f, 500.0f, 0.0f);
GetCharacterMovement()->MaxWalkSpeed = 200.f;
GetCharacterMovement()->MinAnalogWalkSpeed = 20.f;
GetCharacterMovement()->BrakingDecelerationWalking = 2000.f;
```

You'll already be familiar with most of the code from the thief character creation, but you will see some noticeable additions. First of all, we are setting the `AutoPossessAI` property, which lets us define whether the game system will possess the AI character once in the level – we want it to be both in full control when it is spawned at runtime and when it is already in the level when the game starts, so we have opted for a value of `PlacedInWorldOrSpawned`.

Then, we define which controller will be used for the AI system by setting the `AIControllerClass` property; in this case, we are just using the base `AAIController` class, but you can obviously implement your own with additional features.

The last notable thing is the `PawnSense` component creation – as you can see, we are initializing the properties that will make the minion see and hear at a certain distance. You should take note of the `SensingInterval` initialization, which will let us tweak how much time will pass between two sense perceptions. This will make the difference between a very reactive character (i.e., a lower value) or a really dumb one (i.e., a higher one).

Initializing the minion

It's now time to initialize the character when it is added to the game. As you already know, this is usually done from the `BeginPlay()` method. So, just after the `Super::BeginPlay()` declaration, add the following:

```
SetNextPatrolLocation();
```

This call will simply start the patrolling behavior. Then, add the `PostInitializeComponents()` implementation by adding this code to the file:

```
void AUS_Minion::PostInitializeComponents()
{
  Super::PostInitializeComponents();

  if(GetLocalRole() != ROLE_Authority) return;

  OnActorBeginOverlap.AddDynamic(this, &AUS_Minion::OnBeginOverlap);
  GetPawnSense()->OnSeePawn.AddDynamic(this, &AUS_
Minion::OnPawnDetected);
}
```

As you can see, we are using two delegates to react to an Actor overlap, for checking whether we have reached the player character, and to handle the pawn perception to check whether we can see the player character. Also, notice that they are initialized only if the role of this object is authoritative (i.e., the method is being executed on the server).

The next step is to implement these two delegate functions in order to manage the aforementioned events.

Handling the delegate functions

Whenever the minion detects a pawn, it will immediately check whether it is a character and, if the result is successful, it will start chasing it. Let's add the method to handle the delegate in the source file:

```
void AUS_Minion::OnPawnDetected(APawn* Pawn)
{
  if (!Pawn->IsA<AUS_Character>()) return;

  GEngine->AddOnScreenDebugMessage(-1, 5.f, FColor::Red,
TEXT("Character detected!"));

  if (GetCharacterMovement()->MaxWalkSpeed != ChaseSpeed)
  {
    Chase(Pawn);
  }
}
```

The code here is quite straightforward – we just have added a debug message stating that a character has been detected.

The second delegate we need to handle is the overlap, so add the following method implementation:

```
void AUS_Minion::OnBeginOverlap(AActor* OverlappedActor, AActor*
OtherActor)
{
  if (!OtherActor->IsA<AUS_Character>()) return;

  GEngine->AddOnScreenDebugMessage(-1, 5.f, FColor::Yellow,
TEXT("Character captured!"));
}
```

As you can see, we check again whether we have found a character, and after that, we simply display a debug message – it looks like our hero got a little too close to the minions and now they've roped them into joining the Lichlord's undead army! Later on, you'll implement a respawn system to let the player restart the game with a brand-new character.

The next step will be the actual AI's movement through the Navigation Mesh, both for the patrol and chase behaviors.

Implementing the chase and patrol behaviors

It's now time to start implementing the movement control for your AI character – specifically, you'll be implementing the `SetNextPatrolLocation()` function, which will find a new reachable point for the minion, and the `Chase()` function, which will send the minion on a "seek and destroy" mission toward the character. To do so, add the following code to the file:

```
void AUS_Minion::SetNextPatrolLocation()
{
  if(GetLocalRole() != ROLE_Authority) return;

  GetCharacterMovement()->MaxWalkSpeed = PatrolSpeed;

  const auto LocationFound = UNavigationSystemV1::K2_
GetRandomReachablePointInRadius(
      this, GetActorLocation(), PatrolLocation, PatrolRadius);
  if(LocationFound)
  {
    UAIBlueprintHelperLibrary::SimpleMoveToLocation(GetController(),
PatrolLocation);
  }
}

void AUS_Minion::Chase(APawn* Pawn)
{
  if(GetLocalRole() != ROLE_Authority) return;

  GetCharacterMovement()->MaxWalkSpeed = ChaseSpeed;
  UAIBlueprintHelperLibrary::SimpleMoveToActor(GetController(), Pawn);

  DrawDebugSphere(GetWorld(), Pawn->GetActorLocation(), 25.f, 12,
FColor::Red, true, 10.f, 0, 2.f);
}
```

The first function sets the character speed to the patrolling value and uses the `UNavigationSystemV1::K2_GetRandomReachablePointInRadius()` method to find a reachable point in the Navigation Mesh. Then, the AI is simply commanded to reach that location.

The second function does something similar, but the target point will be the character – after all, it is on a mission from the Lichlord to get as many soon-to-be undead heroes as possible!

Implementing the Tick() event

The last thing you need to implement in order to make the patrolling system fully operational is to check whether the AI character has reached its destination; in this case, it will just have to find another point in the Navigation Mesh. As we need to continuously check the distance between the AI and the target point, the best place to write the code is within the `Tick()` event. Let's find the method and, just after the `Super::Tick(DeltaTime)` call, add this piece of code:

```
if(GetLocalRole() != ROLE_Authority) return;

if(GetMovementComponent()->GetMaxSpeed() == ChaseSpeed) return;

if((GetActorLocation() - PatrolLocation).Size() < 500.f)
{
  SetNextPatrolLocation();
}
```

As you can see, the first line checks whether the character is patrolling (i.e., the maximum speed should not equal the chase speed). Then, we are checking that we are near enough (about half a meter) to the patrol location in order to look for another reachable point.

Testing the AI opponent

Now that the enemy AI has been created, you can test it out in the game level. To do this, open the Unreal Engine Editor and, from the Content Browser, drag an instance of the `US_Minion` class (located in the `C++ Classes | UnrealShadows_LOTL` folder) into the level. You should see something similar to *Figure 8.2*:

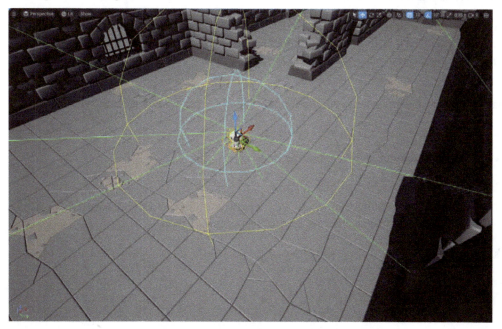

Figure 8.2 – The AI opponent in the level

The gizmos around the character represent the `PawnSense` component – its sight and hearing capabilities. The sight area is represented by a green cone that shows how wide and far the AI can see. The hearing sense is represented by two spheres – a yellow one that shows how far the AI will hear a noise if it is not obstructed by any obstacle, and a cyan one that shows how far the AI will sense noise, even if generated behind an obstacle, such as a wall.

Go into play mode and the opponent should start wandering around the level and over the Navigation Mesh. Whenever a player character enters the minion's line of sight (i.e., the green cone), the enemy will react and start chasing the player at a higher speed.

Once the character has been reached, you will notice that the minion will stop moving – its mission has been completed and it can rest!

As an extra exercise, you may want to add a timer that will check whether the AI is staying still for too long; in that case, it will restart its patrolling system by looking for a new reachable location.

So, in this section, you have created your AI opponent, ready to roam around the dungeon, seeking its next victim. You have created a simple but effective patrolling system and added a perception sense to the AI so that it can intercept the player when they are not stealthy enough.

In the next section, you'll create a spawning system in order to add minions as the game progresses and make things more challenging for the players.

Adding opponents to the level

Now that you have an opponent for your thief hero, it is time to let the system spawn a bunch of them at runtime. You'll be doing this by implementing a spawn system similar to the one used in *Chapter 3, Testing the Multiplayer System with a Project Prototype* – this time, you'll create the spawner in C++ instead.

What we want to implement here is an Actor that will have the following features:

- Spawns a few minions at the start of the game.
- Spawns new minions at predefined intervals.
- Spawns the minions in a selected area.
- Randomly selects a minion type every time it spawns. At the moment, we have just one minion type, but in the following chapters, we will add more variations.

Let's get started.

Creating a spawner class

Start by creating a C++ class that extends from Actor and name it `US_MinionSpawner`. Once created, open the `.h` file and, in the `private` section, add the following declarations:

```
UPROPERTY(VisibleAnywhere, BlueprintReadOnly, Category = "Spawn
System", meta = (AllowPrivateAccess = "true"))
TObjectPtr<class UBoxComponent> SpawnArea;

UPROPERTY()
FTimerHandle SpawnTimerHandle;
```

You should be already familiar with the first declaration from *Chapter 3, Testing the Multiplayer System with a Project Prototype* – we are declaring an area that will be used to randomize the spawned minion location. The second declaration will be used to store a reference of the timer handler used by the spawner to generate new minions at predefined intervals.

Now we are going to declare some properties that will make this class customizable in the level. In the `public` section, add the following property declarations:

```
UPROPERTY(EditAnywhere, BlueprintReadOnly, Category="Spawn System")
TArray<TSubclassOf<class AUS_Minion>> SpawnableMinions;

UPROPERTY(EditAnywhere, BlueprintReadOnly, Category="Spawn System")
float SpawnDelay = 10.0f;

UPROPERTY(EditAnywhere, BlueprintReadOnly, Category="Spawn System")
int32 NumMinionsAtStart = 5;
```

The first property will expose an array that will contain all the spawnable minion types. As stated before, at the moment, we have just one type, but we will add some more later on. The other two properties are self-explanatory, letting us define the spawn timing and how many minions should already be in the level when the game starts.

The last step is to add a `Spawn()` method in the protected section of the header:

```
UFUNCTION()
void Spawn();
```

The header is now finished. Now, let's switch to the `.cpp` and implement some code logic.

Implementing the spawner logic

It's time to implement the spawner features. To do so, open the .cpp file, find the constructor, and add the required includes at the top of the file:

```
#include "US_Minion.h"
#include "Components/BoxComponent.h"
```

Then, add the following piece of code:

```
SpawnArea = CreateDefaultSubobject<UBoxComponent>(TEXT("Spawn Area"));
SpawnArea->SetupAttachment(RootComponent);
SpawnArea->SetBoxExtent(FVector(1000.0f, 1000.0f, 100.0f));
```

You are already well versed in creating components, so let's dive right into the BeginPlay() method and add this code just after the Super::BeginPlay() declaration:

```
if (SpawnableMinions.IsEmpty()) return;
if (GetLocalRole() != ROLE_Authority) return;

for (int32 i = 0; i < NumMinionsAtStart; i++)
{
  Spawn();
}

GetWorldTimerManager().SetTimer(SpawnTimerHandle, this, &AUS_
MinionSpawner::Spawn, SpawnDelay, true, SpawnDelay);
```

First of all, we are checking that there is at least one spawnable minion type – if the array is empty, there is no need to go on with the code. Then, we check that the Actor has the authority to spawn something; as usual, we want the server to be in full control of what's happening.

After that, we call the Spawn() function in a loop, in order to create a starting pool of enemies. The last step is to create a timer, which will call the Spawn() function at an interval defined by the SpawnDelay value.

The last thing to do to have the spawner fully functional is to add the Spawn() function implementation. Let's add it at the end of the file:

```
void AUS_MinionSpawner::Spawn()
{
  FActorSpawnParameters SpawnParams;
  SpawnParams.SpawnCollisionHandlingOverride =
  ESpawnActorCollisionHandlingMethod::AdjustIfPossibleButDont
SpawnIfColliding;
```

```
auto Minion =
  SpawnableMinions[FMath::RandRange(0, SpawnableMinions.Num() - 1)];

const auto Rotation =
  FRotator(0.0f, FMath::RandRange(0.0f, 360.0f), 0.0f);
const auto Location =
  SpawnArea->GetComponentLocation() +
    FVector(
      FMath::RandRange(-SpawnArea->GetScaledBoxExtent().X, SpawnArea-
>GetScaledBoxExtent().X),
      FMath::RandRange(-SpawnArea->GetScaledBoxExtent().Y, SpawnArea-
>GetScaledBoxExtent().Y),
      0.0f);

GetWorld()->SpawnActor<AUS_Minion>(Minion, Location, Rotation,
SpawnParams);
}
```

As long as it may seem, this code is quite straightforward, and you have already done something similar at the start of this book (do you remember the falling fruits?). We are just taking a random minion type from the array, retrieving a random location in the spawn area, and then we are going to spawn the minion at that location. The only thing worth mentioning is SpawnCollisionHandlingOverride, which is set to spawn the Actor, avoiding any collision with other objects in the level.

As an extra exercise, you may add a limit to the number of minions that will be spawned from a single spawner object. This will avoid overcrowding your level and making the game unplayable for your players!

The spawn Actor is ready, so it is time to compile your project and do some proper testing.

Testing the spawner

It is now time to venture into the glories of the Unreal Engine Editor and summon those mischievous minions to frolic throughout the level! Locate the US_MinionSpawner class (found inside the C++ Classes | UnrealShadows_LOTL folder) and drag it into your level to create an instance of it.

Next, position the Actor in a suitable place and resize the **Box Extent** parameters to set a nice size for the minions to be located within. In my case, I opted to place the spawner in the room labeled **SP3** with the **Box Extent** property set to **(900, 400, 100)**, as you can see in *Figure 8.3*:

Figure 8.3 – The spawn area

Then, with the Actor still selected, do the following:

1. Locate the **Spawn System** category in the **Details** panel.

2. Add an element to the **Spawnable Minions** array, which will be labeled as **Index[0]**. From the corresponding drop-down menu, select **US_Minion**.

3. Tweak **Spawn Delay** and **Num Minions at Start** to suit your needs; in my case, I have left the default values, as you can see in *Figure 8.4*:

Figure 8.4 – The spawn settings

You obviously have the freedom to add as many spawner Actors as you feel necessary to balance your game level.

Once you enter the realm of play mode, lo and behold, the undead minions shall materialize before your very eyes, their replication and synchronization across all clients being a testament to the mystical powers of the Lichlord! Well, actually, it's a testament to the power of the Unreal Engine replication system, but you don't want to let your players in on the secret. Keep them in the dark and let them marvel at the seamless magic of your game's performance.

Figure 8.5 displays how the spawner looks in action whenever you test it, but more simply and less poetically:

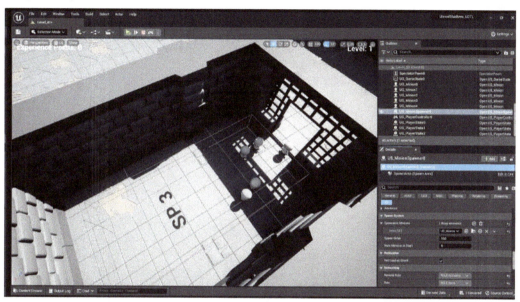

Figure 8.5 – The spawner in action

In this section, you created a fully customizable spawn system that can be used and tweaked for any level in your game. It's time to wrap things up and move on to the next chapter of this adventure-packed multiplayer game.

Summary

In this chapter, you were introduced to the basics of AI in a multiplayer game. First of all, you were given some information on how to create a Navigation System that will let your AI move independently around the level. After that, you created a base minion, which will patrol around seeking the player characters, changing its behavior to a more aggressive stance once it finds them. As a last step, you added spawn points around the dungeon in order to populate the area with worthy opponents.

The most important thing to take away from this chapter is that, with your previously acquired knowledge, everything is correctly synchronized over the network. I promised you that learning things from the start would be a huge advantage in the future! And trust me, putting in the effort and really grasping the basics is now paying off with your project!

In the next chapter, we'll keep on exploring some of the possibilities of implementing worthy opponents for your hero – we will give it a sense of hearing and a health system in order to make it more engaging and, at the very least, defeatable.

9
Extending AI Behaviors

Enhancing an enemy character's behavior in a multiplayer game is a great way of making it more challenging and exciting for players. It can also help create a more immersive experience, as enemies become smarter, faster, and stronger. By introducing new abilities or changing existing ones, you can make your game stand out from other similar titles on the market.

In this chapter, you will learn how to add improvements to your minion's AI behavior – this will involve creating some sort of communication between your hero character's stealth abilities and the undead minion sensing system. Additionally, you will learn how to make your opponents communicate and cooperate with each other, in order to give your thief a hard time.

You will also implement a health system for the AI opponents, make your character attack, and impart some damage on them. Finally, you will create some variations for the minions in order to make them less predictable and more engaging.

By the end of this chapter, you will have improved your understanding of managing AI Actors in a multiplayer game. Additionally, you will have a strong understanding of how to ensure effective communication within a networked environment.

In this chapter, I will guide you through the following sections:

- Making AI opponents more challenging
- Implementing an alert system
- Adding health to the AI
- Adding a weapon system to a character
- Creating AI variations

Technical requirements

To follow the topics presented in this chapter, you should have completed the previous ones and understood their content.

Additionally, if you would prefer to begin with code from the companion repository for this book, you can download the `.zip` project files provided at this book's companion project repository: `https://github.com/PacktPublishing/Multiplayer-Game-Development-with-Unreal-Engine-5`.

You can download the files that are up to date with the end of the last chapter by clicking the `Unreal Shadows – Chapter 08 End` link.

Making AI opponents more challenging

So far, your undead lackey is equipped with a (more or less) keen sense of vision, allowing it to peer into the abyss of the dungeon, scouting for unsuspecting prey. However, even the sneakiest of thieves can unexpectedly bump into a hindrance while tip-toeing through the shadows. The cunning Lichlord knows this all too well and has bestowed upon his minions the added gift of acute hearing, so not even a pin drop goes unnoticed!

In this section, you will implement a noise system based on player character movement. The game logic you will be adding is based on the following requisites:

- The thief character will make a noise when sprinting
- The noise level will be based on the character statistics
- The AI minions will react when they hear a noise

So, open your IDE, as it's time to add a new component feature to your hero!

Making some noise

In order to let your thief character make noise while it's sprinting, you will add a new component – a **pawn noise emitter**. This component will not spawn an actual sound or noise, but it will emit a signal that can be intercepted by the pawn-sensing component you have attached to the minion character.

In order to declare this component, open the `US_Character.h` header file, and in the `private` section, add the following code:

```
UPROPERTY(VisibleAnywhere, BlueprintReadOnly, Category = "Stealth",
meta = (AllowPrivateAccess = "true"))
TObjectPtr<UPawnNoiseEmitterComponent> NoiseEmitter;
```

Now that the component has been declared, it's time to initialize it. Open the `US_Character.cpp` file and add the necessary `include` declaration at the top of the file:

```
#include "Components/PawnNoiseEmitterComponent.h"
```

Then, find the constructor, and just after the `FollowCamera` initialization, add these two lines:

```
NoiseEmitter = CreateDefaultSubobject<UPawnNoiseEmitterComponent>
(TEXT("NoiseEmitter"));
NoiseEmitter->NoiseLifetime = 0.01f;
```

After the component creation, we just initialize its lifetime to a really low value (i.e., 0.01) – this value indicates the time that should pass before the new noise emission overwrites the previous one. As we use the `Tick()` event to emit the noise, and this event is executed every frame, we don't need a high value.

Now, look for the `Tick()` function, and just before its closing bracket, add the following code:

```
if (GetCharacterMovement()->MaxWalkSpeed == GetCharacterStats()-
>SprintSpeed)
{
  auto Noise = 1.f;
  if(GetCharacterStats() && GetCharacterStats()->StealthMultiplier)
  {
    Noise = Noise / GetCharacterStats()->StealthMultiplier;
  }
  NoiseEmitter->MakeNoise(this, Noise, GetActorLocation());
}
```

In the previous code, we verify whether the character is sprinting and proceed further only if the result is affirmative. We then compute the noise, based on a unity value divided by the `StealthMultiplier` character. As you will remember from *Chapter 6, Replicating Properties Over the Network*, this value is declared inside the character statistics data table, and it grows as the character levels up. This means the higher the multiplier, the lower the noise made by the character. After the noise has been evaluated, it is emitted by the `NoiseEmitter` component by using the `MakeNoise()` method.

Now that our character has picked up the skill of making noise while sprinting, it's time we equip our undead minions with some sharp-eared talents and set them to action!

Enabling the hearing sense

The minion character already has the ability to hear noise through the pawn-sensing component, but at the moment, this ability is not used. You'll need to open the `US_Minion.h` header file and add the following declaration to the `protected` section:

```
UFUNCTION()
void OnHearNoise(APawn* PawnInstigator, const FVector& Location, float
Volume);
```

As you can see, this is a simple callback declaration that will be used to handle the hearing of any noise.

Next, add the following method declaration to the `public` section:

```
UFUNCTION(BlueprintCallable, Category="Minion AI")
void GoToLocation(const FVector& Location);
```

This is a simple utility function that we will use to send the minion to the origin of the noise.

Now, open the `US_Minion.cpp` file and look for the `PostInitializeComponents()` implementation. Just before the closing bracket, add the delegate binding for the hearing event:

```
GetPawnSense()->OnHearNoise.AddDynamic(this, &AUS_
Minion::OnHearNoise);
```

Now, implement the `OnHearNoise()` function by adding the following code:

```
void AUS_Minion::OnHearNoise(APawn* PawnInstigator, const FVector&
Location, float Volume)
{
  GEngine->AddOnScreenDebugMessage(-1, 5.f, FColor::Green, TEXT("Noise
detected!"));
  GoToLocation(Location);
  UAIBlueprintHelperLibrary::SimpleMoveToLocation(GetController(),
PatrolLocation);
}
```

Once a noise has been detected, we send the minion to the location where it was generated. As you can see, we don't check whether the noise instigator is our thief character – the Lichlord has commanded his minions to meticulously investigate any and all audible disturbances, leaving no corner unexplored!

Finally, add the implementation for the `GoToLocation()` function:

```
void AUS_Minion::GoToLocation(const FVector& Location)
{
  PatrolLocation = Location;
  UAIBlueprintHelperLibrary::SimpleMoveToLocation(GetController(),
PatrolLocation);
}
```

Here, we just set `PatrolLocation` and send the minion there (it's nothing fancy but extremely useful, as you will see later in the chapter).

The minion is now ready, so compile your project and start some testing.

Testing the hearing sense

To test the brand-new hearing sense feature, start a game session and walk around the minions, paying attention to not enter their sight cone of vision. The minions won't notice the character unless it starts sprinting. At that moment, you should get a debug message, and the minion will start chasing the thief. *Figure 9.1* shows a scenario where the character has carelessly run behind a couple of skeleton minions and has subsequently been detected by their hearing sense.

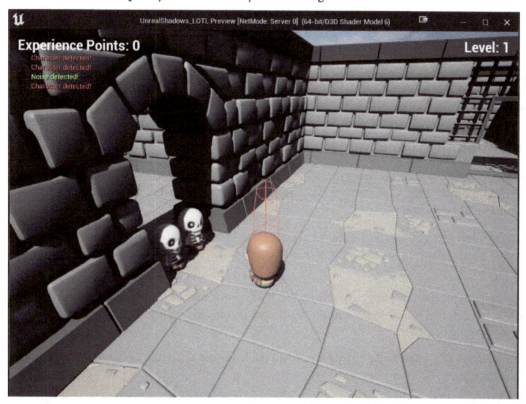

Figure 9.1 – The character has been detected

In this section, you added a new sense to the minion characters; this will make the game more tactical for the players – running around the dungeon like there's no tomorrow won't be an optionable solution!

In the upcoming section, you shall pave the way for a messaging system that enables even the humblest minion to unleash a call to arms upon discovering fresh prey. Oh, you thought heroism was all smooth sailing, did you? Ah, how fallible the human mind can be (smirks the Lichlord).

Implementing an alert system

In this section, you will work on a system that allows an AI character to alert its fellow minions once it detects a player character. At first glance, you might assume that the code logic to alert nearby AI opponents could be implemented directly inside the minion class – it's just a matter of sending them a message, isn't it? But there's more to it than meets the eye, dear reader. It seems the Lichlord has bigger aspirations for communication than you had anticipated. Fear not, for he has dictated that you make use of a Gameplay Framework class that has lurked unnoticed in the shadows until this moment – the Game Mode.

As you will remember from *Chapter 4, Setting Up Your First Multiplayer Environment*, a **Game Mode** is a class that manages a game's rules and settings – this includes tasks such as communicating with AI Actors in the level. Alerting them of a new intruder in the dungeon is definitely a feature we want to have in this class.

Declaring the Game Mode functions

As usual, you will start by declaring the needed functions inside the class header – in this case, you will need just one, called `AlertMinions()`. Open the `US_GameMode.h` header file and declare it in the `public` section:

```
UFUNCTION(BlueprintCallable, Category = "Minions")
void AlertMinions(class AActor* AlertInstigator, const FVector&
Location, float Radius);
```

Although this function may appear pretty simple, it will provide valuable information such as which minion has detected something, the position where to investigate, and the distance at which fellow minions should be alerted.

Now, open the `US_GameMode.cpp` file and add the following `include` declarations at the very top of the code:

```
#include "US_Minion.h"
#include "Kismet/GameplayStatics.h"
```

As you already know, those declarations are needed to properly implement the code you will write in the class. Once you have added those lines, you can add the following method implementation:

```
void AUS_GameMode::AlertMinions(AActor* AlertInstigator, const
FVector& Location, const float Radius)
{
 TArray<AActor*> Minions;
 UGameplayStatics::GetAllActorsOfClass(GetWorld(), AUS_
Minion::StaticClass(), Minions);

 for (const auto Minion : Minions)
```

```
  {
    if(AlertInstigator == Minion) continue;
    if (const auto Distance = FVector::Distance(AlertInstigator
  ->GetActorLocation(), Minion->GetActorLocation()); Distance < Radius)
    {
      if (const auto MinionCharacter = Cast<AUS_Minion>(Minion))
      {
        MinionCharacter->GoToLocation(Location);
      }
    }
  }
}
```

The code looks for all the classes that extend AUS_Minion in the level through GetActorsOfClass() and stores them in an array. After that, it loops through this array, computing the distance between each minion and the alerting one. If the distance is within range (i.e., the Radius property), the AI will be commanded to go to that location and investigate through the GoToLocation() function.

The alert behavior for the Game Mode has been implemented; this means it's now possible for minions to call for assistance whenever they detect an intruder.

Making the AI send alert messages

Sending messages from the AI character is a pretty straightforward task, as the Game Mode is reachable from any Actor in the game as long as it's on the server – as you may already know, this is an awesome feature provided by the Unreal Engine Gameplay Framework. So, let's open the US_Minion.h file and declare the alert radius for the soon-to-be-sent messages in the private section:

```
UPROPERTY(EditDefaultsOnly, BlueprintReadOnly, Category = "Minion AI",
meta = (AllowPrivateAccess = "true"))
float AlertRadius = 6000.0f;
```

Using a configurable radius range will come in handy to create different types of minions – do you want a super-alert, ear-piercing sentinel? Set it to a very high value! Or go for a slimy, self-serving AI that's just in it for the Lichlord's favors and undead promotions by setting it to zero – this way, none of the fellow minions will be alerted and the sentinel will (hopefully) be granted a pat on the head by its lord upon reaching the player character. The choice is yours!

To implement the function, open the US_Minion.cpp file and add the following include at the very beginning of the file:

```
#include "US_GameMode.h"
```

Then, locate the Chase() method. Before its closing bracket, add this code:

```
if(const auto GameMode = Cast<AUS_GameMode>(GetWorld()-
>GetAuthGameMode()))
{
  GameMode->AlertMinions(this, Pawn->GetActorLocation(), AlertRadius);
}
```

As you can see, once the Game Mode has been retrieved, we just send the alert message with the opportune parameters. It's now time to compile the project and do some testing.

Testing the alert implementation

Start a new game session, and once the number of minions is good enough, let your character be detected by one of them. Once alerted, all nearby minions will begin investigating the area, posing a serious danger to the player as more and more AI characters spot them, leading to a potentially dangerous chain reaction.

Figure 9.2 shows one such situation – the player has not been stealthy enough, and AI opponents have started detecting the character while alerting each other.

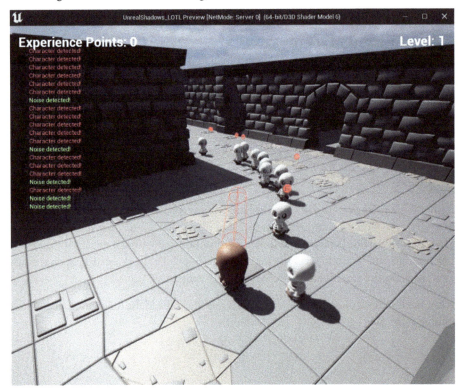

Figure 9.2 – The alert system in action

In this section, you implemented a messaging system for your AI opponents and learned the power of having a centralized place to manage your gameplay logic.

In the next section, you will use the Gameplay Framework damage system to let players defeat enemies. Did you really believe I'd allow the poor thief hero to rot in the Lichlord's grasp without any aid? Well, think again, my dear reader!

Adding health to the AI

In this part of the project, you will add a health system to the minion AI to make it possible to defeat it during gameplay. You will also add a spawn system so that when the opponent is defeated, the player will be rewarded with a well-deserved prize.

To implement such features, we need to open the minion class and start doing some coding – open the US_Minion.h header, and in the private section, add these two declarations:

```
UPROPERTY(EditDefaultsOnly, BlueprintReadOnly, Category="Health", meta
= (AllowPrivateAccess = "true"))
float Health = 5.f;

UPROPERTY(EditDefaultsOnly, BlueprintReadOnly, Category="Pickup", meta
= (AllowPrivateAccess = "true"))
TSubclassOf<class AUS_BasePickup> SpawnedPickup;
```

The first one is used to keep track of the enemy health, while the second one will contain the class of the item pickup that will be spawned once the minion is defeated. Both of them can be modified in a child Blueprint Class (thanks to the EditDefaultsOnly property specifier), so you can build your own variations of the minion.

Now, locate the protected section and add the damage handler declaration:

```
UFUNCTION()
void OnDamage(AActor* DamagedActor, float Damage, const UDamageType*
DamageType, AController* InstigatedBy, AActor* DamageCauser);
```

The header is now complete, so it's time to open the US_Minion.cpp file and implement the health system. As usual, start by adding the needed include declarations at the top of the file:

```
#include "US_BasePickup.h"
```

Next, declare the base pickup that will be spawned when the character is defeated; you'll use the pickup coin you created in *Chapter 6, Replicating Properties Over the Network*. Locate the constructor, and just before the closing bracket, add this code:

```
static ConstructorHelpers::FClassFinder<AUS_BasePickup>
SpawnedPickupAsset(TEXT("/Game/Blueprints/BP_GoldCoinPickup"));
if (SpawnedPickupAsset.Succeeded())
```

```
{
  SpawnedPickup = SpawnedPickupAsset.Class;
}
```

This code logic should be familiar, as we get a Blueprint asset from the project library and assign it the `SpawnedPickup` reference.

Then, we need to implement the damage handler logic. Locate the `PostInitializeComponents()` method and add this line of code:

```
OnTakeAnyDamage.AddDynamic(this, &AUS_Minion::OnDamage);
```

Here, we just bind the `OnDamage` handler to the `OnTakeAnyDamage` delegate. As a last step, we need to implement the `OnDamage()` method, so add this code to your class:

```
void AUS_Minion::OnDamage(AActor* DamagedActor, float Damage, const
UDamageType* DamageType, AController* InstigatedBy,
  AActor* DamageCauser)
{
  Health -= Damage;
  if(Health > 0) return;

  if(SpawnedPickup)
  {
    GetWorld()->SpawnActor<AUS_BasePickup>(SpawnedPickup,
GetActorLocation(), GetActorRotation());
  }
  Destroy();
}
```

What this function does is to subtract the `Damage` value from the `Health` property; if the minion reaches zero health, it will immediately spawn the prize (i.e., the pickup) and then it will destroy itself.

In this section, you created a simple health system for the AI opponent, by adding the `Health` property and keeping track of its value as damage is taken – whenever the minion has been defeated, it will spawn a coin or a similar prize, ready to be picked up by the nearest (or swiftest) character!

Unfortunately for your players, the hapless band of thieving heroes is, at the moment, ill equipped to dispatch the Lichlord's minions in the treacherous underground realm! Fear not, for we shall come to their aid by adding a splendid weapon inventory to their arsenal in the next section.

Adding a weapon system to the character

Your beloved character has been longing for a weapon system ever since you started implementing it. In this section, we shall finally grant its wishes and provide it the ability to wield (not-so) powerful tools of destruction. Let's make our character stronger and more formidable by arming it with an amazing weapon!

Since our character hero is a sneaky thief who prefers to avoid direct combat with stronger and more heavily armored opponents, we will focus on a throwing dagger system.

In order to avoid adding cluttered code in the US_Character class, you'll implement a brand-new component that will handle the weapon logic – this means that you'll work on the following features:

- A component that will be added to the character and handle the player input and dagger spawn logic
- A dagger weapon that will be thrown at runtime and cause damage to the enemy opponents

As a first step, we will create the weapon projectile that will be spawned by the character when attacking during gameplay.

Creating a dagger projectile

The first thing to do is create a projectile class that will serve as a throwable dagger. To do so, in the Unreal Editor, create a new C++ class that will extend Actor, and call it US_BaseWeaponProjectile. Once it has been created, open the US_BaseWeaponProjectile.h file, and in the private section, add the following component declarations:

```
UPROPERTY(VisibleAnywhere, BlueprintReadOnly, Category="Components",
meta = (AllowPrivateAccess = "true"))
TObjectPtr<class USphereComponent> SphereCollision;

UPROPERTY(VisibleAnywhere, BlueprintReadOnly, Category="Components",
meta = (AllowPrivateAccess = "true"))
TObjectPtr<UStaticMeshComponent> Mesh;

UPROPERTY(VisibleAnywhere, BlueprintReadOnly, Category = "Components",
meta = (AllowPrivateAccess = "true"))
TObjectPtr<class UProjectileMovementComponent> ProjectileMovement;
```

As you can see, we will add a collision area to check hits during gameplay, a static mesh for the dagger model, and projectile logic to make the dagger move once it has been thrown.

Remaining in the `private` section, add the Damage property with a base value of 1:

```
UPROPERTY(EditDefaultsOnly, BlueprintReadOnly, Category="Weapon", meta
= (AllowPrivateAccess = "true"))
float Damage = 1.f;
```

Then, in the `public` section, add the usual getter methods for the components:

```
FORCEINLINE USphereComponent* GetSphereCollision() const { return
SphereCollision; }
FORCEINLINE UStaticMeshComponent* GetMesh() const { return Mesh; }
FORCEINLINE UProjectileMovementComponent* GetProjectileMovement()
const { return ProjectileMovement; }
```

Finally, we need to add a handler for when the weapon makes contact with its target. Add the following code to the `protected` section:

```
UFUNCTION()
void OnHit(UPrimitiveComponent* HitComponent, AActor* OtherActor,
UPrimitiveComponent* OtherComp, FVector NormalImpulse,
  const FHitResult& Hit);
```

The header is ready, so we need to implement the logic – open the US_BaseWeaponProjectile.
cpp file and add the necessary `include` declarations at its top:

```
#include "US_Character.h"
#include "US_CharacterStats.h"
#include "Components/SphereComponent.h"
#include "Engine/DamageEvents.h"
#include "GameFramework/ProjectileMovementComponent.h"
```

Then, locate the constructor and add the following code:

```
SphereCollision =
CreateDefaultSubobject<USphereComponent>("Collision");
SphereCollision->SetGenerateOverlapEvents(true);
SphereCollision->SetSphereRadius(10.0f);
SphereCollision->BodyInstance.SetCollisionProfileName("BlockAll");
SphereCollision->OnComponentHit.AddDynamic(this, &AUS_
BaseWeaponProjectile::OnHit);

RootComponent = SphereCollision;

Mesh = CreateDefaultSubobject<UStaticMeshComponent>("Mesh");
Mesh->SetupAttachment(RootComponent);
Mesh->SetCollisionEnabled(ECollisionEnabled::PhysicsOnly);
```

```
Mesh->SetRelativeLocation(FVector(-40.f, 0.f, 0.f));
Mesh->SetRelativeRotation(FRotator(-90.f, 0.f, 0.f));
static ConstructorHelpers::FObjectFinder<UStaticMesh>
StaticMesh(TEXT("/Game/KayKit/DungeonElements/dagger_common"));
if (StaticMesh.Succeeded())
{
 GetMesh()->SetStaticMesh(StaticMesh.Object);
}


ProjectileMovement = CreateDefaultSubobject<UProjectileMovement
Component>("ProjectileMovement");
ProjectileMovement->UpdatedComponent = SphereCollision;
ProjectileMovement->ProjectileGravityScale = 0;
ProjectileMovement->InitialSpeed = 3000;
ProjectileMovement->MaxSpeed = 3000;
ProjectileMovement->bRotationFollowsVelocity = true;
ProjectileMovement->bShouldBounce = false;


bReplicates = true;
```

This code logic is lengthy but straightforward to comprehend – we just create and initialize the necessary components:

`SphereCollision` has some basic values you should be familiar with:

- `Mesh` is set to a dagger model and rotated and positioned in order to align with the overall Actor
- `ProjectileMovement` has gravity disabled and a speed that will move the Actor fast and simulate a real dagger

One thing to mention is that we bind the `OnHit()` method to the `OnComponentHit` delegate through the `AddDynamic` helper macro. Also, note the final line of code that activates replication for the weapon – always keep in mind that Actors are not replicated by default!

Now, add the `OnHit()` implementation:

```
void AUS_BaseWeaponProjectile::OnHit(UPrimitiveComponent*
HitComponent, AActor* OtherActor,
 UPrimitiveComponent* OtherComp, FVector NormalImpulse, const
FHitResult& Hit)
{
 auto ComputedDamage = Damage;
 if (const auto Character = Cast<AUS_Character>(GetInstigator()))
 {
  ComputedDamage *= Character->GetCharacterStats()->DamageMultiplier;
 }
```

```
 if (OtherActor && OtherActor != this)
 {
  const FDamageEvent Event(UDamageType::StaticClass());
  OtherActor->TakeDamage(ComputedDamage, Event,
GetInstigatorController(), this);
 }
 Destroy();
}
```

The code can be divided into three main parts:

- In the first part, we compute the damage, starting from the Damage base value. If the instigator (i.e., the character that spawned the projectile) is US_Character, we get its damage multiplier from the statistics and update the provoked damage. This means the higher the level of the character, the higher the damage.

> **Note**
>
> For a refresher on how character statistics are managed, please take a look back at *Chapter 6, Replicating Properties Over the Network*.

- The second part of the code verifies whether the launched projectile has hit an Actor. If it has, it will then inflict the corresponding amount of damage.

- The last and final part simply destroys the projectile – its mission is finished, and this means it should be removed from the game.

With the projectile all set up and ready to go, it's time to implement some spawn logic so that your thief hero can unleash the full power of this shiny new weapon.

Implementing the weapon component

Let's start by creating a class that will add new features to the character. As you may remember from *Chapter 4, Setting Up Your First Multiplayer Environment*, a component will let you implement reusable functionality and can be attached to any Actor or another component. In this case, we will implement a weapon system, with a **Scene Component**, which has the ability to be placed somewhere inside the parent Actor (i.e., the component has a Transform property) – this will allow you to position the component somewhere inside the character and act as a spawn point for the thrown projectiles.

Let's start by creating the class. To do so, create a new class that extends from a Scene component and call it `US_WeaponProjectileComponent`. Once the creation process has finished, open `US_WeaponProjectileComponent.h`, and in the `private` section, add the following declarations:

```
UPROPERTY(EditDefaultsOnly, BlueprintReadOnly, Category="Projectile",
meta = (AllowPrivateAccess = "true"))
TSubclassOf<class AUS_BaseWeaponProjectile> ProjectileClass;

UPROPERTY(EditAnywhere, BlueprintReadOnly, Category="Input",
meta=(AllowPrivateAccess = "true"))
class UInputMappingContext* WeaponMappingContext;

UPROPERTY(EditAnywhere, BlueprintReadOnly, Category="Input",
meta=(AllowPrivateAccess = "true"))
class UInputAction* ThrowAction;
```

As you can see, we declare the projectile class (i.e., the projectile we previously created, or a subclass of it). Then, we declare the necessary elements that will let us take advantage of the enhanced input system. As we don't want to add dependencies to the main character, we will use a different mapping context from the one used in *Chapter 5, Managing Actors in a Multiplayer Environment* – this will let us implement a flexible combat system and add as many features as we want, without adding clutter to the main character class. Imagine the thrill of watching your sneaky thief hero slipping through the shadows, quietly backstabbing the most despised minions of the dreaded Lichlord! The possibilities for mayhem and mischief will be endless!

Okay, let's stop dreaming and get back to coding. In the `public` section, add a setter for the projectile class that will allow you to change the spawned dagger projectile:

```
UFUNCTION(BlueprintCallable, Category = "Projectile")
void SetProjectileClass(TSubclassOf<class AUS_BaseWeaponProjectile>
NewProjectileClass);
```

This function has nothing to do with throwing things around, but it will be most useful if you plan to add a weapon pickup to your game, in order to improve your character's fighting skills.

Lastly, in the `protected` section, declare the `Throw()` action and its corresponding server call:

```
void Throw();

UFUNCTION(Server, Reliable)
void Throw_Server();
```

This code will let us spawn the thrown daggers during gameplay from the server – always remember that the server should be in command when generating replicated Actors.

Now that the header file is finished, open the US_WeaponProjectileComponent.cpp file to start implementing its features. As usual, locate the top of the file, and add the include declarations for the classes we will use:

```
#include "EnhancedInputComponent.h"
#include "EnhancedInputSubsystems.h"
#include "US_BaseWeaponProjectile.h"
#include "US_Character.h"
```

Then, in the constructor, add this single line of code:

```
ProjectileClass = AUS_BaseWeaponProjectile::StaticClass();
```

Here, we just declare the base projectile that will be spawned when the throw action is triggered; you will obviously be able to change it in the derived Blueprint Classes if you need a different weapon.

Now, locate the BeginPlay() method, and just after the Super::BeginPlay() declaration, add this code:

```
const ACharacter* Character = Cast<ACharacter>(GetOwner());
if(!Character) return;

if (const APlayerController* PlayerController = Cast<APlayerController
>(Character->GetController()))
{
  if (UEnhancedInputLocalPlayerSubsystem* Subsystem = ULocalPlayer:
:GetSubsystem<UEnhancedInputLocalPlayerSubsystem>(PlayerController-
>GetLocalPlayer()))
  {
   Subsystem->AddMappingContext(WeaponMappingContext, 1);
  }

  if (UEnhancedInputComponent* EnhancedInputComponent = Cast<UEnhancedI
nputComponent>(PlayerController->InputComponent))
  {
   EnhancedInputComponent->BindAction(ThrowAction,
ETriggerEvent::Triggered, this, &UUS_
WeaponProjectileComponent::Throw);
  }
}
```

In the previous code, we check that the component owner is our US_Character class, in order to get its controller and initialize the mapping context and its actions. Note that this initialization is done inside the BeginPlay() function, which means that these steps will be done just once – that is, when the game is started – to be sure that there is an Actor owner and a corresponding controller.

Now, implement the throw logic by adding the following method implementations:

```
void UUS_WeaponProjectileComponent::Throw()
{
  Throw_Server();
}

void UUS_WeaponProjectileComponent:: Throw_Server_Implementation()
{
  if (ProjectileClass)
  {
    const auto Character = Cast<AUS_Character>(GetOwner());
    const auto ProjectileSpawnLocation = GetComponentLocation();
    const auto ProjectileSpawnRotation = GetComponentRotation();
    auto ProjectileSpawnParams = FActorSpawnParameters();
    ProjectileSpawnParams.Owner = GetOwner();
    ProjectileSpawnParams.Instigator = Character;

    GetWorld()->SpawnActor<AUS_BaseWeaponProjectile>(ProjectileClass,
ProjectileSpawnLocation, ProjectileSpawnRotation,
ProjectileSpawnParams);
  }
}
```

As you can see, the `Throw()` method simply calls the server-side implementation that will spawn the projectile from the component location. You are already familiar with the spawn action (do you remember the minion spawner?), but there is an important thing to notice this time – we use the `FActorSpawnParameters` structure to set the owner of the projectile and, most importantly, the instigator (i.e., the Actor that spawned the object). This property is used by the projectile to retrieve the character statistics and handle the damage multiplier, code logic we implemented in the previous section.

Lastly, add the setter method that will let you change the weapon spawned by the character:

```
void UUS_
WeaponProjectileComponent::SetProjectileClass(TSubclassOf<AUS_
BaseWeaponProjectile> NewProjectileClass)
{
  ProjectileClass = NewProjectileClass;
}
```

The component has now been properly set – you just need to attach an instance of it to the thief character to make it fully operational.

Attaching the WeaponProjectile component to the character

Now that you have created a weapon component, it's time to add it to the character. Open the US_
Character.h header file, and in the `private` section, add the component declaration:

```
UPROPERTY(VisibleAnywhere, BlueprintReadOnly, Category = "Weapon",
meta = (AllowPrivateAccess = "true"))
TObjectPtr<class UUS_WeaponProjectileComponent> Weapon;
```

And, as usual, add the corresponding getter utility method to the `public` section:

```
FORCEINLINE UUS_WeaponProjectileComponent* GetWeapon() const { return
Weapon; }
```

Then, open the US_Character.cpp source file and include the component class declaration at
the top of the file:

```
#include "US_WeaponProjectileComponent.h"
```

Now, locate the constructor, and just after the noise emitter creation and initialization, add the
following code:

```
Weapon = CreateDefaultSubobject<UUS_
WeaponProjectileComponent>(TEXT("Weapon"));
Weapon->SetupAttachment(RootComponent);
Weapon->SetRelativeLocation(FVector(120.f, 70.f, 0.f));
```

As you can see, after we create the component, we attach it to the root component of the character and
position it at a relative location, set to (120, 70, 0). If you want your character to be left-handed,
you can just use a negative value for the X coordinate (i.e., -120.f).

As hard as it may be to believe, the code to attach the weapon component to the character is complete;
the code logic is already handled in the component itself, so you can sit back, relax, and let everything
fall into place like a well-oiled machine!

You can now switch back to the Unreal Editor and compile your project – once finished, you can
open the **BP_Character** Blueprint, and you will see that the character is now equipped with a
WeaponProjectile component, with **Projectile Class** set to a default value, as depicted in *Figure 9.3*:

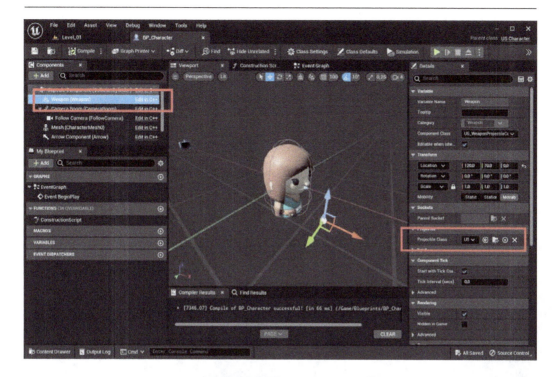

Figure 9.3 – The WeaponProjectile component attached to the character Actor

With the `WeaponProjectile` component attached to the character, the last thing to do is to create a mapping context for the player input and an input action for the throw logic.

Adding an input system for the weapon

In the final part of this section, you will define the mapping context and the input action for the throw interaction. This is something you are already familiar with, as you previously created similar assets in *Chapter 5*, *Managing Actors in a Multiplayer Environment*.

So, without further ado, let's open the Content Browser and navigate to the **Content | Input** folder. We will create the throw action asset in the following steps.

Setting up the input mapping context for the throw interaction

To create the action asset for the throw interaction, follow these steps:

1. Right-click in the Content Browser and select **Input | Input Action**, naming the newly created asset `IA_Throw`.

2. Double-click on the asset to open it, and from the **Value Type** dropdown, select **Digital (bool)**.

3. Double-check that the **Consume Input** checkbox is ticked.

The final result for the throw action asset is shown in *Figure 9.4*:

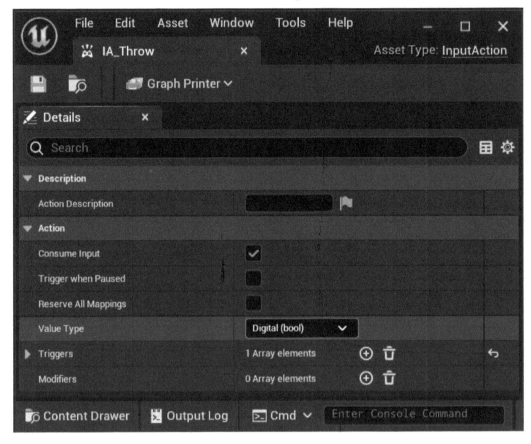

Figure 9.4 – The throw action settings

Now that the action has been set, let's create a mapping context for the weapon interactions.

Setting up the input mapping context for the weapon interactions

To create the weapon context mapping, follow these steps:

1. Right-click in the Content Browser and select **Input | Input Mapping Context**, naming the asset IMC_Weapons. Double-click on the asset to open it.

2. Add a new mapping context by clicking on the + icon next to the **Mappings** field.

3. From the drop-down menu that will be added, select **IA_Throw** to add this action to the mapping context.

4. Click twice on the + icon next to the drop-down menu to add two other control bindings for this action (one is set by default). In the drop-down menu next to each new field, use the following properties:

- The first binding should be set to **Left Ctrl** from the **Keyboard** category

- The second binding should be set to **Gamepad Face Button Right** from the **Gamepad** category

- The third binding should be set to **Left Mouse Button** from the **Mouse** category

The final result for the weapon mapping context should be like the one depicted in *Figure 9.5*:

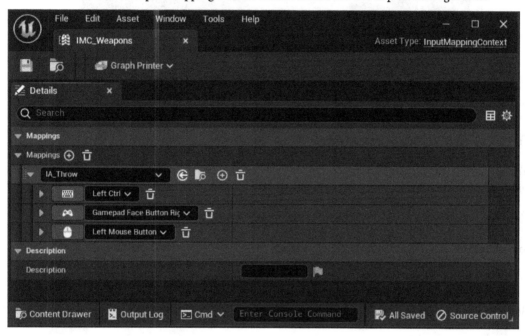

Figure 9.5 – The weapon mapping context settings

Now that the assets are ready, it's time to add them to the character:

1. Open the **BP_Character** Blueprint, select the **Weapon** component, and in the **Details** panel, locate the **Input** category.

2. In the **Weapon Mapping Context** field, assign the **IMC_Weapons** asset.

3. In the **Throw Action** field, assign the **IA_Throw** asset.

Once you have set these properties, your **Input** category should look like the one depicted in *Figure 9.6*:

Figure 9.6 – The updated Input category

Now that the input settings have been properly updated, it's time to do some testing to check that everything works properly.

Testing the weapon system

It's time to show the Lichlord's minions who the boss is and wreak some havoc in their underground lairs! Let's give them a taste of our hero's targeting skills by starting a game session.

During gameplay, your character should be able to spawn a dagger whenever using the throw action – for example, by clicking the left mouse button. The dagger should destroy itself whenever it hits something and provoke damage to the AI minions.

Whenever a minion reaches zero health, it should be removed from the game, and a coin should spawn in the level. Collecting enough coins will make your character level up, and consequently, the character itself will provoke additional damage when hitting any enemy.

Figure 9.7 shows the character throwing some daggers during gameplay:

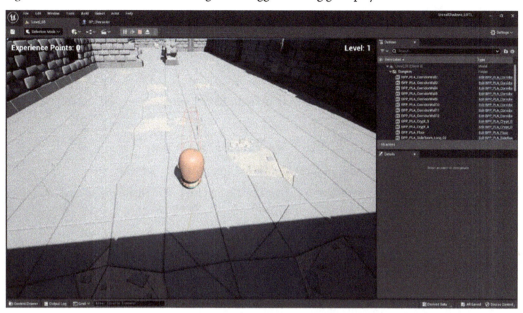

Figure 9.7 – The dagger attack in action

In this section, you implemented a weapon system through a new component that is attached to your character and a projectile Actor that can be spawned in the game and properly replicated through the network.

In the upcoming section, you will introduce some diverse variations of the AI opponents, with the aim of enhancing the game's variety and overall enjoyability.

Creating AI variations

Now that we've got the AI opponents all set up and ready to go for some epic battles, let's add some more variations to AI minions and make things more interesting and engaging. If a project has been well planned, changing the behavior of an AI – even a basic one such as the one we created in this chapter – is usually just a matter of adjusting some settings!

In this section, you'll create a new AI opponent, starting from the basic US_Minion class, and you will tweak its property in order to give it different behavior.

Creating an AI sentinel

While watching mindless minions wander around a dungeon cluelessly may cause a chuckle or two, it is certainly not enough for the Lichlord's devious plans. He wants to be sure that each and every corner of his realm is safe and well guarded. This means you will craft some undead sentinels that will have keen senses and be more territorial.

Let's start by creating a Blueprint Class, inheriting from the basic minion. Open the Content Browser and complete the following steps:

1. In the Blueprints folder, right-click and select **Blueprint Class**.

2. From the window that pops up, select **US_Minion** from the **All Classes** section.

3. Name the newly created Blueprint BP_MinionSentinel, and then double-click on it to open it.

4. In the **Details** panel, locate the **Minion AI** category and apply the following settings:

    - Set **Alert Radius** to a value of 6000,0

    - Set **Patrol Speed** to a value of 60,0

    - Set **Chase Speed** to a value of 20,0

    - Set **Patrol Radius** to a value of 1000,0

    - The final settings for this category are shown in *Figure 9.8*:

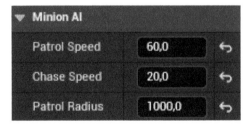

Figure 9.8 – The sentinel Minion AI settings

5. Then, in the **AI** section, apply the following settings:

    - Set **Hearing Threshold** to a value of 600,0

    - Set **LOSHearing Threshold** to a value of 1000,0

    - Set **Sight Radius** to a value of 2500,0

    - Set **Peripheral Vision Angle** to a value of 60,0

The final settings for this category are shown in *Figure 9.9*:

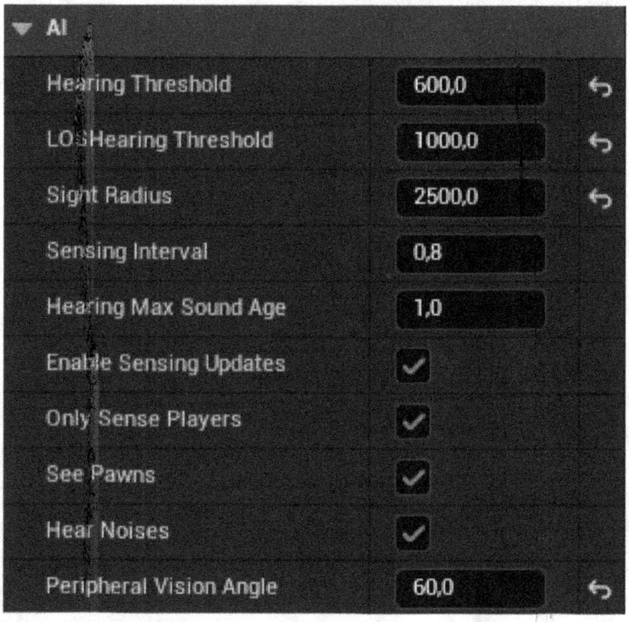

Figure 9.9 – The sentinel AI settings

With these settings, you will create a minion that will patrol an approximately small area, changing direction frequently and moving very slowly. Its senses will be keen, and its alert radius will be larger than a regular minion. When an intruder has been spotted, the sentinel will slow down, calling for help, letting its more aggressive counterparts handle the chase. It's not one for combat, but it's still on the lookout for any suspicious activity!

6. As a final touch, you can add a couple of glowing eyes for this darkness-gazing undead character by changing **Element 5** in the mesh **Materials** list to the **M_Base_Emissive** material asset, as shown in *Figure 9.10*:

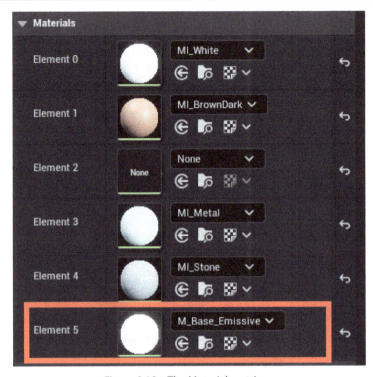

Figure 9.10 – The Materials settings

The final result of the sentinel (with some dramatic lightning add-ons) can be seen in *Figure 9.11*:

Figure 9.11 – The sentinel added to the scene

As you can see, you have created a new AI with just a couple of tweaks to the **Details** panel. Let's create another one, a more aggressive undead minion.

Creating an AI miniboss

You can actually use the same process that worked in the previous subsection to create a new AI that will deal with hero intruders in a totally different way. It's like getting creative with a recipe and making something new and unexpected but still (dangerously) delicious!

Open the Content Browser and complete the following steps:

1. In the `Blueprints` folder, right-click and select **Blueprint Class**.
2. From the window that pops up, select **US_Minion** from the **All Classes** section.
3. Name the newly created Blueprint `BP_MinionMiniboss`, and then double-click on it to open it.
4. In the **Details** panel, locate the **Minion AI** category and apply the following settings:

    - Set **Alert Radius** to a value of `100,0`
    - Set **Patrol Speed** to a value of `100,0`
    - Set **Chase Speed** to a value of `400,0`
    - Set **Patrol Radius** to a value of `50000,0`
    - The final settings for this category are shown in *Figure 9.12*:

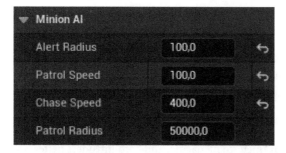

Figure 9.12 – The miniboss Minion AI settings

5. Then, in the **AI** section, apply the following settings:

    - Set **Hearing Threshold** to a value of `200,0`
    - Set **LOSHearing Threshold** to a value of `400,0`
    - Set **Sight Radius** to a value of `200,0`
    - Set **Peripheral Vision Angle** to a value of `20,0`

The final settings for this category are shown in *Figure 9.13*:

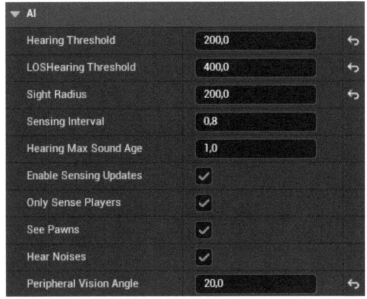

Figure 9.13 – The miniboss AI settings

This AI opponent has been set to a really dull behavior while patrolling (low perception, slower movement, etc.), but it will become dangerously fast once alerted.

Also, the miniboss started to look a bit dull, so the Lichlord has decided to give it a literal armor makeover. To do this, follow these steps:

1. Select the **Mesh** component and change the **Skeletal Mesh Asset** property to the **skeleton_warrior** asset.

2. Change the **Mesh** scale to a value of **1.2** to make it bigger.

3. Set the **Health** property to a value of **20** to make it more damage-resistant.

This foe is about to go from "meh" to menacing, and hero intruders better watch out! The final result of the miniboss, compared with a base minion, is shown in *Figure 9.14*:

Figure 9.14 – The miniboss minion

The beauty of it all is that you can get really creative with your enemy opponents and test out all sorts of different behaviors and tactics. And if something just isn't working for you, no worries! Just delete it and start afresh with something new in just a few short minutes.

As an additional nice touch to the AI, why not use the pickup spawn system we added earlier in this chapter to spice up the game? Depending on how rare or dangerous the defeated minion is, you could have it spawn different types of coins!

Once you have your undead army ready to go, you can get back to your enemy spawner and add the Blueprints to the system – something we will do in the next subsection.

Updating the minion spawner

As you may have guessed, adding your brand-new minion varieties is just a matter of putting their Blueprints inside a spawner. To do so, select the spawner you previously added to the level, and in the **Details** panel, locate the **Spawnable Minions** array property in the **Spawn System** category – there should already be one item in the list, **US_Minion**.

Add as many items as you wish, selecting the spawnable minions you need for that particular spawn area. *Figure 9.15* shows my setup for the main spawner area in the level:

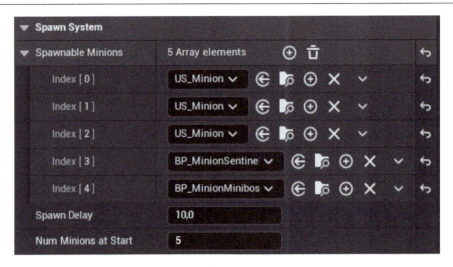

Figure 9.15 – The spawn area setup

As you can see, I chose to work with five elements, allocating a 20% chance for each to be added to the level every time the Spawn() method is called. Since the basic minion utilizes three of these elements, there is a 60% chance that it will appear as an opponent, compared to the sentinel and miniboss, which only have a 20% probability of spawning.

Once you are happy with your setup, you can test the game. *Figure 9.16* shows my spawner in action at the start of the game:

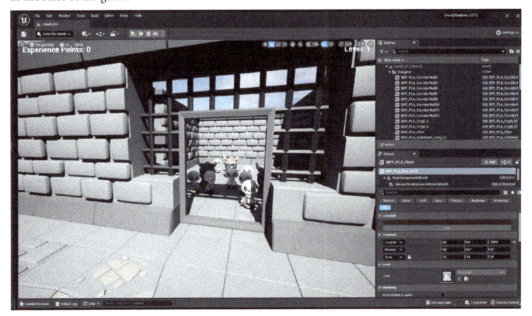

Figure 9.16 – The spawner at the start of the game

In this final section, you created some variations for the base minions; by changing some of their base properties, you changed the way they behave during gameplay, making your level more engaging and diverse.

Summary

In this chapter, you actively worked to improve the behavior of your enemy AIs within the level. The focus was on developing new features that make the gaming experience even more engaging and challenging for players. You actually improved the Lichlord's minions' sense of hearing to make them even more alert and perceptive when it comes to spotting those poor thieving heroes.

On the flip side, you also implemented a health system for the minions and added some pretty sharp (literally!) tools to the player's arsenal that they can use to take down those nasty foes! Finally, you created some enemy variations to make the dungeon less boring and more engaging for the player.

As you can see from what you have built here, if you plan ahead, improving gameplay can be a walk in the park! By taking the time to carefully map out your strategies and implement the right features, you can make gameplay engaging and immersive for players while also achieving your desired results.

In the next chapter, we will improve the overall look and feel of the game by adding animations and prisoners to rescue. Additionally, I will provide you with some tips on how to take your game to the next level, but let's be clear – I'm not going to code it all for you! I believe in your ability to create something amazing, and I can't wait to see what you come up with!

10
Enhancing the Player Experience

One of the best ways to improve a video game is to add a good look and feel to it. A great-looking game will create an immersive experience that will engage players and make them want to keep coming back for more.

For this reason, it's important for developers to focus on tweaking visual and audio feedback until everything looks just right! It might take some time, but getting these last touches right will make sure your video game has an awesome look and feel – something that players won't forget anytime soon!

Keeping this in mind, the following chapter will concentrate on improving certain aspects, such as using different animations together and synchronizing them over the network, or adding **non-player characters** (**NPCs**) to interact with – features that your protagonist has longed for a considerable amount of time.

Additionally, you'll be providing a purpose for your players to fight for: the daring rescue of some imprisoned comrades!

Finally, I'll share some additional ideas to help guide you in completing your multiplayer game. This book may not have enough pages to cover every detail, but that shouldn't stop your creativity and imagination from taking flight!

By the end of this chapter, you will possess a sleek and robust prototype for your multiplayer game and be well equipped and prepared to embark on the next phase – learning how to optimize it.

In this chapter, I will guide you through the following sections:

- Animating the character
- Adding NPC Actors
- Making further improvements to the game

Technical requirements

To follow the topics presented in this chapter, you should have completed the previous ones and understood their content.

Additionally, if you would prefer to begin with code from the companion repository for this book, you can download the `.zip` project files provided:

`https://github.com/PacktPublishing/Multiplayer-Game-Development-with-Unreal-Engine-5`

You can download the files that are up to date with the end of the last chapter by clicking the `Unreal Shadows - Chapter 09 End` link.

Animating the character

So far, your hero has been exploring the dungeon and searching for hidden treasures while avoiding enemies, but there's something missing that will really bring it to life – a proper animation system.

In this section, I'll guide you through the creation of simple animations that will work on the networked environment of your project. This will involve creating Blueprints specifically designed for the animation system and establishing their connection to your character class – you will be creating the needed animation assets and then adding the needed code to make everything work properly.

Creating the animation assets

Animating characters in Unreal Engine involves creating **Animation Blueprints** that handle the motion and logic of character movement and actions. This book doesn't prioritize this topic – in fact, it's not usually the main focus for game programmers! However, having some basic knowledge of how things work under the hood will be a good addition to your game development arsenal.

To create a simple but fully functional animation system for the player character, we will need three assets:

- An asset to control the movement transitions from idle to walk to run, and vice versa

- An asset used to play the throw animation

- A Blueprint to control the two aforementioned assets

To get started, we first need a folder to put all the assets in. So, open the Unreal Editor and, in **Content Drawer**, create a new folder called `Animations`. Once it is created, you will be ready to add the first asset.

Creating the movement Blend Space

In Unreal Engine, a **Blend Space** is a special asset that allows for the blending of animations based on the values of two inputs. It allows multiple animations to be blended by plotting them onto a one- or two-dimensional graph. Animators and game developers often use blend spaces to create smooth and realistic transitions between different animations for characters in games.

In our case, we will need to blend three animations – the idle, walk, and sprint ones – that will be managed depending on the character's speed.

To create this Blend Space, complete the following steps:

1. Inside the `Animations` folder, right-click and select **Animation | Blend Space**. Then, from the **Pick Skeleton** window that will pop up, select **rogue_Skeleton**, as depicted in *Figure 10.1*:

Figure 10.1 – Blend Space creation

2. Name the newly-created asset BS_WalkRun and double-click it to open the **Blend Space Editor** window.

3. In **Asset Details**, locate the **Axis Settings** category. Then, in the **Horizontal Axis** section, do the following:

   - Set the **Name** value to Speed

   - Set the **Maximum Axis** value to 500

4. Leave the **Vertical Axis** section as it is (i.e., set to **None**), as we won't use it.

   What we have done here is initialize the main setting values for the animation blend, exposing the **Speed** property that will be used by the controlling Blueprint we will be adding later.

   Now, you will be adding the animation assets that will be blended together.

5. Locate the **rogue_Idle** animation in the **Asset Browser** and drag it into the graph at the center of the editor. This will create a point in the coordinate system of the diagram.

6. Select the point and set its **Speed** property to 0 and its **None** property to 0.

   You should get a graph that looks like the one depicted in *Figure 10.2*:

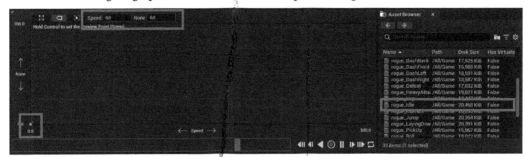

Figure 10.2 – Idle animation settings

Now, we will add two more assets to the graph – one for the walk animation and one for the run animation.

7. Drag the **rogue_Walk** asset into the graph and set its **Speed** property to 45 and its **None** property to 0.

8. Again, drag the **rogue_Walk** asset into the graph and set its **Speed** property to 100 and its **None** property to 0.

9. Drag the **rogue_Run** asset into the graph and set its **Speed** property to 500 and its **None** property to 0.

The complete Blend Space asset can be seen in *Figure 10.3*:

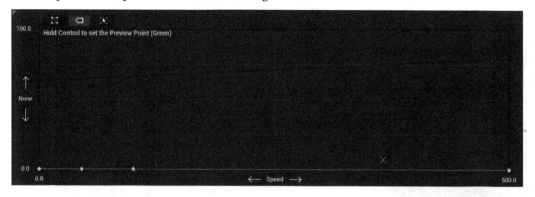

Figure 10.3 – Complete blend space

To test the animation blends on the character, you can simply press the *Ctrl* key and hover the mouse on the zone of the graph you want to check – you will see the character start a walk-and-move cycle, the animation assets blending seamlessly. The Blend Space is complete, so we can now start creating the asset that will handle the throw animation.

Creating the throw Animation Montage

An **Animation Montage** is a type of asset that enables the combination of multiple animations and their selective play from a Blueprint. Animation Montages are commonly used for creating complex animation sequences such as attack combos, cutscenes, and other interactive gameplay elements. In our project, we will use one to play the single-throw animation from the controlling Blueprint.

To create the Animation Montage, complete the following steps:

1. Inside the `Animations` folder, right-click and select **Animation | Animation Montage**. Then, from the **Pick Skeleton** window that will pop up, select **rogue_Skeleton**.

2. Name the newly created asset `AM_Throw` and double-click it to open the **Animation Montage Editor** window.

3. From the **Asset Browser**, drag the **rogue_Throw** asset – in the **DefaultGroup.DefaultSlot** line – onto the timeline at the center of the editor.

The final result for the Animation Montage is shown in *Figure 10.4*:

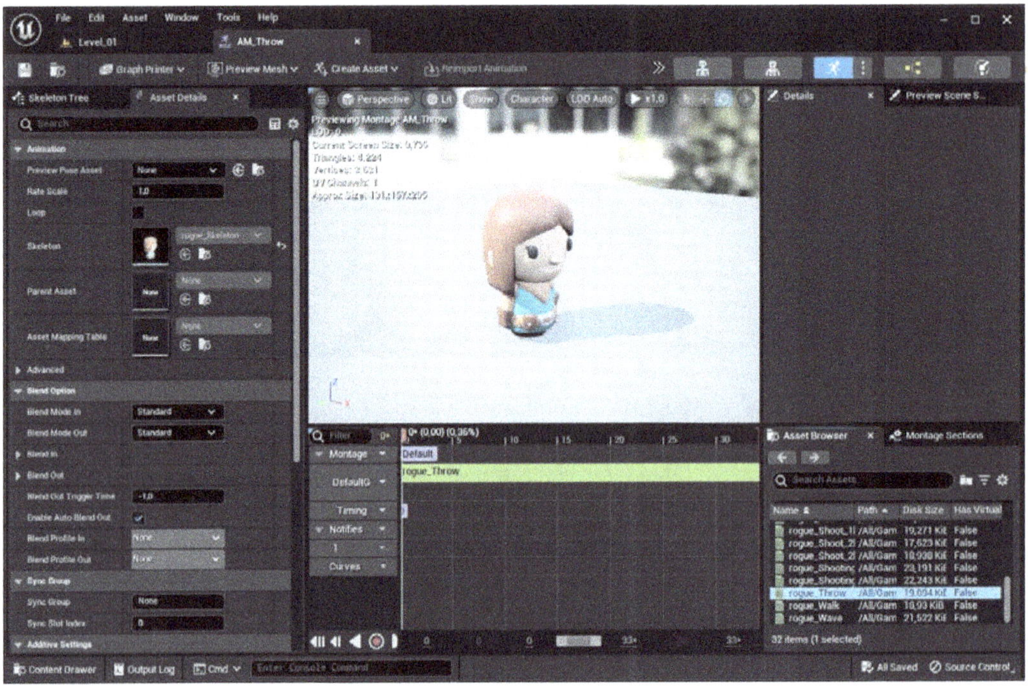

Figure 10.4 – Throw Animation Montage

This Montage and the previous **Blend Space** asset will be controlled by a dedicated Blueprint that we are going to add to the project in the next steps.

Creating the character Animation Blueprint

An **Animation Blueprint** is a specialized type of Blueprint that is used to create and control complex animation behaviors for Actors in the game. It defines how animations should be processed and blended together, as well as how animation inputs should be mapped.

In our case, we need to control the Blend Space **Speed** parameter in order to let the character walk and run when needed, and start the throw Animation Montage when the character is attacking.

To create the Animation Blueprint, complete the following steps:

1. Inside the `Animations` folder, right-click and select **Animation | Animation Blueprint**. Then, from the **Create Animation Blueprint** window that will pop up, select **rogue_Skeleton**, as depicted in *Figure 10.5*:

Figure 10.5 – Animation Blueprint creation

2. Name the newly-created asset AB_Character and double-click it to open the editor window.

    If you are not already familiar with Animation Blueprints, you will notice some similarities to a regular Blueprint class, such as the **My Blueprints** and **Event Graph** tabs. If it is not already selected, open **Event Graph** to start some Visual Scripting code and then continue with the following steps.

3. Add an **Event Blueprint Initialize Animation** node.

4. Click and drag from the **Return Value** outgoing pin of **Try Get Pawn Owner** (which will already be present in the graph) and add a **Cast To US_Character** node.

5.   Connect the event execution pin to the cast node incoming execution pin.

6. From the **As US Character** outgoing pin of the cast node, click and drag, selecting the **Promote to Variable** option – this will create a variable and add a corresponding **Set** node to the graph that will be automatically connected to the cast node. Name the variable Character.

7. From the outgoing pin of the **Set Character** node, click and drag to add a **Character Movement** getter node.

8. From this getter node outgoing pin, click and drag and select **Promote to Variable**. Name the variable `Movement Component` and connect the **Set Movement Component** node that will be automatically added to the graph to the execution pin of the **Set Character** node.

The final graph is shown in *Figure 10.6*:

Figure 10.6 – Event Blueprint Initialize Animation graph

This visual script is executed when the Blueprint is initialized and basically sets the variables you will need later on, during gameplay.

Now, locate the **Event Blueprint Update** animation node that should be already present in the graph.

9. From the **Variables** section, drag a getter node for the **Character** property. Right-click it and select the **Convert to Validated Get** option; this will change the node into an executable one that will check whether the **Character** variable is valid.

10. Connect the **Event Blueprint Update Animation** execution pin to the incoming execution pin of the **Get Validated Character** node.

11. In the **Variables** section, create a new variable of type **float** and call it `CharacterSpeed`. Drag a **Set** node for this variable into the graph.

12. From the **Variables** section, drag a **Get** node for the **Movement Component** variable.

13. Click and drag from the outgoing pin of the **Movement Component** node and create a **Get Velocity** property node.

14. Click and drag from the outgoing pin of the **Get Velocity** node and create a **Vector Length XY** node.

15. Connect the outgoing pin of the **Vector Length XY** node to the incoming pin of the **Set Character Speed** node.

The final result of the graph is shown in *Figure 10.7*:

Figure 10.7 – Event Blueprint Update graph

This Visual Scripting code basically tracks the velocity magnitude of the character and stores it in the **Character Speed** variable, which will be used in the following steps to blend the movement animation.

Next, select the **AnimGraph** tab of the editor, which will display a single **Output Pose** – this node represents the final animation pose of the character. We now need to tell the graph how to animate the character.

16. Drag the **Character Speed** property from the **Variables** section to create a getter node.

17. Click and drag from the **Character Speed** outgoing pin and create a **Blendspace Player** '**BS_WalkRun**' node.

18. Click and drag the outgoing pin of the **Blendspace Player** '**BS_WalkRun**' node and create a **Slot 'Default Slot'** node – we will use this node from the C++ code to execute the throw Animation Montage.

19. Connect the outgoing pin of **Slot 'Default Slot'** to the incoming pin of the **Output Pose** node.

The final result of the AnimGraph is depicted in *Figure 10.8*:

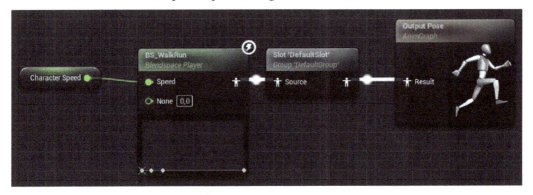

Figure 10.8 – AnimGraph

With this final step, the Animation Blueprint is complete; now, you just need to connect it to the character Blueprint to make it work.

Adding the Animation System to the character

To add the animation system to the character, you just have to declare the Animation Blueprint inside the Blueprint class. To do so, open the **BP_Character** Blueprint and select the **Mesh** property. Then, in the **Details** panel, locate the **Anim Class** property. From the drop-down menu next to it, select **AB_Character** as shown in *Figure 10.9*:

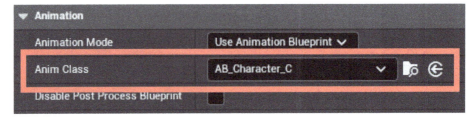

Figure 10.9 – Animation Blueprint assigned to the Blueprint class

If you test the game right now, you should see the character starting the animation loop and reacting to the player input when walking and running. However, the run animation will be weirdly jumpy and buggy – this is happening because these animations are not replicated and are just checking the character speed to update.

From a technical point of view, the speed value (i.e., MaxWalkSpeed) is just stored in the server instance of the character, but the client will have its own MaxWalkSpeed value. While this may be acceptable if you are just moving an Actor around, as the server will be constantly updating the Actor position, animating a Skeletal Mesh component based on its speed is a totally different beast. In fact, the Animation System is using the local value (i.e., the client one) and the system will continuously conflict between server and client data, resulting in a broken animation.

That's why we need to move the start-and-stop sprint logic we implemented in *Chapter 7, Using Remote Procedure Calls (RPCs)*, from the server to the client and call the corresponding methods as multicast ones so that all the clients will be aware of this change.

To do so, open the US_Character.h header file and add the following client declarations:

```
UFUNCTION(NetMulticast, Reliable)
void SprintStart_Client();

UFUNCTION(NetMulticast, Reliable)
void SprintEnd_Client();
```

As you can see, we used the NetMulticast specifier in order to let all the clients know that the character has started sprinting. Additionally, this call needs to be a Reliable one so you are guaranteed to send all the data to the recipients without any packet loss.

> **Note**
>
> For a refresher on RPCs and the NetMulticast specifier, please refer to *Chapter 7, Using Remote Procedure Calls (RPCs)*.

Now, open the US_Character.cpp file and locate SprintStart_Server_Implementation() and SprintEnd_Server_Implementation(). You are going to move all the content of both methods to the corresponding client-side calls. To do so, remove all the content (i.e., the code in between the brackets) and, in SprintStart_Server_Implementation(), add the client-side call:

```
SprintStart_Client();
```

For the SprintEnd_Server_Implementation() method, add the following:

```
SprintEnd_Client();
```

After that, move the previously removed code to the client-side implementations:

```
void AUS_Character::SprintStart_Client_Implementation()
{
  if (GetCharacterStats())
  {
```

```
    GetCharacterMovement()->MaxWalkSpeed = GetCharacterStats()-
>SprintSpeed;
    }
}

void AUS_Character::SprintEnd_Client_Implementation()
{
  if (GetCharacterStats())
  {
    GetCharacterMovement()->MaxWalkSpeed = GetCharacterStats()-
>WalkSpeed;
  }
}
```

The overall behavior will then be as follows:

- The client controlled by the player receives the movement inputs and sends this data to the server

- The server handles this input and sends the update request to all clients

- All the clients update the MaxWalkSpeed value accordingly

Once you have compiled the project, try testing the game – our character can now move and sprint like a pro, and you'll get to see their animations shine in all their glory!

For some extra practice, try working on the minion character and implementing the same animation logic. This is the true meaning of summoning a bunch of bones to a fully-fledged, reanimated minion, and who knows? The Lichlord might just reward you with a surprise or two for a job well done!

Adding the throw animation

What's missing at the moment is the throw animation and, in this case, network synchronization is something we really want – every connected player in the game will need to see the character animation whenever it is throwing the dagger in the dungeon, and this animation should be played at the same time for all clients.

The first thing to do is to ensure that the WeaponProjectile component will be properly replicated. To do so, open the US_Character.cpp file. Then, in the constructor, locate the Weapon component initialization, and add the following line of code:

```
Weapon->SetIsReplicated(true);
```

Next, open US_WeaponProjectileComponent.h and, in the private section, add the following Animation Montage reference:

```
UPROPERTY(EditDefaultsOnly, BlueprintReadOnly, Category="Projectile",
meta=(AllowPrivateAccess = "true"))
UAnimMontage* ThrowAnimation;
```

After that, in the protected section, add the following declaration:

```
UFUNCTION(NetMulticast, Unreliable)
void Throw_Client();
```

This is the throw method that will be executed from the client side. Notice that we are RPC multicasting to all clients with the Unreliable property specifier – even though we want this animation synchronized over the network, it is just an aesthetic add-on, so we can afford to lose the data over the network. The other clients won't see the animation, but the dagger will be spawned anyway.

With the header declarations complete, open the US_WeaponProjectileComponent.cpp file and add the client-side throw method:

```
void UUS_WeaponProjectileComponent::Throw_Client_Implementation()
{
  const auto Character = Cast<AUS_Character>(GetOwner());
  if (ThrowAnimation != nullptr)
  {
    if (const auto AnimInstance = Character->GetMesh()-
>GetAnimInstance(); AnimInstance != nullptr)
    {
      AnimInstance->Montage_Play(ThrowAnimation, 1.f);
    }
  }
}
```

As you can see, the code will get the owner of this component and, if it is of the US_Character type, will play the Animation Montage.

This method will be called from its server-side counterpart, so locate the Throw_Server_Implementation() method. We could just execute the method call, but we need to give a slight delay to the spawn logic because the throw animation will take some time to complete, and spawning the dagger ahead of time would return ugly visual feedback to the player. To do so, remove all the content of the function and replace it with the following code:

```
if (ProjectileClass)
{
  Throw_Client();
  FTimerHandle TimerHandle;
```

```
GetWorld()->GetTimerManager().SetTimer(TimerHandle, [&]()
{
  const auto Character = Cast<AUS_Character>(GetOwner());
  const auto ProjectileSpawnLocation = GetComponentLocation();
  const auto ProjectileSpawnRotation = GetComponentRotation();
  auto ProjectileSpawnParams = FActorSpawnParameters();
  ProjectileSpawnParams.Owner = GetOwner();
  ProjectileSpawnParams.Instigator = Character;

  GetWorld()->SpawnActor<AUS_BaseWeaponProjectile>(ProjectileClass,
ProjectileSpawnLocation, ProjectileSpawnRotation,
ProjectileSpawnParams);
}, .4f, false);
}
```

Here, we have just moved the spawn logic inside a timer handle to delay the spawn process while calling the client-side throw logic, in order to start the animation immediately.

> **Note**
>
> Unreal Engine provides more advanced methods for synchronizing animations beyond simply delaying method calls, such as **Animation Notifies** (https://docs.unrealengine. com/5.1/en-US/animation-notifies-in-unreal-engine/). However, for the purpose of this book, the delay method is a quick and dirty solution that will suffice for our needs.

As the last step, open the **BP_Character** Blueprint, select the **Weapon** component and, in the **Details** panel, look for the **Throw Animation** property and assign the **AM_Throw** montage you have already created.

You can now test the game and the character should throw the dagger and synchronize correctly with the throw animation.

In this section, you have dipped your toes into the mystical realm of animation (although you're not quite ready to battle the Lichlord just yet) and conjured up a basic animation system that networked players will appreciate. In the next section, you're about to bring some friendly characters to life and add even more fun to your game by giving players someone to rescue.

Adding NPC Actors

While taking a leisurely stroll in the underground and dodging or stabbing zombies can be amusing, let's not forget the big bucks the king's shelling out for us. We've got a rescue mission on our hands – liberate his knights from the Lichlord's dungeons before they're turned into undead abominations. Time to get down to business, my fearless developer!

In this section, you'll create an Actor Blueprint that will serve as a prisoner your beloved thief needs to rescue (in order to get more experience points). To implement such a system, you will make good use of the `Interactable` interface you implemented in *Chapter 7, Using Remote Procedure Calls (RPCs)*.

Creating the NPC character

The NPC you will be creating is a simple, replicated Actor that will cheer when the player has interacted with it and will grant some experience points. The first things we need are the Animation Montages that will play the idle and cheer animations. To do so, complete the following steps:

1. In the `Animations` folder, add a new **Animation Montage** asset based on the **knight_Skeleton** asset and call it `AM_KnightIdle`.

2. Add the **knight_Idle** animation to the **DefaultGroup.DefaultSlot** section of the montage.

3. Add another **Animation Montage** asset based on the **knight_Skeleton** asset and call it `AM_KnightCheer`.

4. Add the **knight_cheer** animation to the montage.

    With these two animation assets ready, you can start creating the prisoner Blueprint. Open the `Blueprints` folder and complete the following steps.

5. Create a new Blueprint based on the **Actor** class and name it `BP_KnightPrisoner`. Double-click it to open it.

6. In the **Components** panel, add a **Skeletal Mesh** component.

7. In the **Details** panel, tick the **Replicates** property in order to replicate the Actor over the network.

8. Create an **Integer** variable and call it `EarnedXp`. Set its **Default Value** to `20`. Tick the **Instance Editable** property to make the variable public.

9. Create an **Anim Montage Object Reference** variable and call it `MontageIdle`. Set its **Default Value** to **AM_KnightIdle**. Tick the **Instance Editable** property.

10. Create another **Anim Montage Object Reference** variable and call it `MontageCheer`. Set its default value to **AM_KnightCheer**. Tick the **Instance Editable** property.

With these base settings available, you can start adding some Visual Scripting to the Event Graph in order to make the Actor fully functional. You will start from the **Begin Play** event to start the idle animation. To do so, complete the following steps:

1. Add an **Event BeginPlay** node to the graph.

2. From the **Components** panel, drag into the graph a reference of the **Skeletal Mesh** component.

3. From the **Variables** panel, drag a getter node for the **MontageIdle** variable.

4. From the **Event BeginPlay** execution pin, create a **Play Animation** node.

5. Connect the **Skeletal Mesh** pin to the **Target** pin of the **Play Animation** node.

6. Connect the **Montage Idle** pin to the **New Anim to Play** pin of the **Play Animation** node.

7. Tick the **Looping** property of the **Play Animation** node.

    The final result for this part of the graph is shown in *Figure 10.10*:

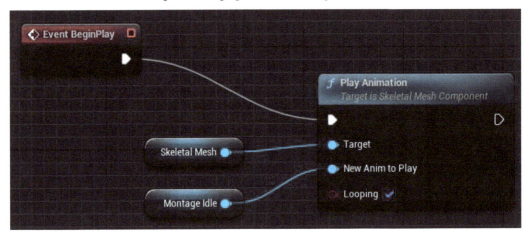

Figure 10.10 – Event BeginPlay graph

Then, create a custom event that will start the cheer animation when the prisoner is rescued by the player character. This event needs to be executed as a **Multicast** event in order to start the animation on all clients. To do so, complete the following steps:

1. Right-click on the graph and create a **Custom Event** node, naming it CharacterCheer. With the event selected, locate the **Replicates** property in the **Details** panel and, from its drop-down menu, select **Multicast**, leaving the **Reliable** checkmark unticked, as shown in *Figure 10.11*:

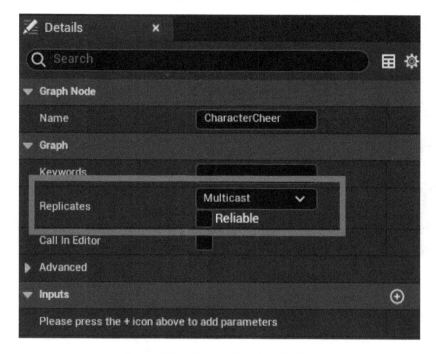

Figure 10.11 – Custom Event replication

2. From the **Components** panel, drag into the graph a reference to the **Skeletal Mesh** component.

3. From the **Variables** panel, drag a getter node for the **MontageCheer** variable.

4. From the **Event BeginPlay** execution pin, create a **Play Animation** node.

5. Connect the **Skeletal Mesh** pin to the **Target** pin of the **Play Animation** node.

6. Connect the **Montage Idle** pin to the **New Anim to Play** pin of the **Play Animation** node.

7. Tick the **Looping** property of the **Play Animation** node.

The final result for this part of the graph is shown in *Figure 10.12*:

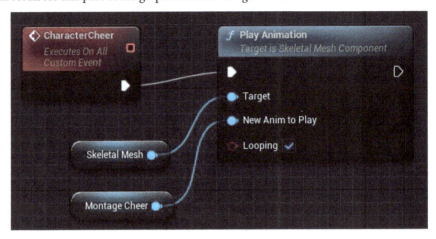

Figure 10.12 – CharacterCheer Custom Event

The last step needed to make the Actor work properly is to make it interactable with the player character by implementing the US_Interactable interface. To do so, complete the following steps:

1. Open the **Class Settings** panel and locate the **Interfaces** category.

2. In **Implemented Interfaces**, add the **US_Interactable** interface.

3. In the **My Blueprint** panel, locate the **Interfaces** category and right-click the **Interact** method, selecting **Implement event**. An **Event Interact** node will be added to the Event Graph.

4. Click and drag from the event **Character Instigator** pin to add a **PlayerState** node and connect its **Target** pin to the **Character Instigator** pin of the **Event Interact** node.

5. Click and drag from the outgoing pin of the **PlayerState** node and create a **Cast To US_ PlayerState** node. Connect its incoming execution pin to the outgoing execution pin of the **Event Interact** node.

6. Click and drag from the **As US PlayerState** of the cast node and create an **Add Xp** node. Connect its incoming execution pin to the **Success** execution pin of the cast node.

7. From the **Variables** panel, drag a getter node for the **EarnedXp** variable. Connect its outgoing pin to the **Value** pin of the **Add Xp** node.

8. Click and drag from the outgoing pin of the **Add Xp** node and create a **Character Cheer** node to complete the graph, as shown in *Figure 10.13*:

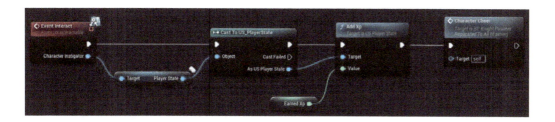

Figure 10.13 – Interaction graph

You may have noticed that we didn't use any authority checks in the previous graph; this is because we know that this event will only be called on the server.

The Blueprint is now complete, so it's time to do some testing.

Testing the NPC Actor

To test the Blueprint, you can drag an instance of it into the level and start a gameplay session. The thief character should be able to reach the NPC and, if we use the interaction button, the animation should show them cheering. The hero who liberates the NPC characters will receive a well-deserved pool of experience points as a reward. Time to level up and become an even greater hero!

Figure 10.14 shows the final result of the NPC Actor, once it has been liberated by the thief hero:

Figure 10.14 – A liberated Actor during gameplay

Well, it seems we now have a new prisoner to play with! But why settle for one when we can have variations? Feel free to get creative and give our captive some fresh looks to keep things interesting. By creating child Blueprints and changing the Actor's Skeletal Mesh component and Animation Montages, you will be able to make good use of the barbarian and mage models available in the project. You may even create a rogue prisoner variation – who says we can't go off-script a little? The king may have paid us to rescue his knights and warriors, but hey, a skilled hero or two in the Thief Guild never hurt anyone!

Congratulations – you've completed this part of the adventure. Now it's time to let your imagination run wild and add your own game logic! In the next section, I won't be teaching you any new techniques, but I'll provide you with some fresh ideas to enhance the gameplay and make it more exciting.

Making further improvements to the game

Now that you have solid knowledge of how the Unreal multiplayer system works, it's time to unleash your creativity and bring your own ideas to life, making your game truly unique and personalized. In this section, I will give you some hints on how to spice up your project, but don't hesitate to add your own twist to make it uniquely yours.

Let's make some noise!

Currently, the minions' hearing senses are only utilized to detect when a character is running. Why not tweak the system and let other elements in the game alert the Lichlord's minions?

Unfortunately, `PawnNoiseEmitterComponent` can only be used on, well... pawns, so you cannot attach it to other Actors (it simply won't work); however, in *Chapter 9, Extending AI Behaviors*, you built a strong system to alert enemy minions that makes use of the Game Mode. As the Game Mode can be reached by any Actor in the level, you can exploit the `AlertMinions()` function and send messages that will call for help when activated.

One of the best ways to use this method is through traps – whenever the player character steps into one such device, all the minions around will be alerted. Some examples of this kind of game feature include the following:

- *Creaking doors*: Whenever the character opens a door, it will make a creaking or squeaking sound that will alert the Lichlord's servants to the intruders.

- *Traps*: Some dungeon areas will be more protected than others – set some mechanical devices that will rally all nearby enemies. After all, this is just a matter of creating a collision area and calling a method in the Game Mode!

- *Magical items*: Create some magical artifact that can be interacted with by the player. The Lichlord is a sneaky one: he cast an alert spell, which condemned the hapless thief hero to their inevitable fate. Whenever the character tries to use that juicy item, an alarm will be sent to nearby minions, alerting them. Think of the possibilities! You can even use the floating book we created at the beginning of the project.

I need a key!

Opening doors in a dungeon can be a fun game, but things can get even more interesting when you come across a locked door. Why not give it a try and see what other surprises lie in wait?

In *Chapter 7, Using Remote Procedure Calls (RPCs)*, you created the US_Interactable interface and made use of the Interact() method. However, the interface also exposes the CanInteract() method, which can be used to check whether the Actor can be interacted with.

A door may implement a system that will only return true to the CanInteract() method if the player character has a key – this means creating a key pickup item and adding the US_Character system to track whether they have one or more keys to use. These locked doors can be used to keep the NPCs locked in some cellars and only able to be freed if the corresponding key is found somewhere in the level.

Watch out for the Lichlord! His prisoners are double-locked up tighter than a merchant's coin purse in the deepest and most heavily guarded cells of his dungeon!

Improve your arsenal, my hero!

While it's nice to have a pointy dagger to throw at your hated opponents, it's even nicer to have a magical one that will inflict more damage, or even defeat enemies with a single hit. You can implement a pickup Blueprint that will make good use of the SetProjectileClass() function you implemented in the US_WeaponProjectileComponent class.

Upon picking up the item, the character will be granted a variant of the US_BaseWeaponProjectile class with augmented damage. You can even think about letting defeated enemies drop weapon pickups instead of coins!

As an additional feature, you may even think to create throwing rocks that will send alert messages upon hitting the ground – just remember to enable gravity for the projectile. Having items that can be thrown and that will make noise to alert minions and direct them far away from the player characters will add some fresh gameplay logic that will improve the overall game experience.

Get ready for a wickedly clever twist, and use your quick wit to dazzle the Lichlord's mindless servants! With brains like yours, who needs brawn?

You are not a machine gun

Currently, players have the ability to throw an unlimited number of daggers during gameplay. While this may be enjoyable initially, it will ultimately disrupt the balance of the game and result in a monotonous experience over time.

To make things more interesting (and in favor of the Lichlord's shadowy plans), limit the players to just one throwing dagger projectile at a time. Once the character has thrown the weapon, it won't be able to throw it again until the dagger has been recovered.

Implementing this feature is quite straightforward – once the character throws the projectile, set the `ProjectileClass` weapon component to a `null` value so that the character won't be able to spawn any more objects. Upon hitting something, the thrown weapon will spawn a dagger pickup (see the previous subsection) before destroying itself. This will force the character to get to the dropped weapon and pick it up in order to attack again.

As an alternative feature, you may give your character a limited number of knives and use a count variable to check whether the character has any knives available every time the player tries to throw one.

Whoever said life in the dungeon would be a walk in the park obviously never encountered a horde of undead monsters while armed with a simple (and single!) weapon.

No time to waste

At the moment, your characters can walk around calmly and take their time in rescuing the prisoners. Why not spice things up by adding a time counter? The Lichlord is hosting a grand celebration with the intention of transforming the king's knight into a loyal member of his undead army! Your hero must hurry up before it is too late!

You can make good use of the `US_GameMode` class and create a time manager that will start as soon as the first player enters the dungeon – if the players can't free every captive from the dungeon, they'll be royally out of luck and the game will be a total flop. It looks like it's all or nothing for this quest!

Tables, tables everywhere!

As your project progresses, it will become increasingly difficult to keep track of all the variations in enemies and weapons. To ease the pain, you can use the struct and data table system introduced in *Chapter 6, Replicating Properties Over the Network,* to create dedicated structures for the throwing weapons and AI opponents.

Let your creative side run wild and come up with a ton of amazing Blueprint options based on the stats you like best – get ready for your hero adventurers to embark on thrilling journeys full of surprises in your game!

Need some help?

As you may have noticed from the previous subsections, once you become familiar with your game, the potential outcomes become limitless. You can add any new gameplay logic and test it until you are happy.

On my end, I'll be working on creating exciting new features for the game and storing them in my own GitHub repository. Feel free to check in from time to time to see what wild and crazy ideas I've come up with! The link to the repository is `https://github.com/marcosecchi/unrealshadows-ltol`.

And if you come up with a clever idea, feel free to contact me and tell me about it – if time permits, I will try to implement it and upload it to the repository in order to make this project grow!

Summary

Throughout this chapter, you fine-tuned the gameplay logic and added the finishing touches. You began by incorporating some nice animations for character movements and attacks, elevating the game's overall appeal.

Additionally, you created someone for the players to rescue: a prisoner Actor that can be interacted with and that will grant the thief hero some well-deserved experience points.

Last but not least, I shared a few fresh ideas to take your gameplay to the next level. By incorporating these ideas, you can make the game truly your own and one of a kind. So, get creative and have fun!

Get ready for the next chapter, where you'll dive into debugging and testing a networked game. This will take your development skills to the next level, something that's necessary if you want to become a top-notch multiplayer programmer!

11
Debugging a Multiplayer Game

Debugging an application is a crucial aspect of programming in general, and this holds particularly true when dealing with multiplayer game programming. The debugging process helps developers identify and resolve any issues that may arise when running a networked application or game. By understanding the basics of network debugging, programmers can ensure their games run smoothly and efficiently on all platforms.

When it comes to debugging networks with Unreal Engine, there are several tools available to help make the process easier for programmers. The first step in this process is setting up logging within your project settings so that you can track errors as they occur during the development or testing phases of your game's life cycle.

Additionally, developing an emulated multiplayer environment can be a highly effective method of replicating real-life scenarios, while simultaneously assessing the operational efficacy of your systems.

What's more, tools such as the Network Profiler will provide detailed insights into critical metrics such as connection speeds and latencies, enabling the identification of potential issues and areas that require improvement.

As you progress through this chapter, you will acquire a comprehensive understanding of the optimization techniques, enabling you to fine-tune the performance of your project and ensure a seamless multiplayer game experience. Furthermore, you will learn how to effectively isolate and troubleshoot any existing issues that may disrupt the overall gameplay experience.

So, in this chapter, I will guide you through the following sections:

- Introducing network debugging
- Emulating a networked environment
- Using the Network Profiler
- Improving performance and bandwidth utilization

Technical requirements

To follow the topics presented in this chapter, you should have completed the previous ones and understood their content.

Additionally, if you would prefer to begin with code from the companion repository for this book, you can download the `.zip` project files provided in this book's companion project repository: `https://github.com/PacktPublishing/Multiplayer-Game-Development-with-Unreal-Engine-5`.

You can download the files that are up to date with the end of the previous chapter by clicking the `Unreal Shadows - Chapter 10 End` link.

Introducing network debugging

Network testing and debugging is an essential skill for any professional working on multiplayer games. It requires a deep understanding of networking protocols and technologies, as well as an ability to identify and diagnose problems quickly. Additionally, it involves troubleshooting both client-side issues on the user's device and server-side issues on the game's servers. By mastering this skill, you can ensure that games are running smoothly with minimal latency for all players involved.

As you embark on the development of a networked game, it is imperative to consider the following obstacles that come with creating a seamless and engaging multiplayer experience for your audience, as opposed to a single-player game:

- You will need to debug multiple running instances of the project
- Network communication, by its nature, may be unreliable and unstable, and different clients may have different issues
- A client will work differently as opposed to a server

Unreal Engine comes equipped with a range of dedicated tools and workflows specifically designed for debugging networked applications. By following the guides provided in this chapter, you will gain valuable insights into how to effectively utilize these tools, as well as learn expert tips and best practices for troubleshooting any common networking problems that you may encounter.

Before I delve into how Unreal Engine's debugging tools operate, it's essential to have a basic understanding of game debugging.

Explaining game debugging

The process of **debugging** involves testing every part of the project to make sure everything works as expected and identifying any areas where improvements can be made – this will ensure optimal performance and stability for players when they're playing your games. Debugging also includes checking the code functionality across different platforms and devices (for example, mobile platforms, desktop, or VR devices), running automated tests on builds before deployment, and so on.

In the end, good debugging practices will allow you to find small details that might otherwise go unnoticed and cause serious problems in development if they're not addressed early on!

In the previous chapters, you utilized many debug tools provided by Unreal Engine – probably the most used one has been the `GEngine->AddOnScreenDebugMessage()` command, which adds the capability of showing messages on the screen.

Some other tools for debugging are purely visuals – such as `DrawDebugSphere()`, which you used in *Chapter 7, Using Remote Procedure Calls (RPC)*, to show the position of the Actors your player character can interact with.

If you are familiar with tools such as Microsoft Visual Studio, JetBrains Rider, or any other programming IDE, you will most probably know how important it is to use **breakpoints** – points in the code where the execution of the code can be temporarily stopped so that you can inspect a program's data and state.

Debugging a multiplayer game – due to its very specialized nature – needs some more tools to inspect what is happening behind the scenes. In the following subsections, I will introduce you to some of these tools to help you improve your multiplayer programming expertise.

Introducing multiplayer options

Since *Chapter 3, Testing the Multiplayer System with a Project Prototype*, you have used the most common tool for testing a multiplayer environment by selecting **Listen Server Net Mode** and choosing the number of players to emulate. These settings are just part of the **Multiplayer Options** category that can be tweaked in the project settings. To see the full range of options, from the main menu, do the following:

1. Select the **Window | Editor Preferences** option and locate the **Level Editor | Play** setting.
2. Look for the **Multiplayer Options** category, as shown in *Figure 11.1*:

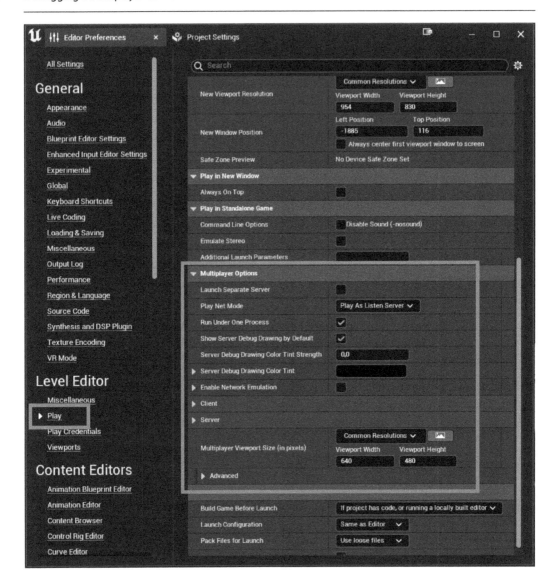

Figure 11.1 – The Multiplayer Options category

This category offers a plethora of options for customizing and debugging your game – you have already used **Play Net Mode** and **Play Number of Clients** (located in the **Client** subsection), even if you set these values from another part of the Unreal Editor (that is, the main toolbar). But there's much more than this!

As an example, you can locate the **Multiplayer Viewport Size (in pixels)** option and, from the **Common Resolutions** dropdown, select the client display resolution. This will let you test the look and feel of your game once it's played on your target devices. *Figure 11.2* shows the look of the game once played on a **720x1280 Razer Phone** device:

Figure 11.2 – The smartphone display emulation

Hey, I know our project wasn't originally designed to be played on a smartphone, but you get the idea anyway, right?

Later in this chapter, I will demonstrate some additional features within the **Multiplayer Options** section – for instance, the traffic emulation settings – that will enhance your proficiency during the debugging phase of your project.

Logging in a networked environment

As you may already know, in Unreal Engine – or any programming environment – **logging** can be used to debug and track the flow of code at runtime. Logging is a widely used practice in software development, and multiplayer development is no exception. Unreal Engine offers a wide variety of log categories and some of them are dedicated to networking.

The **Output Log** window keeps track of all the messages and can be opened by clicking on the dedicated button at the bottom of Unreal Engine, as shown in *Figure 11.3*:

Figure 11.3 – The Output Log activation button

Additionally, all log messages are saved in a `.log` file located in your project folder (that is, `[Your Project Folder]/Saved/Logs/`).

Each log message is categorized and can be filtered – as an example, *Figure 11.4* shows the log window after I resized the game viewport from the editor:

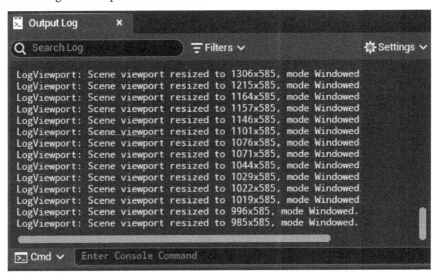

Figure 11.4 – The log window open

The most common category you will be using while network debugging is **LogNet**, which includes the majority of network logs.

> **Note**
>
> For an exhaustive list of all the log categories available in a networked environment, check out the official documentation: `https://docs.unrealengine.com/5.1/en-US/logging-for-networked-games-in-unreal-engine/`.

Filtering the LogNet category

Now that you have some basic knowledge of the network log system, you can try playing the game and checking the **Output Log** window to see what's happening under the hood. To do this, follow these steps:

1. Open your project in Unreal Engine and click on the **Output Log** button at the bottom of the editor. Optionally, you can click the **Dock in Layout** button to dock the window inside the editor and make it non-collapsible.

2. Once the log window is open, locate the **Filters** button and click on it to open all the filters. You will notice that the LogNet category is not shown. To enable it, you need to start a game session – once in Play Mode, you will notice that the category is visible.

3. From the **Filters** list, click on the **Categories** section and untick the **Show All** option to deselect all the categories, and then locate the **LogNet** category to enable it, as shown in *Figure 11.5*:

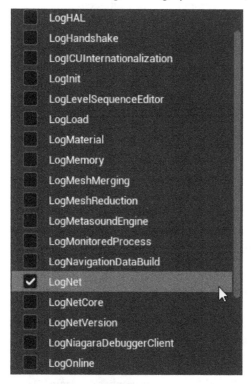

Figure 11.5 – The log categories filter

Once you have enabled only the **LogNet** category, you will get a filtered log list, as depicted in *Figure 11.6*:

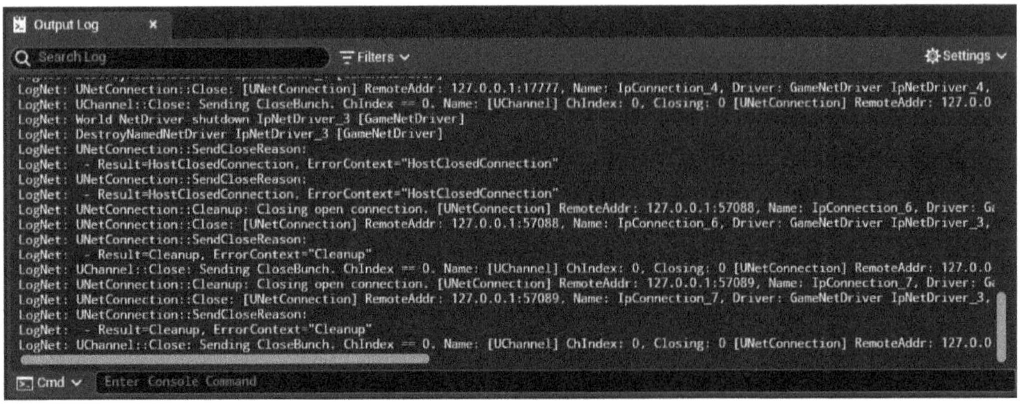

Figure 11.6 – The LogNet output

As you can see, there's a lot of stuff going on here, and it depends on your game session.

As an extra exercise, take some time and read the log messages. You probably won't understand much at first sight but, as time goes by, this kind of communication with Unreal Engine will become familiar to you.

In the next subsection, you will learn how to create a log category so that you can easily track what's happening inside your application.

Creating a custom log category

Usually, when you are caught up in the whirlwind of a project, the temptation is to use log messages without worrying too much about categorizing them. This is a mistake that, of course, will be paid for in the long run. Creating customized categories for your logs is simple, and there are no good reasons not to do it.

To define a custom category, you need to use the DECLARE_LOG_CATEGORY_EXTERN macro inside a header and, in the corresponding source file, introduce the DEFINE_LOG_CATEGORY macro. Additionally, the category name must be named with a Log prefix – for instance, LogMyApp. As an example, in the next few steps, you will be creating a custom log category for your game, named LogUnrealShadows, which you can then use anywhere in your project.

So, open your programming IDE and create a new empty class named US_CustomLogs – you won't need an Unreal class, just a regular C++ one.

Then, open the US_CustomLogs.h file and remove the class declaration as you won't be using it. After that, add the following line of code:

```
DECLARE_LOG_CATEGORY_EXTERN(LogUnrealShadows, Display, All);
```

This macro declares `LogUnrealShadows` as a new log category to be used in your project. The verbosity for this category is set to `Display`; this means that the message will be printed to the console and the log file – if you need to print the message just in the log file and not in the console, you can use the `Log` value instead.

Now, open the `US_CustomLogs.cpp` file and define the log category by adding the following line of code:

```
DEFINE_LOG_CATEGORY(LogUnrealShadows);
```

This macro will let you use the `LogUnrealShadows` category anywhere in your project. Once in Play Mode, you will be able to select the `LogUnrealShadows` category from the **Output Log** filter, as shown in *Figure 11.7*:

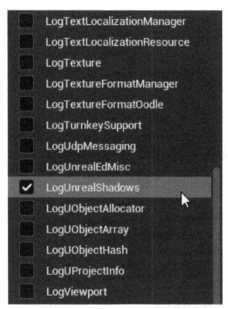

Figure 11.7 – The LogUnrealShadows category

Now that the category has been defined, you can use it to add your logs in the game – to do this, you can use the `UE_LOG()` macro. As an example, open the `US_GameMode.cpp` file and add the needed `include` declaration:

```
#include "US_CustomLogs.h"
```

Then, to log an alert message inside the `AlertMinions()` function class, you must add the following line of code:

```
UE_LOG(LogUnrealShadows, Display, TEXT("Alerting Minions"));
```

Figure 11.8 shows the aforementioned message in the **Output Log** panel once a character has been detected:

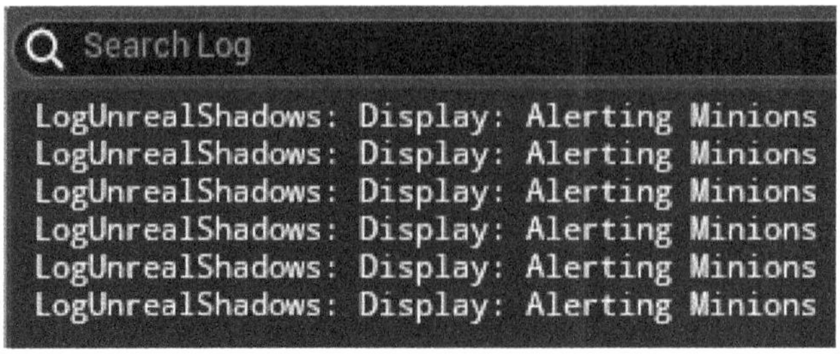

Figure 11.8 – The custom message in the Output Log panel

This section introduced you to some of the key debugging tools that are available in Unreal Engine and explained how to effectively utilize them. In the upcoming section, you'll be presented with how to simulate a networked environment on your personal computer, providing you with the ability to test your project under conditions where major issues may arise during execution.

Emulating a networked environment

Creating a replica of a multiplayer network environment can be an effective way to simulate real-world scenarios and test the performance of your systems. By leveraging Unreal's capabilities, you'll be able to test multiple connections on a single machine and provide a realistic experience that will give you an accurate idea of your game behavior once it has been deployed online.

Network emulation is an important feature that helps you simulate lag and packet loss for both servers and clients. This is especially important in identifying and troubleshooting networking issues. Unreal Editor, the command line console, and configuration files all offer configurable settings for network emulation to ensure that it can be tailored precisely to your needs.

Enabling network emulation

Network emulation can be enabled from the **Editor Preferences** window, in the **Level Editor | Play** section. To enable this tool, locate the **Multiplayer Options** category and tick the **Enable Network Emulation** option, as depicted in *Figure 11.9*:

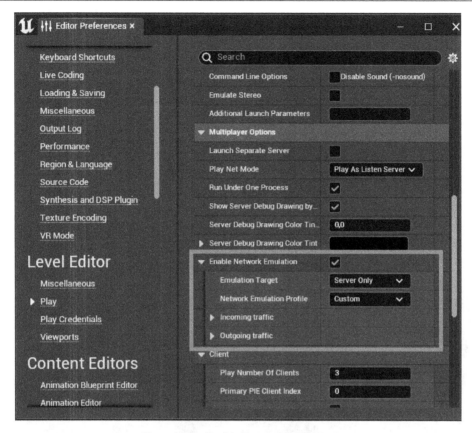

Figure 11.9 – Enable Network Emulation

Selecting this option will enable a set of options you can use to test different situations during a multiplayer session. Firstly, you can select which target to emulate through the **Emulation Target** property – there are three options for this:

- **Server Only**: This option will emulate just the server's behavior over the network
- **Clients Only**: This option will emulate just the client's behavior over the network
- **Everyone**: This option will emulate both the client's and the server's behavior over the network

Secondly, you have access to **Network Emulation Profile**, which will let you select different scenarios for a networked game – there are three options for this:

- **Average**: This option will emulate a regular multiplayer game
- **Bad**: This option will create a worst-case scenario, with a high time lag and a lot of data packets lost during the networked game
- **Custom**: This option will let you customize the emulation experience with your own values

The aforementioned profiles will initialize a set of values for the **Incoming Traffic** and the **Outgoing Traffic** values of the client or the server (or both), depending on the **Emulation Target** selection. *Figure 11.10* shows the expanded profile options with the custom option selected:

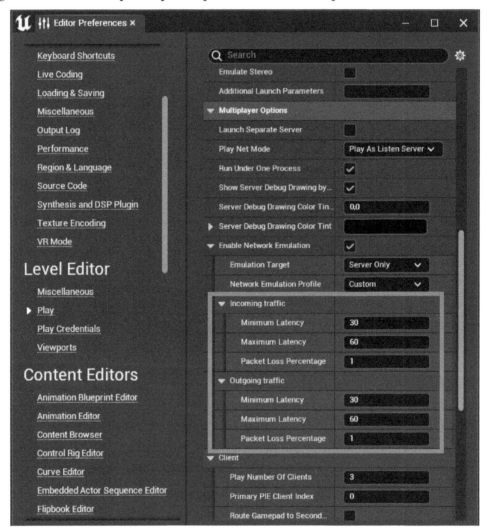

Figure 11.10 - The emulation profiles expanded

In the next subsection, I will present you the meaning of most of the settings for this section of the **Multiplayer Options** category.

Explaining the Incoming Traffic option

Activating the **Incoming Traffic** option will introduce delays or loss in the reception of packets during playtime. You can modify the following properties:

- **Minimum Latency**: This indicates the minimum amount of time lag in milliseconds
- **Maximum Latency**: This indicates the maximum amount of time lag in milliseconds
- **Packet Loss Percentage**: This indicates the chance that a packet will be lost before being received

As an example, a typical bad situation of incoming traffic will have a latency of about 100 to 200 milliseconds and a probability of losing incoming data of about 5%. To create a similar scenario, your settings may have the following values:

- **Minimum Latency** may be set to a value of 100 milliseconds
- **Maximum Latency** may be set to a value of 200 milliseconds
- **Packet Loss Percentage** may be set to a value of 5%

Explaining the Outgoing Traffic option

Similarly, activating the **Outgoing Traffic** option will introduce delays or losses when you're sending packets during playtime. You can modify the following properties:

- **Minimum Latency**: This indicates the minimum amount of time lag in milliseconds
- **Maximum Latency**: This indicates the maximum amount of time lag in milliseconds
- **Packet Loss Percentage**: This indicates the chance that a packet will be lost before being received

As an example, you may simulate an average situation (that is, one that is not optimal but still acceptable) by having a latency of about 30 to 60 milliseconds and a probability of losing data of about 1%. Your settings may have the following values:

- **Minimum Latency** may be set to a value of 30 milliseconds
- **Maximum Latency** may be set to a value of 60 milliseconds
- **Packet Loss Percentage** may be set to a value of 1%

You've now learned about all the ways you can simulate a real networked game environment. It's now time to put that knowledge to the test and try it out with your multiplayer game! The Lichlord is getting a bit restless and is eagerly waiting for you. It's best not to keep him waiting too long, so let's not waste any time!

Testing the game with network emulation

Testing a game in a networked emulation is quite straightforward once you have understood the aforementioned elements – select your preferred settings and run the game. We will be emulating the game under different network scenarios, so open the project you have been working on in the previous chapters and get ready to do some testing.

Testing the game under average conditions

In this scenario, you will be testing one of the default profiles available in the **Editor Preferences** area and checking the game's behavior. To do so, follow these steps:

1. Open **Editor Preferences** and locate the **Play | Multiplayer** category.

2. Tick the **Enable Network Emulation** checkbox and set **Emulation Target to Everyone**; with this option, we will be testing both the client and the server network traffic.

3. In the **Network Emulation Profile** drop-down menu, select **Average**. The settings are shown in *Figure 11.11*:

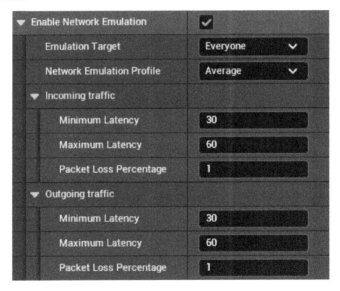

Figure 11.11 – Network emulation with the Average profile

With this profile set up, start a **Play as a Listen Server** game session and analyze your game. You should see the game work almost smoothly, with no lag or synchronization issues. This is because we opted for a very low percentage of packet loss (that is, 1%) and a lag latency for both the server and the clients that will be in the range of 30 to 60 milliseconds.

What we have here is an acceptable game scenario and the player experience will be nice and smooth. Now, let's try using some harsh conditions to see how the game behaves.

Testing the game under the worst conditions

In this second test, you'll be testing a worst-case scenario, where the network will have a high percentage of packet loss and the traffic latency will emulate a bad network bandwidth. To do so, follow these steps:

1. Open **Editor Preferences** and locate the **Play | Multiplayer** category.

2. Tick the **Enable Network Emulation** checkbox and set **Emulation Target to Everyone**; with this option, we will be testing both the client and the server network traffic.

3. From the **Network Emulation Profile** drop-down menu, select **Custom**.

4. For both the **Incoming Traffic** and **Outgoing Traffic** categories, do the following:

   • Set the **Minimum Latency** value to 450.

   • Set the **Maximum Latency** value to 550.

   • Set the **Packet Loss Percentage** value to 10. The settings are shown in *Figure 11.12*:

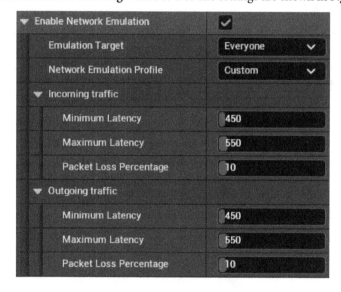

Figure 11.12 – Network emulation in a worst-case scenario

With this profile set up, start a **Play as a Listen Server** game session and analyze your game. You will experience an almost broken experience! The same character will seem to move completely out of sync in the different windows and the same thing will stay true for your character attack.

But notice that I said "almost" – as the server is authoritative and we are using reliable RPCs for the most important operations, such as throwing daggers, the game will go on flawlessly from an execution point of view. This means that the same character position will – sooner or later – be synchronized on all clients and the daggers will always be thrown, no matter the packet loss percentage.

If you want to test a totally broken game, try setting **Packet Loss Percentage** to a value of 100, meaning that no packet will be received by the server or the clients. When entering Play Mode, the client won't even start and all you will get will be a black screen. But this means the Lichlord has laid down a wickedly powerful enchantment on the network, stranding your fearless gang of thieves in a mystical quagmire. Unless some tech-savvy wizard at the King's court can conjure a nifty counter-magic to unweave the spell, that is!

In this section, you learned how to test your game in a networked emulation environment directly from your trusty computer. One of the most powerful features available is the ability to simulate data loss and network lags – this means checking the player experience under any scenario, including a worst-case one, where the player will have an almost totally broken experience due to bad networking technology.

In the next section, you will be presented with another important topic in improving your game – how to profile a networked application.

Using the Network Profiler

Unreal Engine's **Network Profiler** is a powerful standalone tool capable of analyzing and optimizing the performance of multiplayer game networks. A Profiler session will give you detailed insights into connection speeds, latency times, and other important metrics that can be used to identify potential issues or areas of improvement. By leveraging this information, you will be able to get optimal network performance and achieve a nicer user experience. In this section, I will guide you through the main features of this tool.

As stated previously, the Network Profiler is a standalone application that can be found in your Unreal Engine executable folder. Depending on your engine installation, the location path may vary, but it is usually located at [Your PC]/Programs Files/Epic Games/UE_5.1/Engine/Binaries/DotNET/NetworkProfiler.exe.

The Network Profiler application is shown in *Figure 11.13*:

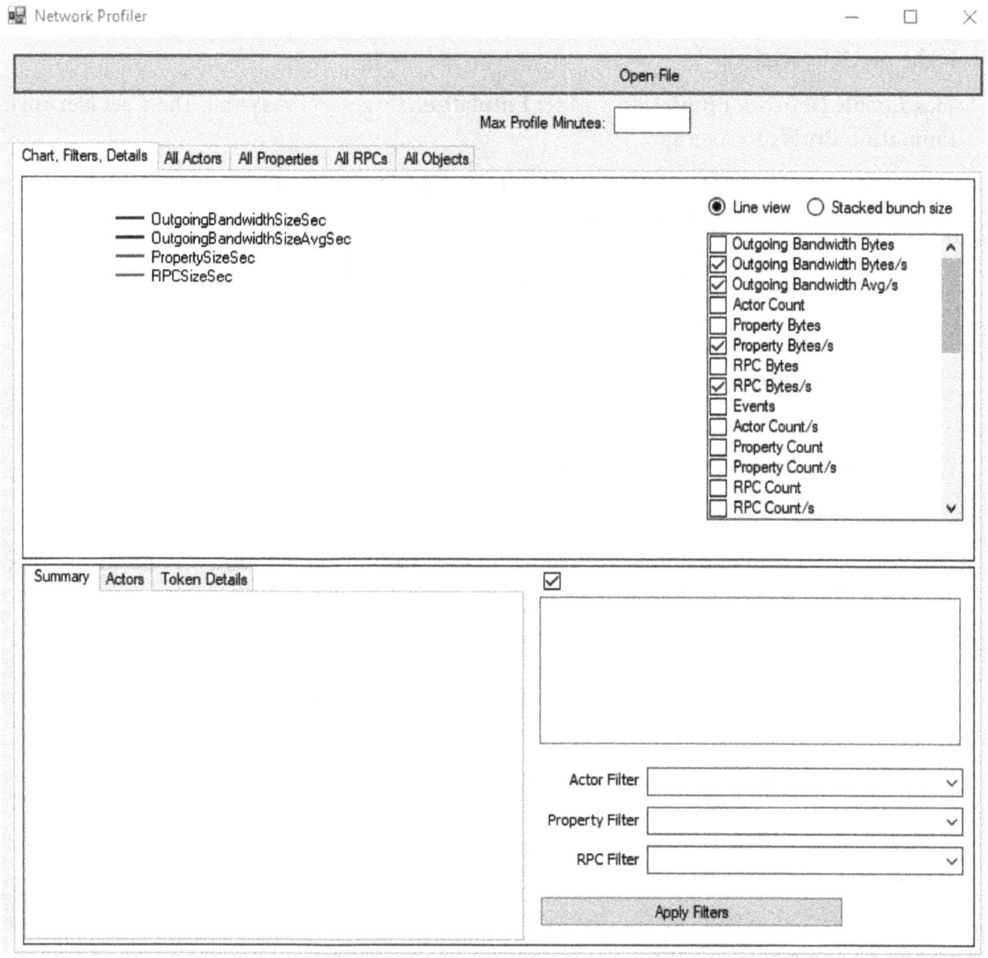

Figure 11.13 – The Network Profiler application

In the following section, I will show you how to record a network session and peek into its data through the Network Profiler.

Recording a profiling session

To use the Network Profiler, you need to collect some data for it to analyze. To accomplish this, you'll need to work with an engine version that has stat tracking enabled, such as a debugger or editor built for non-debug configurations – in our case, we will be recording the data directly from the Unreal Engine Editor with the default **Average** emulation profile.

To record a profiling session, follow these steps:

1. Open the **Play | Multiplayer Options** category in the **Editor Preferences** window, as explained in the previous section.

2. Tick **Enable Network Emulation** and set **Emulation Target** to **Everyone**. Then, set **Network Emulation Profile** to **Average**.

3. Start your game and locate the **Console Command** prompt located at the bottom of the editor (or at the bottom of any **Output Log** window that's open), as depicted in *Figure 11.14*:

Figure 11.14 – The Console Command prompt

4. Inside the prompt, enter this command:

    ```
    netprofile enable
    ```

    This will start a profile recording session and the **Output Log** window should display the following message:

    ```
    LogNet: Network Profiler: ENABLED
    ```

5. Play your game for a couple of minutes and then enter the following command. This will close the profiling session:

    ```
    netprofile disable
    ```

6. This command will close the profiling session and save a `.nprof` file with all the recorded data in your project folder at the following location:

    ```
    [Your Project folder]/Saved/Profiling
    ```

    As an alternative, you can just use the `netprofile` command, which will toggle the Profiler every time it is used.

Once you have saved your profiling session, you can open it with the profiling tool.

Analyzing a profiling session

After launching the Profiler application, you can click the **Open** button and navigate to the `Profiling` folder to open the session you have recorded. An example session is depicted in *Figure 11.15*:

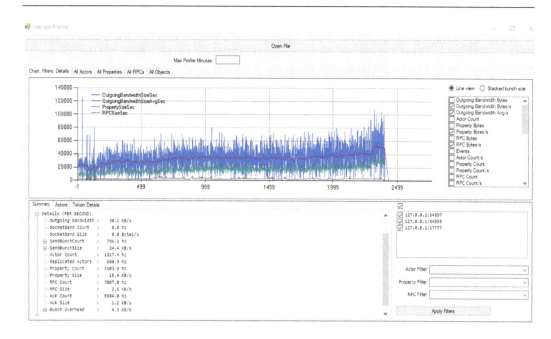

Figure 11.15 – A profiling session example

You will see a lot of information here, including a graph containing all the networking information. Let's focus on the bottom-right section, where you will see a list of IP addresses, as shown in *Figure 11.16*:

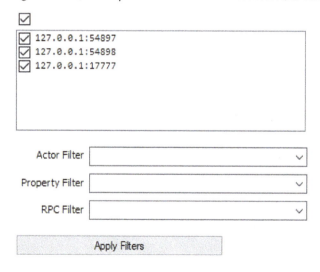

Figure 11.16 – The list of server and client IP addresses

This list represents the clients and the server that were profiled during the session – as you can see, in my example, I have a server (using port **17777**) and two clients (using ports **54897** and **54898**). You can select the client or the server you need to analyze and click the **Apply Filters** button to show just its profiled data. Additionally, you can enable some of the drop-down menus that will let you filter additional data, such as a single Actor type in the game. An example of this is the **BP_Character** Blueprint Class.

Once you have selected the client or the server you need to analyze, you can select a portion of the graph that represents a group of frames during gameplay just by clicking and dragging on the chart data, as shown in *Figure 11.17*:

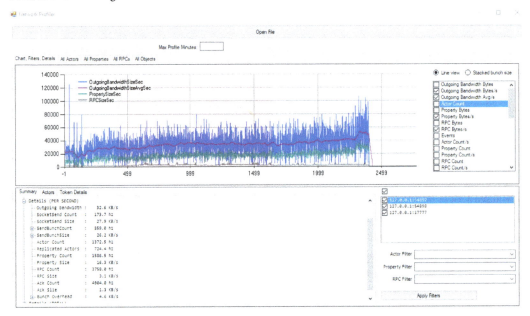

Figure 11.17 – A selected portion of the chart data

If needed, you can even select a single frame by just clicking on the graph. *Figure 11.18* shows the frame selection in the graph chart:

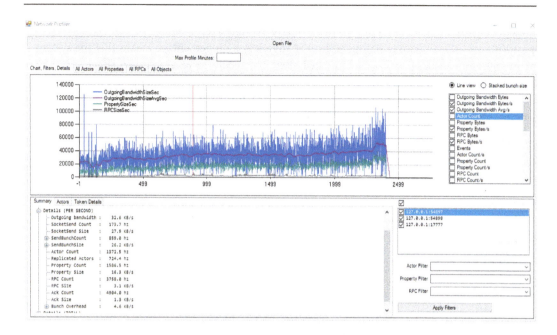

Figure 11.18 – A single frame in the chart data

Now, select the **Actors** tab, located at the bottom left of the application; you will be presented with all the Actors that were replicated during the selected frame range. My profiled record is shown in *Figure 11.19*:

Actor	MS	KB/s	Bytes	Count	Update HZ	Rep HZ	Waste
US	0.07	8.26	201	18	757.40	420.78	44.44
BP_Character	0.02	0.00	0	6	252.47	0.00	100.00
BP_MinionMiniboss	0.02	1.93	47	6	252.47	84.16	66.67
BP_MinionSentinel	0.01	1.89	46	2	84.16	84.16	0.00
GameplayDebuggerCategoryReplicator	0.01	0.00	0	2	84.16	0.00	100.00
BP_WoodenDoor	0.00	0.00	0	2	84.16	0.00	100.00
BP_KnightPrisoner	0.00	0.00	0	2	84.16	0.00	100.00

Figure 11.19 – The Actors tab

One of the most interesting columns here is **MS**, which shows how many milliseconds were needed to replicate an Actor. Using this value, you can determine whether the Actor is taking an excessive amount of time to replicate and then proceed to investigate the underlying causes of this issue.

Another really important column to consider is **Waste**. Its values represent the percentage – in terms of performance – lost by not updating replicated values. A high percentage means that the system kept on replicating values that were not updated often. If this column reaches values above 80%, you should probably consider changing the `NetUpdateFrequency` value (that is, the time interval that will pass when updating data over the network) of your Actor to a higher value to update its values less often.

If you select one of the Actors, you will get detailed information on the replicated properties during the analyzed time range. As an example, *Figure 11.20* shows the `BP_WoodenDoor` data in a time range of about 1 minute:

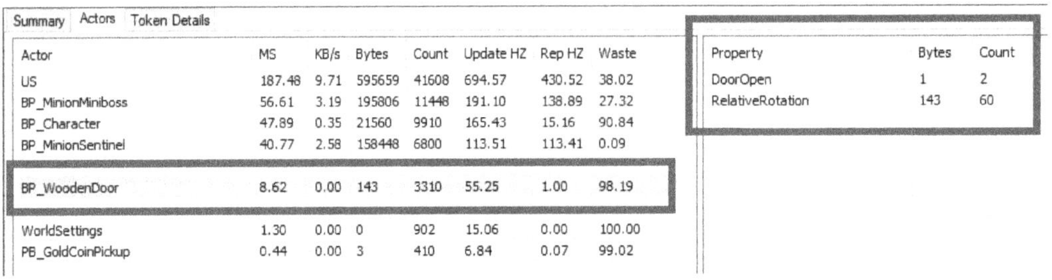

Summary	Actors	Token Details								Property	Bytes	Count
Actor		MS	KB/s	Bytes	Count	Update HZ	Rep HZ	Waste		DoorOpen	1	2
US		187.48	9.71	595659	41608	694.57	430.52	38.02		RelativeRotation	143	60
BP_MinionMiniboss		56.61	3.19	195806	11448	191.10	138.89	27.32				
BP_Character		47.89	0.35	21560	9910	165.43	15.16	90.84				
BP_MinionSentinel		40.77	2.58	158448	6800	113.51	113.41	0.09				
BP_WoodenDoor		8.62	0.00	143	3310	55.25	1.00	98.19				
WorldSettings		1.30	0.00	0	902	15.06	0.00	100.00				
PB_GoldCoinPickup		0.44	0.00	3	410	6.84	0.07	99.02				

Figure 11.20 – The profiled data for the BP_WoodenDoor Blueprint

During gameplay, one of the characters interacted with the door, so you can see the **DoorOpen** property replicated twice – one for the starting value and one for when the character was opened – and **60** replications for the **RelativeRotation** property – when the opening animation was activated.

What's wrong here is the **98.19%** value for **Waste**. Imagine adding dozens of doors to a big dungeon level! Such a waste of networked traffic. I should probably consider getting back to the door and changing `NetUpdateFrequency` to a higher value.

On the positive side, take a look at the **Waste** value for the **BP_MinionMiniboss** Actor, as depicted in *Figure 11.21*:

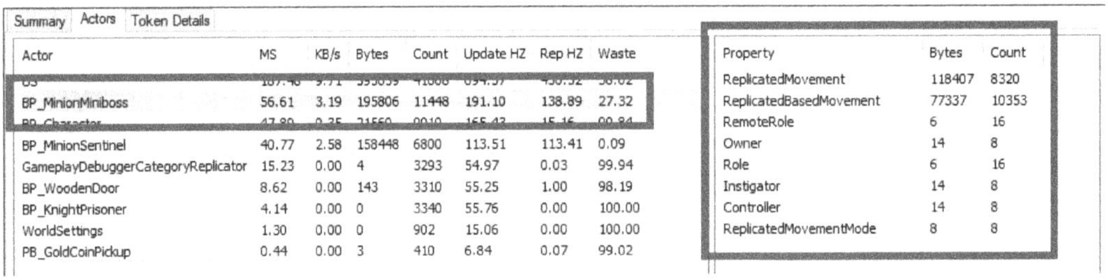

Summary	Actors	Token Details								Property	Bytes	Count
Actor		MS	KB/s	Bytes	Count	Update HZ	Rep HZ	Waste		ReplicatedMovement	118407	8320
US		187.48	9.71	595659	41608	694.57	430.52	38.02		ReplicatedBasedMovement	77337	10353
BP_MinionMiniboss		56.61	3.19	195806	11448	191.10	138.89	27.32		RemoteRole	6	16
BP_Character		47.89	0.35	21560	9910	165.43	15.16	90.84		Owner	14	8
BP_MinionSentinel		40.77	2.58	158448	6800	113.51	113.41	0.09		Role	6	16
GameplayDebuggerCategoryReplicator		15.23	0.00	4	3293	54.97	0.03	99.94		Instigator	14	8
BP_WoodenDoor		8.62	0.00	143	3310	55.25	1.00	98.19		Controller	14	8
BP_KnightPrisoner		4.14	0.00	0	3340	55.76	0.00	100.00		ReplicatedMovementMode	8	8
WorldSettings		1.30	0.00	0	902	15.06	0.00	100.00				
PB_GoldCoinPickup		0.44	0.00	3	410	6.84	0.07	99.02				

Figure 11.21 – The profiled data for the BP_Miniboss Blueprint

I have achieved a nice **27.32%** for 1 minute of gameplay! But pay attention... this does not mean that I have spent fewer resources on this Actor replication. This indicates that I'm utilizing the available resources more efficiently.

Now, open the **All RPCs** tab located at the top of the application; you will get a list of the remote procedure calls that were used during the selected frame range. *Figure 11.22* shows my situation for the example I have used so far:

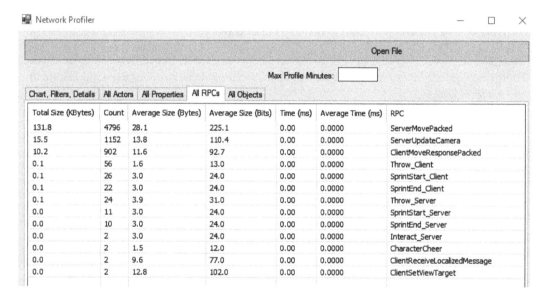

Figure 11.22 – The RPC profiling window

As you can see, you can analyze how many times a remote call was made and the cost of calling it – this additional information can help you optimize your code and streamline your program's performance.

In this section, I presented you with one of the most important tools when working on a multiplayer game – the Network Profiler. With a strong knowledge of how to use it, you will be able to analyze various aspects of your game's network performance, such as the frequency and cost of remote calls, as well as potential bottlenecks. This information can help you identify areas where you can optimize your game's performance while providing a smoother and more enjoyable experience for players.

In the next section, I'll share some tips with you that I hope will be useful in improving your multiplayer project and help you avoid common issues that can arise once your game is played online.

Improving performance and bandwidth utilization

Although Unreal Engine strives to maximize the efficiency of replicating Actors, it is typically a time-consuming process that can negatively impact performance. To facilitate this task, there are a few steps that you can take to optimize replication and make it more efficient. In this section, I will give you some advice on how to improve performance and avoid bottlenecks that may stop your game from working efficiently.

Turning on replication only when necessary

When replicating Actors, the server performs various checks, such as relevance, frequency of updates, and dormancy, among others. Avoid turning on replication on Actors that won't need this feature to put them off these checks.

If you really need Actor replication, consider fine-tuning `NetUpdateFrequency` for less important (or less frequently changing) Actors. This property will set the maximum update frequency over the network for the Actor. As an example, a background Actor such as an NPC may update at a very slow rate – say every 0.5 seconds – while a fast-moving enemy may need an update every 0.2 seconds.

In some cases, you may want to implement custom net relevancy rules (or override available variables), which can help in reducing network load at runtime.

Avoiding invoking RPCs that are not required or essential

An RPC that could have been avoided is considered an unnecessary RPC and should be avoided.

As an example, server-specific logic does not have to be included in a server RPC if you can ensure that a non-replicated function will run only on the server.

Another example is a method call on a client – if you can guarantee that the client is locally controlled (that is, by using `APawn::IsLocallyControlled()`), you can avoid using an RPC.

Distinguishing between reliable and unreliable RPCs

As you already know from *Chapter 7, Using Remote Procedure Calls (RPCs)*, any replicated method can either be reliable or unreliable and, by default, RPCs are unreliable.

Making the right choice between the two options may change the way your game will behave radically. To help you with this, here's a list of the pros and cons of reliable and unreliable RPCs:

- **Reliable RPCs**:

  - **Pro**: Functions will arrive at their destination in the same order as they were sent

  - **Con**: Functions will consume more bandwidth and may lead to longer latency

- **Unreliable RPCs:**

  - **Pro**: Functions will result in lower bandwidth usage compared to reliable calls; this makes them good candidates for functions that need to be called frequently.

  - **Con**: Functions may not successfully reach their destination or may arrive with gaps in the RPC calls, even though they will be processed in the correct order.

As an example, you should refrain from sending reliable events too frequently, such as on the `Tick()` event, since the engine's buffer of reliable events may become overloaded and disconnect the associated player. This kind of call is safer to use with an unreliable function – for instance, on non-critical cosmetic events, such as spawning sound and visual effects.

Validating data

If you are using C++, RPCs are the only way to pass data from the client to the server and vice versa, so it is a good habit to validate it whenever needed. The concept behind having a validation function for an RPC is that if it discovers any invalid parameters, it can signal the system to disconnect the client or server that initiated the RPC call. To ensure responsiveness, it's preferable to retrieve data directly from the client and validate it on the server side.

Remembering that the GameMode exists only on the server

This may seem like a pretty basic topic, but you should always keep in mind that the GameMode is a non-replicated Actor and that it runs only on the server. This means that, whenever you will try to get it from a client, you will get a `null` value. Consequently, calling an RPC on it is simply nonsense as it will run locally only on the server.

Using a naming convention for RPCs

As your project grows in size, keeping track of which functions are RPCs and which are not can become challenging; this means that using a good naming convention may be a time-saver. You can use a `_Server` and `_Client` suffix, as I showed you during the previous chapters, or you can opt for a `Server_` and `Client_` prefix. You can even differentiate between `_Client` and `_Multicast` RPCs if you wish.

If you're working with a team, this is typically a requirement. However, even if you're working solo, you'll find this convention to be useful in the long run.

As you may have noticed, improving your game is a constant journey that never truly ends. You'll always be tweaking things, analyzing data, and identifying any obstacles. With the tips I've mentioned, I hope to make this process a little less stressful for you!

Summary

In this chapter, I talked about a really important topic in game programming – making sure that your game works properly and fixing any issues that come up. In earlier chapters, we covered some tools for finding and fixing problems in Unreal Engine, but now, I've given you some even stronger and more helpful tools that you can use to make your game development even better. First of all, you learned how to configure **Multiplayer Options** from **Editor Preferences**, after which you created a log category to properly set custom messages when debugging. You were then presented with how to emulate a real multiplayer environment on a single PC by testing network issues such as packet loss or low bandwidth.

Next, I presented the Network Profiler, a standalone piece of software that will let you read and analyze a multiplayer session to help you find possible issues and bottlenecks in your code.

Lastly, I gave you some advice on how to improve your project even more.

Testing and debugging a game before release can help ensure that it runs smoothly and offers a positive experience to players. Additionally, being equipped with the right tools and knowledge for debugging can make the process faster and easier, saving valuable time and resources during development. Understanding how to debug a multiplayer game is crucial because the involvement of multiple players can create technical challenges that are more intricate, such as synchronization and latency issues.

In the upcoming chapter, we'll get back to our project (and the wicked machinations of the Lichlord!). Our goal this time around? Mastering the art of managing a gameplay session to ensure an unforgettable experience for our future, enthusiastic players. Let's make sure they keep coming back for more, shall we?

Part 4:
Deploying Your Game Online

In the last part of the book, you will become acquainted with the more intricate elements of the Unreal Engine multiplayer system. You will begin by delving into game session management and progress to constructing a deployable build of your game. Finally, you will gain insight into cloud services, which can enhance the appeal of your game to players.

This part includes the following chapters:

- *Chapter 12, Managing Multiplayer Sessions*
- *Chapter 13, Handling Data During a Session*
- *Chapter 14, Deploying Multiplayer Games*
- *Chapter 15, Adding Epic Online Services (EOS)*

12

Managing Multiplayer Sessions

As you already know from previous chapters, a game session is represented by a server with multiple players all connected to it.

Unreal Engine provides a solid framework for creating, destroying, and handling game sessions. By having a strong grip on how to handle a multiplayer session, programmers can ensure their games will provide a nice and flawless experience to all players involved.

In this chapter, you will be presented with the main concepts needed to manage a game session, starting from the basic setup to creating one. Then, you'll learn how to let clients search for available sessions and how to join them. By the end of this chapter, you will have built a user interface that will be used later to handle the Unreal Engine multiplayer session system.

Through the next few sections, I will present the following topics:

- Understanding game sessions
- Preparing a project game session
- Creating a session
- Joining a session

Technical requirements

To follow the topics presented in this chapter, you should have completed *Chapter 11, Debugging a Multiplayer Game*, and understood its content.

Additionally, if you would prefer to begin with code from the companion repository for this book, you can download the `.zip` project files provided in this book's companion project repository: `https://github.com/PacktPublishing/Multiplayer-Game-Development-with-Unreal-Engine-5`.

You can download the files that are up to date with the end of the previous chapter by clicking the `Unreal Shadows - Chapter 11 End` link.

Understanding game sessions

During a **game session**, players can participate in online games by connecting to remote servers or even using their computers as dedicated servers. The Unreal Engine game session system offers a wide range of impressive online capabilities, such as a server browser, player limits, server search over the network, and much more. It's easy to use and only requires a few commands to activate. Whether running on a player's machine or a dedicated server, game sessions provide a way for players to connect and immerse themselves in the virtual world of the game. In this chapter, we will focus on setting up a local network environment, leaving the dedicated server setup to the next chapter.

However, before we begin working on sessions, I need to introduce you to the Online Subsystem and its unique characteristics.

Introducing the Online Subsystem

In Unreal Engine, the **Online Subsystem** is a system that offers a standard method of accessing the features of online services such as Epic Online Services, Steam, Xbox Live, and others. This is especially useful in game development scenarios where multiple platforms or online services are supported. In such cases, the Online Subsystem eliminates the need for developers to make code changes by enabling the use of configuration adjustments for each supported service. This ensures that the coding process and development efforts are streamlined, efficient, and consistent across all supported platforms and services.

The core purpose of the Online Subsystem is to manage asynchronous communication with a diverse range of online platforms. As network speeds, server delays, and backend service runtimes are typically unknown to local machines, interactions with such systems are highly unpredictable in terms of duration. To address this issue, the Online Subsystem leverages delegates for all remote operations, ensuring that they are always executed when any supported asynchronous feature is utilized. Delegates serve a dual purpose by enabling the system to respond to requests as they complete, as well as allowing developers to query runtime requests. By providing a single code path to follow, delegates negate the need for developers to write custom code to handle various success or failure conditions.

Supported features are grouped into service-specific, modular interfaces. For instance, the **Leaderboard** interface encompasses all aspects related to leaderboard access – such as the ability to register personal scores or times, as well as check the leaderboards for scores from players across the globe or within your friends' lists – while the **Purchase** interface covers the process of making in-game purchases and handling past purchases history. Each feature set on every supported online service has an associated interface, allowing developers to write code that is agnostic to the online service being employed, promoting consistency across services.

Epic Games provides a list of plugins that allow developers to work on the Online Subsystem, including dedicated plugins for the most common and used platforms. *Figure 12.1* shows a portion of the many elements available in Unreal Engine's **Plugins | Online Platform** section:

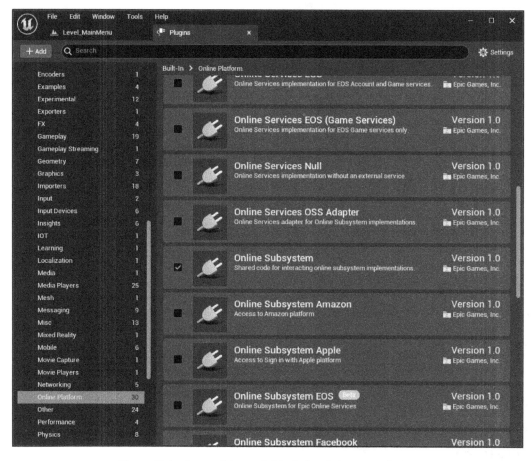

Figure 12.1 – Some of the available Online Subsystem plugins

In this chapter, we will use the default Online Subsystem, which offers the most basic operations to handle a session, including its creation, destruction, and joining. In *Chapter 15*, *Adding Epic Online Services (EOS)*, we'll dive into more detail regarding more advanced Online Subsystem features. Let's start by learning how to manage the most basic session operations.

Understanding session commands

So, how can a multiplayer session be managed and operated? There are four main operations you can use to handle a session:

- **Create Session**
- **Destroy Session**

- **Find Session**
- **Join Session**

Let's take a closer look at each of them and analyze them in detail.

Create Session

The **Create Session** command constitutes the starting point of the session process. Once a session is created successfully, it becomes discoverable by other instances of the game, which can subsequently join it. The **Create Session** command allows you to specify key aspects, such as the number of players allowed in the session itself and LAN mode, which lets you manage an internet-based game or a LAN game.

Destroy Session

If you are hosting a session (that is, you created a session), **Destroy Session** will close it so that it is no longer available for discovery and joining. Connected clients will be immediately disconnected from the session. If you are a client who's connected to a session, calling this command is the way to go to leave the session and, consequently, the game.

Find Session

By using the **Find Session** command, you can retrieve a comprehensive list of currently created and accessible game sessions. Upon a successful call of this method, the returned objects can be queried to obtain important information such as the server's name, ping, and player count. As for the **Create Session** command, you can opt for an internet-based game or a LAN-based one.

Join Session

After identifying the desired session, you can initiate a **Join Session** call to join the game. Upon successful connection to the server, the game will automatically transition to the server's map and allow you to participate in the ongoing gameplay.

Understanding connection errors

As you already know, network operations always pose the risk of encountering errors, and it's critical for games to handle them appropriately. Instances such as the host leaving the session (or crashing), temporary internet connection issues, or other unforeseen problems are common examples.

Any failures associated with the aforementioned session functions will be communicated through appropriate events or, in the case of Blueprints, dedicated execution pins, allowing the developer to configure the game response accordingly. This will guarantee a positive experience for the players, even during critical situations.

Now that you have a grasp of how to make and oversee multiplayer game sessions, let's head back into Unreal Engine and apply this knowledge to our project! In the next few sections, you will create a user interface that lets you host a session and expose it to the network or join one.

Preparing a project game session

In this chapter and the next, we will create a new level that will serve as a starting point for your game and will let players host a session or join one. As mentioned previously, in this chapter, we will focus on creating a LAN-hosted game – this means that all players will be connected to the same local network – leaving the trickier details of hosting a game over the internet to the next chapter.

The level will be pretty simple and will contain the following elements:

- A user interface widget that will do the following:

  - Let the player create and host a session

  - Let the player find and join hosted sessions

- A 3D model of the character that the player will use to change skin colors

In this chapter, we will focus on creating the user interface – including all the needed widgets – leaving the level creation and the skin handling to the next one.

This interface will concentrate on the primary session functions and not on its visual aspect. However, you can decide on the style and look based on your personal preference – just let your creativity run free!

To create our user interface, we will use UMG again – you used it in *Chapter 6, Replicating Properties Over the Network*. One of the main advantages of using the UMG system is that you can create a custom widget and use it to compose the full interface. This will let you separate elements into logical blocks and keep the overall system clean and reusable.

We will start by creating the needed elements for creating and joining a session. By the end of this chapter, we will put everything together in a main menu interface.

To get started, we will need four main components:

- A **Create Session** widget, which will help us in handling the session creation

- A **Find Sessions** widget, which will let us look for available sessions and list them in the user interface

- A **Session Item Renderer** widget, which will be used to show each session's information and will let us join a session

- A **Main Menu** widget, which will let us display the previous widgets on the screen

Let's start creating these widgets by opening the Unreal project and navigating to the `Content | Blueprints` folder. The first widget we will be adding is **Create Session**.

Creating a session

In this section, you will be creating a user interface widget that will let you manage session creation. In particular, the **Create Session** widget will do the following:

- Let the player select how many players are allowed to connect in a single session
- Create the session with the click of a button
- Open the game level and start the game

The first thing we must do is create the actual widget so, in the `Blueprints` folder of the Content Browser, do the following:

1. Right-click and select **User Interface | Widget Blueprint**. In the pop-up window that appears, select **User Widget**, as shown in *Figure 12.2*:

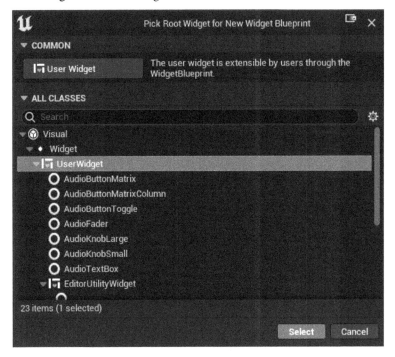

Figure 12.2 – The user widget creation window

2. Name the newly created widget `WB_CreateSession` and double-click on it to open it.

Now, we will add the visual elements.

Adding the visual elements

Once the editor is open, select the **Designer** view and do the following:

1. From the **Palette** panel, drag a **Canvas Panel** item into the main window. Then, from the **Details** panel, name the item `CreateSessionPanel`.

2. From the **Palette** panel, drag an **Image** item – which will work as a background color – onto the **Canvas** panel and, in its **Details** panel, do the following:

    *   Name it `Background`.

    *   Set its **Color** and **Opacity** values to `(0, 0, 0, 0.4)`.

    *   While holding the *Ctrl* and *Shift* keys, click the **Anchors** drop-down menu and select the bottom-right button to make the background stretch over the entirety of the **Canvas** panel. The selection button is shown in *Figure 12.3*:

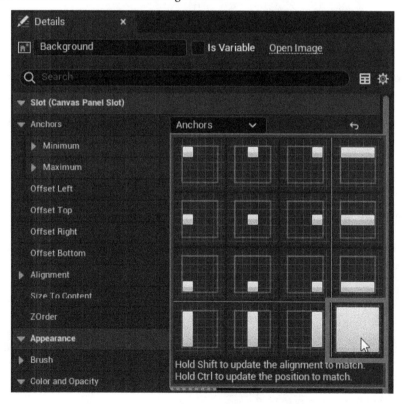

Figure 12.3 – The background anchors selection

3. From the **Palette** window, drag a **VerticalBox** item onto the **Canvas** panel and, in its **Details** panel, do the following:

- Name it Container

- While holding the *Ctrl* and *Shift* keys, click the **Anchors** drop-down menu and select the bottom-right button to make the background stretch over the entirety of the **Canvas** panel

At this point, you have created the container for the widget – nothing fancy, but it's fully functional. The widget hierarchy can be seen in *Figure 12.4*:

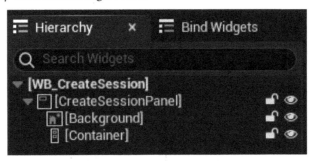

Figure 12.4 – The partial CreateSession widget hierarchy

We are now going to add the working elements that will allow the player to create the session. To do so, follow these steps:

1. From the **Palette** window, drag a **Text** component into the **Container** item (that is, the vertical box) and do the following:

- Name it TitleLabel

- Set its **Padding** property to 5.0

- Set the **Text** property to **Create Session**

2. From the **Palette** window, drag a **Border** component inside the **Container** item and do the following:

- Name it Separator

- Set its **Padding** property to 10.0

3. From the **Palette** window, drag a **Text** component inside the **Container** item and do the following:

- Name it MaxPlayersLabel

- Set its **Padding** property to 5.0

- Set the **Text** property to **Max Players**

4. From the **Palette** window, drag a **SpinBox** component into the **Container** item and do the following:

    - Name it `MaxPlayersSpinBox`

    - Set its **Padding** property to `10.0`

    - Enable the **Minimum Value** property and set its value to `1`

    - Enable the **Maximum Value** property and set its value to `5`

    - Set both **Min Fractional Digit** and **Max Fractional Digit** to 0

    - Double-check that the **Is Variable** checkbox is selected

5. From the **Palette** window, drag a **Button** component into the **Container** item and do the following:

    - Name it `CreateSessionBtn`

    - Set its **Padding** property to `5.0`

    - Double-check that the **Is Variable** checkbox is selected

6. From the **Palette** window, drag a **Text** component inside into **CreateSessionBtn** item and do the following:

    - Name it `CreateSessionLabel`

    - Set its **Text** property to **Create**

    - Set its **Justification** property to **Align Text Center**

The final structure of the widget is shown in *Figure 12.5*:

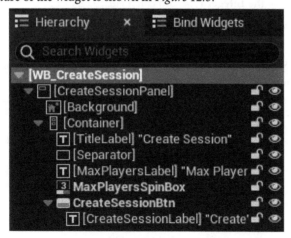

Figure 12.5 – The final CreateSession widget hierarchy

The **Designer** view for the widget is shown in *Figure 12.6*:

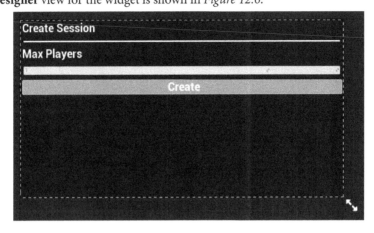

Figure 12.6 – The Designer view of the CreateSession widget

With this layout, the player will be able to select the maximum number of players hosted in a session and start the session itself.

Implementing the Visual Scripting logic

Now that the visual part of the widget is finished, you can start adding the Visual Scripting logic. Open the **Graph** panel by clicking the **Graph** button and, in the **Variables** panel, you should already have two variables – **CreateSessionBtn** and **MaxPlayersSpinBox**. Then, complete the following steps:

1. Add a new variable of the **Integer** type and call it MaxPlayers.

2. Select the **MaxPlayersSpinBox** variable and, in the **Events** panel, click on the **On Value Changed** + button to create an event.

3. Select the **CreateSessionBtn** variable and, in the **Events** panel, click on the **On Clicked** + button to create an event.

The previous steps will create two events that will handle the corresponding user interactions, as shown in *Figure 12.7*:

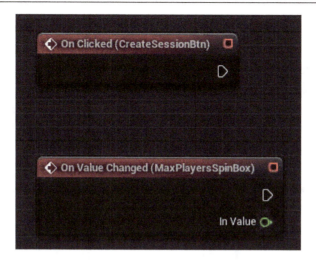

Figure 12.7 – The CreateSession graph events

We will start by handling the spin box change event, which will simply have to assign its value to the **MaxConnections** variable. To do so, follow these steps:

1. From the **Variables** panel, drag a **Set Max Players** node.

2. Connect the outgoing execution pin of the **On Value Changed (MaxPlayersSpinBox)** event to the incoming execution pin of the **Set Max Players** node.

3. Connect the **In Value** pin of the event node to the **Max Players** pin of the **Set** node. This will automatically create a **Truncate** node to convert the spin box float value into an integer.

    The final result of this part of the graph is shown in *Figure 12.8*:

Figure 12.8 – The spin box Event Graph

We can now start working on the session creation part of the graph, which will be fired whenever the **CreateSessionBtn** button is clicked.

4. Add a **Create Session** node and a **Get Player Controller** node to the graph.

5. From the **Variables** panel, drag a **Get Max Players** node.

6. Connect the outgoing execution pin of the **On Clicked (CreateSessionBtn)** event to the incoming execution pin of the **Create Session** node.

7. Connect the **Return Value** pin of the **Get Player Controller** node to the **Player Controller** pin of the **Create Session** node.

8. Connect the outgoing pin of the **Max Players** node to the **Public Connections** pin of the **Create Session** node.

9. Enable the **Use LAN** checkbox of the **Create Session** node.

10. Add an **Open Level (by Name)** node to the graph and expand its advanced properties by clicking on the down arrow at the bottom of the node itself. Set its properties to the following values:

    - Add a value of `Level_01` to the **Level Name** input field (or insert any game level you would like to load)

    - Leave the **Absolute** value checked

    - Add a value of `listen` to the **Options** input field to open the level as a listen server

11. Connect the **On Success** execution pin of the **Create Session** node to the incoming execution pin of the **Open Level (by Name)** node.

12. Optionally, connect the **On Failure** execution pin of the **Create Session** node to a **Print String** node; this will show an error message. This will trace any failure that may pop up during the creation of a session in the **Output Log** window.

The final graph is shown in *Figure 12.9*:

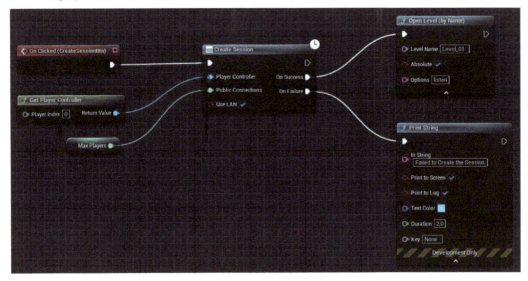

Figure 12.9 – The Create Session Event Graph

The graph you have just created is simple but does a lot of things, including creating a session on a LAN, setting a maximum of players per session, and opening the game level to start the actual multiplayer session.

In the next section, we will work on an interface that will let the player search for and join existing sessions.

Joining a session

In this section, we will work on a couple of widgets that will display a list of sessions available in the network and let the players join them. We will need two widgets: **Session Item Renderer** and **Find Session**. The first one will be used to display a single session's information, while the second one will be responsible for using the first one as a list of available sessions.

Creating the SessionItemRenderer widget

The widget you will create will have the following features:

- Displays the available server name
- Displays the maximum number of available connections, along with the number of connected players
- Provides a join button to let the player enter the session

The first thing we must do is create the widget. So, in the Content Browser area, follow these steps:

1. Right-click and select **User Interface | Widget Blueprint**. In the pop-up window that appears, select **User Widget**.
2. Name the newly created widget WB_SessionItemRenderer and double-click on it to open it.

Once again, we will start by adding the user interface elements.

Adding the visual elements

Once the editor is open, select the **Designer** panel and do the following:

1. From the **Palette** panel, drag a **Horizontal Box** item – a widget that aligns items horizontally – into the main window and, from the **Details** panel, name it Container.
2. From the **Palette** window, drag a **Text** item into the horizontal box container and, in the **Details** panel, do the following:

    - Name it ServerNameLabel and tick the **Is Variable** checkbox to make this item available in the Event Graph area

- Set the **Size** property to `Fill` and the **Padding** property to `5.0`

- Set the **Text** property to `Server Name`

3. From the **Palette** window, drag another **Text** item into the horizontal box container and, in the **Details** panel, do the following:

    - Name it `NumPlayersLabel` and tick the **Is Variable** checkbox to make this item available in the Event Graph area

    - Set the **Padding** property to `5.0`

    - Set the **Text** property to `0/0`

4. From the **Palette** window, drag a **Button** item into the horizontal box container and, in the **Details** panel, do the following:

    - Name it `JoinBtn` and double-check that the **Is Variable** checkbox is ticked

    - Set the **Padding** property to `5.0`

5. From the **Palette** window, drag a **Text** item onto the **JoinBtn** item and, in the **Details** panel, do the following:

    - Name it `JoinLabel`

    - Set the **Text** property to `Join Session`

The final structure of the widget is shown in *Figure 12.10*:

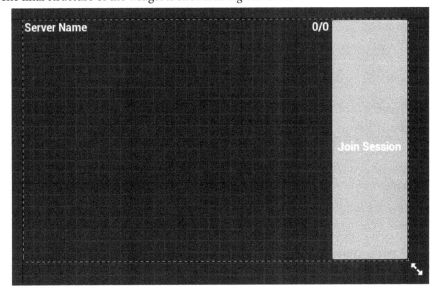

Figure 12.10 – The hierarchy view of the SessionItemRenderer widget

The **Designer** view for the widget is shown in *Figure 12.11*:

Figure 12.11 – The Designer view of the SessionItemRenderer widget

With this layout, the player will be able to see the information for each available session and the join button.

Now that the visual part of the widget is finished, you can start adding the Visual Scripting logic.

Implementing the Visual Scripting logic

Open the **Graph** panel by clicking the **Graph** button and do the following:

1. In the **Variables** panel, you should already have three variables – **JoinBtn**, **NumPlayersLabel**, and **ServerNameLabel**. In the Designer graph, all of them have been marked as **Is Variable**.

2. Add a new variable of the **Blueprint Session Result** type and do the following:

    *   Call it `SearchResult`

    *   In its **Details** panel, enable the **Instance Editable** and **Expose on Spawn** properties to make this property accessible from other Blueprints

You should be already familiar with the **Instance Editable** property, but **Expose on Spawn** may be new to you. Enabling it will show a pin for this property when spawning this Blueprint – this will help us later on in initializing the data when we add this renderer to the list of available sessions.

Now that the variables have been set up, it's time to add some Visual Scripting. We will start by implementing the **Join Session** logic. To do so, follow these steps:

1. With the **JoinBtn** variable selected, add an **On Clicked (JoinBtn)** event by clicking on the **On Clicked** + button in the **Events** panel.

2. Add a **Join Session** node to the graph and connect its incoming execution pin to the outgoing execution pin of the **On Clicked (JoinBtn)** event.

3. Add a **Get Player Controller** node to the graph and connect its **Return Value** pin to the **Player Controller** pin of **Join Session Node**.

4. From the **Variables** panel, drag a **Get Search Result** node into the graph and connect its pin to the **Search Result** node of the **Join Session** node.

The final result for this part of the graph is shown in *Figure 12.12*:

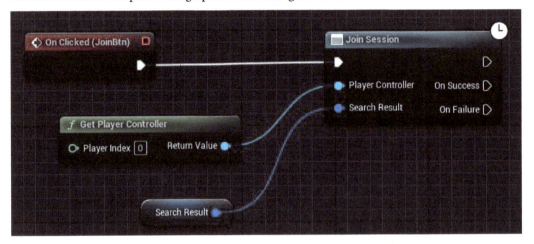

Figure 12.12 – The Join Session graph

As you can see, joining a session is quite straightforward once you have the session data (that is, the search result); this data will be obtained during the **Find Session** procedure we'll add later.

Please notice that we don't need to open any level after joining a session as we did for the **Create Session** widget; this will happen automatically once we are connected to the host.

To complete this widget, we need to show the search result data in the labels we have previously created and, as we have previously exposed this data on spawn, we will have it already available at construction time. Let's complete the widget's Visual Scripting by looking for the **Event Construct** event node in the graph – it should already be available by default. Then, perform the following steps:

1. To keep things clean, add a **Sequence** node with two outgoing pins (the default setup) and connect its incoming execution pin to the outgoing execution pin of the event node.

2. From the **Variables** panel, drag a **Get Server Name Label** node and a **Get Search Result** node.

3. From the **Server Name Label** outgoing pin, click and drag to create a **SetText (Text)** node.

4. Connect the **SetText (Text)** incoming execution pin to the **Then 0** execution pin of the **Sequence** node.

5. From the **Search Result** outgoing pin, click and drag to add a **Get Server Name** node.

6. Connect the **Get Server Name** outgoing pin to the **In Text** pin of the **SetText (Text)** node. This will automatically create a **To Text (String)** node that will convert the text into the correct type.

So far, the graph should be like *Figure 12.13*:

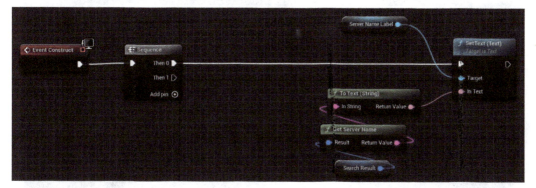

Figure 12.13 – The first part of the Event Construct event node

The previous graph simply gets the available server's name from the search result data and displays it in the corresponding label. We are going to do something similar with the number of connected players. To do so, keep on working on the same graph and continue with these steps.

7. From the **Variables** panel, drag a **Get Num Players Label** node and a **Get Search Result** node.

8. From the **Num Players Label** outgoing pin, click and drag to create a **SetText (Text)** node.

9. Connect the **SetText (Text)** incoming execution pin to the **Then 1** execution pin of the **Sequence** node.

10. From the **Search Result** outgoing pin, click and drag to add a **Get Current Players** node. Repeat this step, but this time, add a **Get Max Players** node.

11. Add an **Append** node (from the **String** category) to the graph. Add an additional pin to this node by using the **Add pin** button – you should now have three incoming pins in total. Do the following operations for the three pins:

   - Connect the incoming **A** pin to **Return Value** of the **Get Current Players** node. This will automatically add a node converted for the type.

   - Insert a / character into the input field for the **B** pin.

   - Connect the incoming **C** pin to **Return Value** of the **Get Max Players** node. This will automatically add a node converted for the type.

12. Connect the **Append** node's outgoing pin to the **In Text** pin of the **SetText (Text)** node. This will automatically create a **To Text (String)** node that will convert the text into the correct type.

This portion of the graph will look like *Figure 12.14*:

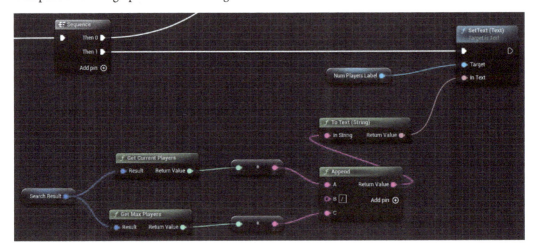

Figure 12.14 – The second part of the Event Construct event node

This widget is now complete and contains all the logic to show a session's information and join it.

We are now going to create the third widget, which will allow us to search the network for available sessions.

Creating the FindSessions widget

The **FindSessions** widget will have the following features:

- Let the player find available sessions through the click of a button
- Show a list of the available sessions
- If required, display information messages

The first thing we must do is create the actual widget. So, in the Content Browser area, do the following:

1. Right-click and select **User Interface | Widget Blueprint**. In the pop-up window that appears, select **User Widget**.

2. Name the newly created widget WB_FindSessions and double-click on it to open it.

As usual, you will start by adding the visual elements to the widget.

Adding the visual elements

Once the editor is open, select the **Designer** panel and follow these steps:

1. From the **Palette** panel, drag a **Canvas Panel** item into the main window. From the **Details** panel, name the item `FindSessionsPanel`.

2. From the **Palette** window, drag an **Image** item – that will work as a background color – inside the **Canvas** panel and, in its **Details** panel, do the following:

    - Name it `Background`

    - Set its **Color** and **Opacity** values to `(0, 0, 0, 0.4)`

    - While holding the *Ctrl* and *Shift* keys, click the **Anchors** drop-down menu and select the bottom-right button to make the background stretch over the entirety of the **Canvas** panel

3. From the **Palette** window, drag a **VerticalBox** item onto the **Canvas** panel and, in its **Details** panel, do the following:

    - Name it `Container`

    - While holding the *Ctrl* and *Shift* keys pressed, click the **Anchors** drop-down menu, and select the bottom-right button to make the background stretch over the entirety of the **Canvas** panel

    At this point, you will have created the container for the widget – nothing fancy, but fully functional. The widget hierarchy can be seen in *Figure 12.15*:

Figure 12.15 – The partial FindSessions widget hierarchy

Now, we are going to add the working elements that will allow the player to find the network sessions.

4. From the **Palette** window, drag a **Button** component into the **Container** item (that is, the vertical box) and do the following:

    - Name it `FindSessionsBtn`

    - Set its **Padding** property to `10.0`

    - Double-check that the **Is Variable** checkbox is selected

5. From the **Palette** window, drag a **Text** component into the **FindSessionBtn** item and do the following:

    - Name it `FindSessionsLabel`

    - Set the **Text** property to `Find Sessions`

6. From the **Palette** window, drag a **Border** component into the **Container** item and do the following:

    - Name it `Separator`

    - Set its **Padding** property to `10.0`

7. From the **Palette** window, drag a **ScrollBox** component – a widget that will let you list items with a side scroll bar – into the **Container** item and do the following:

    - Name it `SessionsScrollBox`

    - Set its **Padding** property to `10.0`

    - Set its **Size** property to **Fill**

    - Double-check that the **Is Variable** checkbox is selected

8. From the **Palette** window, drag a **Text** component into the **Container** item and do the following:

    - Name it `SessionMessage` and tick the **Is Variable** property to expose this item in the graph.

    - Set its **Padding** property to `10.0`

    - Set the **Text** property to **No Session Available**

    The final structure of the widget is shown in *Figure 12.16*:

Figure 12.16 – The final FindSessions widget hierarchy

The **Designer** view for the widget is shown in *Figure 12.17*:

Figure 12.17 – The final FindSessions widget Designer view

With this layout, the player will be able to click the **Find Sessions** button to search the network for available sessions and display them in a selectable list. You now need to open the **Graph** panel and add some Visual Scripting logic.

Implementing the Visual Scripting logic

This part will be a bit more complex than the rest as there will be a lot going on; in particular, the code logic will have to do the following:

- Search for available networks over the LAN
- Display a list of available sessions through the **SessionItemRenderer** widget
- Display error messages
- Enable and disable the search button, depending on the circumstances

As a first step, I need you to check that, in the **Variables** panel, there are three references to the items you will be using: **FindSessionBtn**, **SessionMessage**, and **SessionScrollBox**. Then, follow these steps:

1. Add a new variable called `SessionResults` of the **Blueprint Session Result** type and make it an **Array** – this will contain a list of the sessions that have been found in the network.

2. Select **FindSessionBtn** and, in the **Events** panel, add an **On Clicked** event by clicking the + button next to the corresponding element.

3. Connect the outgoing execution pin of **On Clicked (FindSessionBtn)** to a **Sequence** node with two execution pins (that is, the default ones).

Now, to keep things clean, you'll be creating some functions that will do some of the minor operations:

- **AddItemRenderer** to add a session item to the list
- **EnableSearchButton/DisableSearchButton** to make the search button interactable or not, depending on the situation
- **GetSessionResultMessage** to compose the resulting message of a search

Let's create these now.

Creating the AddItemRenderer function

We'll start from the first function by clicking on the + button in the **Functions** section of the **My Blueprint** window. Follow these steps:

1. Name the function `AddItemRenderer` and, in the **Details** panel, do the following:

    - In the **Input** section, add an input of the **Blueprint Session Result** type and name it `SearchResult`
    - With the function node selected, look for the **Graph** section of the **My Blueprint** window and set **Access Specifier** to **Protected**

2. Add a **Get Player Controller** node to the graph.

3. Add a **Create Widget** node to the graph and do the following:

    - Connect its incoming execution pin to the outgoing execution pin of the **Add Item Renderer** function node
    - From the drop-down menu of the **Class** pin, select **WB_SessionItemRenderer**
    - Connect the **Owning Player** pin to **Return Value** of the **Get Player Controller** node
    - Connect the **Search Result** pin to the **Search Result** pin of the **Add Item Renderer** function node

4. Drag a **Get Session Scroll Box** node from the **Variables** panel onto the graph.

5. Add an **Add Child** node to the graph and do the following:

    - Connect its incoming execution pin to the outgoing execution pin of the **Create Widget** node
    - Connect the **Content** pin to the **Return Value** pin of the **Create Widget** node
    - Connect the **Target** pin to the **Session Scroll Box** getter node

The final graph for the **AddItemRenderer** function is shown in *Figure 12.18*:

Figure 12.18 – The AddItemRenderer function

We can now start creating the function that will enable the search button when requested.

Creating the EnableSearchButton function

Let's start by creating the function by clicking on the + button in the **Functions** section of the **My Blueprint** window. Follow these steps:

1. Name the function `EnableSearchButton` and, with the function node selected, look for the **Graph** section of the **My Blueprint** window and set **Access Specifier** to **Protected**.

2. From the **Variables** panel, drag a **FindSessionsBtn** node.

3. Add a **Set Is Enabled** node to the graph and do the following:

   - Connect its incoming execution pin to the outgoing execution pin of the **Enable Search Button** function node

   - Connect the **Target** pin to the **Find Session Btn** getter

   - Tick the **In Is Enabled** checkbox

The final graph for this function is shown in *Figure 12.19*:

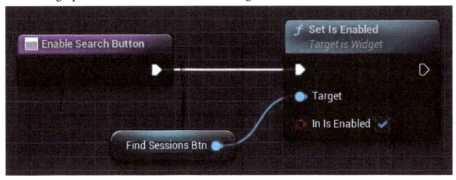

Figure 12.19 – The EnableSearchButton function

The function that will disable the button is almost identical to the previous one, so let's create it.

Creating the DisableSearchButton function

Let's start by creating the function by clicking on the + button in the **Functions** section of the **My Blueprint** window. Follow these steps:

1. With the function node selected, look for the **Graph** section of the **My Blueprint** window and set **Access Specifier** to **Protected**.

2. From the **Variables** panel, drag a **FindSessionsBtn** node.

3. Add a **Set Is Enabled** node to the graph and do the following:

   - Connect its incoming execution pin to the outgoing execution pin of the **Enable Search Button** function node

   - Connect the **Target** pin to the **Find Session Btn** getter

   - Leave the **In Is Enabled** checkbox unticked

The final graph for this function is shown in *Figure 12.20*:

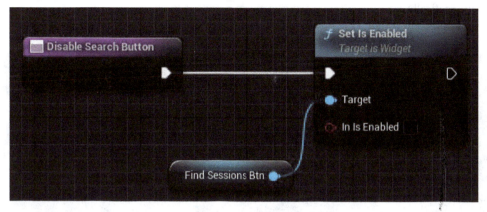

Figure 12.20 – The DisableSearchButton function

We need just one last function – the one that will compose the sessions message.

Creating the GetSessionResultMessage function

Let's start by creating the function by clicking on the + button in the **Functions** section of the **My Blueprint** window. Follow these steps:

1. Name the function `GetSessionsResultMessage` and do the following:

    - With the function node selected, look for the **Graph** section of the **My Blueprint** window, tick the **Pure** attribute, and set **Access Specifier** to **Protected.**

    - Add an **Output** value of the **Text** type and call it `ReturnValue`; this will add **Return Node** to the graph.

2. From the **Variables** panel, drag a **Get Session Results** node.

3. From the outgoing pin of the **Session Results** getter, click and drag to add a **Length** node.

4. Add an **Append** node (from the **String** category) to the graph and add an additional pin to this node by using the **Add pin** button – you should now have three incoming pins in total. Do the following operations for the three pins:

    - Insert in the **A** pin and input `Found:`

    - Connect the **B** pin to the outgoing pin of the **Length** node; this will automatically create a converter node in between

    - Insert in the **C** pin and input `sessions`

5. Connect the outgoing pin of the **Append** node to **Return Value** of **Return Node**; this will automatically create a **To Text (String)** converter node in between.

The final graph for this function is shown in *Figure 12.21*:

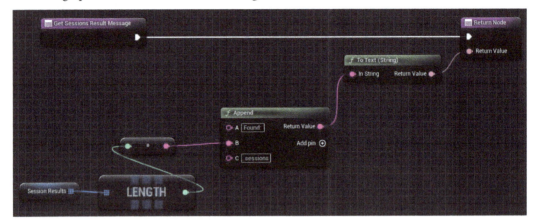

Figure 12.21 – The GetSessionsResultMessage function

The last function has been created, so it's time to get back to the main Event Graph and create the search and result logic.

Implementing the Event Graph

The main graph will need to look for the available sessions in the network and expose them in the widget list. To start with this Visual Scripting logic, follow these steps:

1. Locate the **On Clicked (FindSessionBtn)** event and add a **Sequence** node to the outgoing execution pin.

2. From the **Variables** panel, drag a **SessionsScrollBox** node and, from its outgoing pin, click and drag to add a **Clear Children** node.

3. Connect the **Clear Children** incoming execution pin to the **Then 0** outgoing execution pin of the **Sequence** node.

4. From the **Functions** panel, drag a **Disable Search Button** function and connect its incoming execution pin to the outgoing execution pin of the **Clear Children** node.

5. From the **Variables** panel, drag a **Session Message** node and, from its outgoing pin, click and drag to add a **Set Text** node (from the **Content** category).

6. Connect the incoming execution pin of the **Set Text** node to the outgoing pin of **Disable Search Button**.

7. Insert **Search Session…** into the **Text** field of the **Set Text** node.

This first part of the graph essentially cleans the sessions list from previous search results, disables the search button to avoid multiple clicks, and displays a message. This is shown in *Figure 12.22*:

Figure 12.22 – The first part of the FindSessions graph

The second part of the graph will be responsible for searching the network sessions and showing the actual results.

8. Add a **Get Player Controller** node to the graph.

9. Add a **Find Sessions** node to the graph and do the following:

    - Connect its incoming execution pin to the **Then 1** outgoing execution pin of the **Sequence** node

    - Connect the **Player Controller** pin to the **Return Value** pin of the **Get Player Controller** node

    - Set **Max Results** to 10

    - Tick the **Use LAN** checkbox to enable it

10. From the **Variables** panel, drag a **Set Session Results** node and connect its incoming execution pin to the **On Success** execution pin of the **Find Sessions** node.

11. From the **Functions** panel, drag a **Get Sessions Result Message** node.

12. From the **Variables** panel, drag a **Session Message** getter node and do the following:

    - From its outgoing pin, click and drag to add a **Set Text** node (from the **Content** category)

    - Connect its **Text** pin to the **Return Value** pin of the **Get Sessions Result Message** node

    - Connect its incoming execution pin to the outgoing execution pin of the **Set Session Results** node

13. From the **Variables** panel, drag a **Get Session Results** node. From its outgoing pin, click and drag to add a **For Each Loop** node. Connect the incoming **Exec** pin of the **For Each Loop** node to the outgoing pin of the **Set Text** node.

14. From the **Functions** panel, drag an **Add Item Renderer** node to the graph and do the following:

    - Connect its incoming execution pin to the **Loop Body** execution pin of the **For Each Loop** node

    - Connect its **Search Result** pin to the **Array Element** pin of the **For Each Loop** node

15. From the **Functions** panel, drag an **Enable Search Button** node onto the graph and connect its incoming execution pin to the **Completed** execution pin of the **For Each Loop** node.

This second part of the graph looks for a list of available sessions in the network, displays a result message, and adds the results to the session list. The graph is shown in *Figure 12.23*:

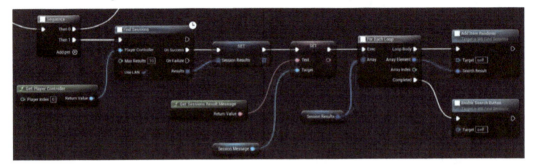

Figure 12.23 – The second part of the FindSessions graph

The last part of the graph will just show an error message if the search results with a failure.

16. From the **Variables** panel, drag a **Session Message** getter node and, from its outgoing pin, click and drag to add a **Set Text** node (from the **Content** category).

17. In the **Text** input field, add the following text: `Error searching for available sessions`.

18. Connect its incoming execution pin to the **On Failure** outgoing execution pin of the **Find Sessions** node.

19. Connect its outgoing execution pin to an **Enable Search Button** node to make the button clickable again.

This part of the graph is self-explanatory and is depicted in *Figure 12.24*:

Figure 12.24 – The third part of the FindSessions graph

We have finally completed this widget and we are now ready to put things together in the **Main Menu** widget.

Creating the Main Menu widget

The **Main Menu** widget – the fourth and last one – simply acts as a container for the **Create Session** and **Find Sessions** ones. To create it, follow these steps:

1. Right-click inside the Content Browser area and select **User Interface | Widget Blueprint**. In the pop-up window that appears, select **User Widget**.

2. Name the newly created widget WB_MainMenu and double-click on it to open it.

3. From the **Palette** window, drag a **Canvas Panel** item into the **Designer** view.

4. From the **Palette** menu, drag a **WB Create Session** item onto the **Canvas** panel and place it somewhere you think is appropriate.

5. From the **Palette** menu, drag a **WB Find Sessions** item onto the **Canvas** panel and place it somewhere you think is appropriate.

   The **Designer** view for this widget should look similar to the one shown in *Figure 12.25*:

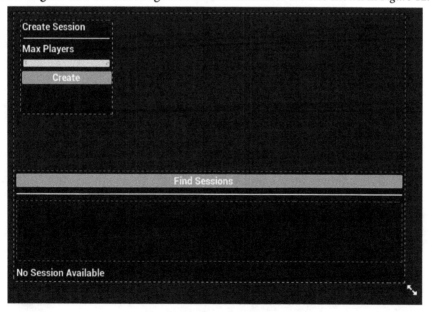

Figure 12.25 – The MainMenu widget

In this section, you created the user interface for the main menu level, which is composed of reusable widgets. Each widget contains dedicated logic for creating sessions and joining them.

Summary

This chapter introduced you to the primary session commands within Unreal Engine's Online Subsystem, providing you with the tools necessary to create, join, and manage multiplayer game sessions with ease. Armed with this knowledge, you have created a user interface that harnesses these features and puts them to practical use.

If you want to take your multiplayer game from being just a basic prototype to a fully functional and complete gaming experience, then you must learn how to use these features. Trust me – having this knowledge under your belt will make all the difference and help you create some truly awesome multiplayer games!

In the next chapter, we'll take these helpful widgets and use them to create the main menu for the game. We'll also create the needed Gameplay Framework classes, as well as a cool system for customizing the character's appearance!

13
Handling Data During a Session

To work on a multiplayer game, you need a solid system in place to manage the flow of data between levels. This means tracking variables – such as character inventory or health – to keep players up to date with the information they need. In short, an effective multiplayer game requires careful management of data to ensure a smooth, engaging experience for all players.

In this chapter, you'll be adding the final touches to the previous chapter's session system by creating a system that will serve as an entry point for the players. This means working on a new level that will let the player create a session – if they're starting the game as a server – or look for available sessions in the network – if they're playing as a client.

Additionally, you will learn how to customize the player character – by adding skin variants – and how to send this data from the session selection level to the actual game level. This will make your character special and even more cool and colorful than before!

By the end of the chapter, you will be able to host a local network game session with a computer acting as a listen server and other PCs connecting to it as clients and have different skins for every player in the game.

In this chapter, I will guide you through the following sections:

- Creating the main menu level
- Handling data during a session
- Making further improvements

Technical requirements

To follow the topics presented in this chapter, you should have completed *Chapter 12, Managing Multiplayer Sessions*, and understood its content.

Additionally, if you would prefer to begin with the code from the companion repository for this book, you can download the `.zip` project files provided in this book's companion project repository: `https://github.com/PacktPublishing/Multiplayer-Game-Development-with-Unreal-Engine-5`.

You can download the files that are up to date with the end of the previous chapter by clicking the `Unreal Shadows - Chapter 12 End` link.

Creating the main menu level

In this section, you'll be working on creating a new level that will serve as a starting point for creating a game session or joining one. You'll be leveraging the power and flexibility of the previously created user interface by adding the needed Gameplay Framework classes, such as a dedicated GameMode and a player Pawn.

First things first, let's open up your programming IDE and start writing some code!

Creating the Pawn

In this subsection, you'll be creating a Pawn that will show the character model and activate the user interface through its controller. This Actor will also be used to show the character model when the player enters the main menu level.

So, from the Unreal Engine Editor, create a new C++ class extending from **Pawn** and call it `US_MainMenuPawn`. Once the class has been created, open the `US_MainMenuPawn.h` header file and add the following code just after the `GENERATED_BODY()` macro:

```
UPROPERTY(VisibleAnywhere, BlueprintReadOnly, Category = "Arrow", meta
= (AllowPrivateAccess = "true"))
TObjectPtr<class UArrowComponent> Arrow;

UPROPERTY(VisibleAnywhere, BlueprintReadOnly, Category = "Camera",
meta = (AllowPrivateAccess = "true"))
TObjectPtr<class UCameraComponent> Camera;

UPROPERTY(VisibleAnywhere, BlueprintReadOnly, Category = "Camera",
meta = (AllowPrivateAccess = "true"))
TObjectPtr<USkeletalMeshComponent> Mesh;
```

Then, in the `protected` section, add the corresponding getter functions:

```
FORCEINLINE UArrowComponent* GetArrow() const { return Arrow; }
FORCEINLINE UCameraComponent* GetCamera() const { return Camera; }
FORCEINLINE USkeletalMeshComponent* GetMesh() const { return Mesh; }
```

All of the previous code is quite straightforward, and you should already be familiar with it from the previous chapters; we are declaring the needed components – an arrow, a camera, and a mesh – and then we are exposing the corresponding getter methods.

Next, open the `US_MainMenuPawn.cpp` file and add the needed `include` declarations:

```
#include "Camera/CameraComponent.h"
#include "Components/ArrowComponent.h"
```

Then, locate the constructor and add the following code:

```
Arrow = CreateDefaultSubobject<UArrowComponent>(TEXT("Arrow"));
RootComponent = Arrow;

Camera = CreateDefaultSubobject<UCameraComponent>(TEXT("Camera"));
Camera->SetupAttachment(RootComponent);
Camera->SetRelativeLocation(FVector(450.f, 90.f, 160.f));
Camera->SetRelativeRotation(FRotator(-10.f, 180.f, 0.f));

Mesh = CreateDefaultSubobject<USkeletalMeshComponent>(TEXT("Mesh"));
Mesh->SetupAttachment(RootComponent);
Camera->SetRelativeLocation(FVector(0.f, -30.f, 90.f));
static ConstructorHelpers::FObjectFinder<USkeletalMesh>
SkeletalMeshAsset(TEXT("/Game/KayKit/Characters/rogue"));
if (SkeletalMeshAsset.Succeeded())
{
  Mesh->SetSkeletalMesh(SkeletalMeshAsset.Object);
}
```

We are not adding anything new here. As normal, we are just adding a list of components for the Actor, including a utility arrow element, the mesh, and the camera.

Now that the basic `Pawn` class has been created, it's time to implement a Blueprint from it and add the previously created user interface. So, return to the Unreal Engine Editor and, in the **Blueprints** folder, create a new Blueprint class extending from **US_MainMenuPawn** and call it `BP_MainMenuPawn`. Then, open the Blueprint and, in the Event Graph, complete the following steps:

1. Add a **Get Player Controller** node.
2. Add a **Create Widget** node to the graph and connect its incoming execution pin to the outgoing execution pin of the **Event BeginPlay** node.

3. From the **Class** drop-down menu, select the **WB_MainMenu** class.

4. Connect the **Owning Player** pin to the **Return** value of the **Get Player Controller** node.

5. From the outgoing execution pin of the **Create Widget** node, click and drag to add an **Add to Viewport** node. Then, connect the **Target** pin to **Return Value** of the **Create Widget** node.

6. Click and drag from **Return Value** of the **Get Player Controller** node to add **Set Show Mouse Cursor**. Then, tick the **Show Mouse Cursor** checkbox and connect the incoming execution pin to the outgoing execution pin of the **Add to Viewport** node.

The final graph is depicted in *Figure 13.1*:

Figure 13.1 – The final graph for the BP_MainMenuPawn Blueprint

The BP_MainMenuPawn Blueprint is complete and ready to go, so we can now move on to working on the GameMode class.

Creating the GameMode

It's now time to create the GameMode that will handle the main menu level. In the **Blueprints** folder, create a new Blueprint class extending from **GameMode** and call it BP_MainMenuGameMode.

Next, open the Blueprint. Then, in the **Details** panel, locate the **Classes** category and, in the **Default Pawn Class** drop-down menu, select **BP_MainMenuPawn**, as shown in *Figure 13.2*:

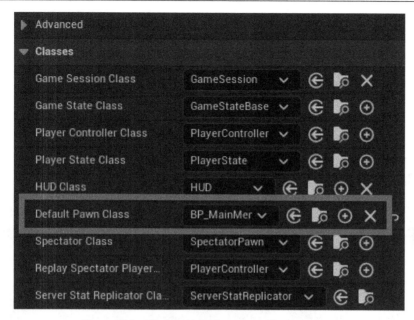

Figure 13.2 – The BP_MainMenuGameMode settings

The GameMode is now ready; we just need to create a new level and use it to show the session user interface.

Creating the level

Creating the main menu level is quite straightforward:

1. Open the Content | Maps folder.

2. From the main menu, select **File | New Level**, select the **Basic** template, and call it Level_MainMenu.

3. Open the level and, in the **Worlds Settings** panel, locate **GameMode Override**. In the corresponding drop-down menu, select **BP_MainMenuGameMode**.

4. In the **Editor** main menu, select **Edit | Project Settings** and, in the newly opened window, locate the **Maps & Modes** section. Then, from the **Editor Template Map Overrides** drop-down menu, select **Level_MainMenu**.

Congratulations, you've made it through this section and built your game's starting level! With this, your players can now create and host game sessions like a boss on their LAN or join in on the action as a client. Let's start testing these features by playing the game.

Testing the session system

To start testing a game session, open the **Level_MainMenu** map and play with these settings:

- Set **Net Mode** set to **Play Standalone**
- Set **Number of Players** set to 3

You will see the user interface you've created so far, as depicted in *Figure 13.3*:

Figure 13.3 – The user interface

From this interface, you will be able to create a session, like so:

1. From the **Max Players** spinner, set the maximum number of players to **3** or more.
2. Click the **Create** button; you will start the game and see the game level.

Then, to join a session, follow these steps:

1. Select one of the other opened clients and click the **Find Session** button; this operation will start the server search and, after a while, you should see the list of available servers in the LAN, along with the number of players already connected. *Figure 13.4* shows a game where there is a player already connected (that is, the listen server) with a maximum of 3 players:

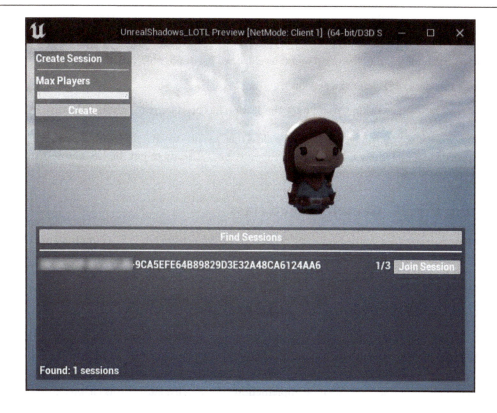

Figure 13.4 – The session search result

2. Click the **Join Session** button to, well... join the session. Your character will be teleported to the game level and you will be able to start playing.

In this section, you were introduced to session management and learned how to create, search for, and join sessions in a multiplayer game.

Brace yourself because, in the upcoming section, you'll be spicing up your game with an extra dose of customization. That's right – get ready to add skin variants that will make each player's character truly one of a kind. It's time to get creative and let your imagination run wild!

Handling data during a session

In this section, you'll be working on a new topic: passing data from one level to another when joining a session. You already possess almost all the knowledge necessary to perform this task – you just need to put things together.

What we need to do here is create a skin system for the character model that will do the following:

- Select a random skin in the main menu level from a list of possible variants
- Store this data while joining a session
- Update the character skin variant once the session has been joined

In the following steps, you will be working on a class that has remained inactive until this point, but that will prove to be incredibly useful moving forward. So, get ready to put the **US_GameInstance** class to work and see what it can do!

Updating the US_GameInstance class

You may have forgotten but, at the beginning of this project, you created the **US_GameInstance** class. This class offers a couple of interesting peculiarities:

- It is persistent across levels
- It is unique for each client (that is, it is not replicated over the network)

These features make it an awesome candidate for transporting data between levels while keeping them locally. You can use it to pass things such as the experience points gained by a player or their actual equipment. In our case, we will be using it to store a really simple piece of information: an index of the selected skin of the character (we'll be implementing the skin list later in this chapter).

Open the US_GameInstance.h header file and, in the `public` section, add this declaration:

```
UPROPERTY(BlueprintReadWrite)
int32 SkinIndex;
```

As easy as it may seem, it's all we need to pass the skin selection from one level to another!

In the next few steps, we will be creating a data structure to handle the character skin variants.

Adding the CharacterSkins data

In this subsection, you'll be creating a data structure similar to the one you created in *Chapter 6*, *Replicating Properties Over the Network*, but this time, you will be storing just material references that will be used to change the character's mesh colors.

The character model has six materials, as shown in *Figure 13.5*:

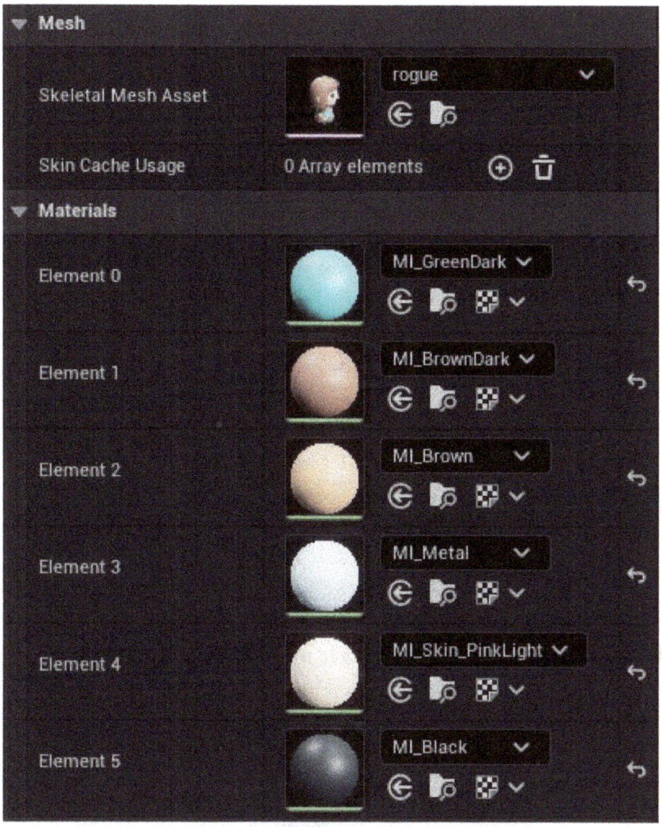

Figure 13.5 – The character model materials

For the character customization, we will only need four of them - specifically, **Element 0**, **Element 1**, and **Element 2**, all of which will change the character's hair and clothes, and **Element 4**, which will change the character's skin.

Creating the structure

To create the structure that will contain the skin data, open your programming IDE and create a file named US_CharacterSkins.h. Then, inside that file, add the following code:

```
#pragma once

#include "CoreMinimal.h"
#include "Engine/DataTable.h"
#include "US_CharacterSkins.generated.h"
```

```
USTRUCT(BlueprintType)
struct UNREALSHADOWS_LOTL_API FUS_CharacterSkins : public
FTableRowBase
{
  GENERATED_BODY()

  UPROPERTY(BlueprintReadWrite, EditAnywhere)
  UMaterialInterface *Material4;

  UPROPERTY(BlueprintReadWrite, EditAnywhere)
  UMaterialInterface *Material0;

  UPROPERTY(BlueprintReadWrite, EditAnywhere)
  UMaterialInterface *Material1;

  UPROPERTY(BlueprintReadWrite, EditAnywhere)
  UMaterialInterface *Material2;
};
```

As you can see, we are creating a data structure from FTableRowBase – the structure that will let us create data tables – and then we are declaring the four material references. As a side note, remember that the UNREALSHADOWS_LOTL_API API identifier may change, depending on your project name.

In the next steps, you will be creating the actual skin data out of this structure by generating a data table.

Creating the data table

Now that you have created a data structure, you are ready to create the actual data from it. To create your skin data table, follow these steps:

1. Open your **Blueprints** folder in the Content Browser, right-click, and select **Miscellaneous | Data Table**.

2. In the **Pick Row Structure** pop-up window, select **US_CharacterSkins** from the drop-down menu.

3. Click the **OK** button to generate the data table and name it DT_CharacterSkins.

4. Double-click on the newly created asset to open it. You will get an empty dataset; create your character skin rows by using any material from the project (or create custom materials!).

During the development phase, I like to create debug skins that will help me identify each unique character. In this case, I used a single color for all the elements in a row set (that is, all green, all red, or all blue), as shown in *Figure 13.6*:

Figure 13.6 – The Skins data table

Once you are satisfied with the skin system and you have battle-tested it, you will need some more realistic skins for your thief character; this process will be as easy as creating a new data table with the skin colors of your choice and setting this table as the selected one in the **Pawn** variable.

Now that you have a skin catalog asset, you can start adding code to the main menu Pawn class to set its skins at runtime.

Updating the US_MainMenuPawn class

In this section, you'll be enhancing your character's appearance by assigning a random skin. Every time players connect to the main menu level, their character will be allotted a unique set of colors for their skin, taken from the previously created data table. So, get ready to see a little more variety in your game!

As I mentioned previously, you dealt with this in *Chapter 6, Replicating Properties Over the Network*, but as the old saying goes, practice makes perfect!

With your programming IDE, open the US_MainMenuPawn.h header file and, in the implicit private section, add the data table and skin declarations:

```
UPROPERTY(EditAnywhere, BlueprintReadOnly, Category = "Character
Data", meta = (AllowPrivateAccess = "true"))
class UDataTable* CharacterSkinDataTable;

struct FUS_CharacterSkins* CharacterSkin;
```

Next, in the public section, add the getter method for the selected character skin:

```
FORCEINLINE FUS_CharacterSkins* GetCharacterSkin() const { return
CharacterSkin; }
```

And in the protected section, declare a function that will handle the skin randomization process:

```
void RandomizeCharacterSkin();
```

Now, you can open the US_MainMenuPawn.cpp file to start adding the skin handling implementation. First of all, declare the needed includes:

```
#include "US_CharacterSkins.h"
#include "US_GameInstance.h"
```

Then, add the RandomizeCharacterSkin() implementation:

```
void AUS_MainMenuPawn::RandomizeCharacterSkin()
{
 if(CharacterSkinDataTable)
 {
  TArray<FUS_CharacterSkins*> CharacterSkinsRows;
  CharacterSkinDataTable->GetAllRows<FUS_CharacterSkins>(TEXT("US_
Character"), CharacterSkinsRows);

  if(CharacterSkinsRows.Num() > 0)
  {
   const auto NewIndex = FMath::RandRange(0, CharacterSkinsRows.Num()
- 1);
   CharacterSkin = CharacterSkinsRows [NewIndex];

   Mesh->SetMaterial(4, CharacterSkinsRows[NewIndex]->Material4);
   Mesh->SetMaterial(0, CharacterSkinsRows[NewIndex]->Material0);
   Mesh->SetMaterial(1, CharacterSkinsRows[NewIndex]->Material1);
   Mesh->SetMaterial(2, CharacterSkinsRows[NewIndex]->Material2);

    if (const auto GameInstance = Cast<UUS_
GameInstance>(GetGameInstance()))
```

```
    {
      GameInstance->SkinIndex = NewIndex;
    }
  }
}
```

As you can see, we are retrieving all the data rows from the table reference and, after checking that there is at least one item in the table, we get a random row and set the pawn mesh materials to its included data. This will update the pawn shown in the level. After that, we retrieve the game instance as a UUS_GameInstance type and assign the previously randomized index to the SkinIndex property.

As a last step, we will be adding the randomization call when the game is started. So, in the BeginPlay() method, add the following code:

```
if(IsLocallyControlled())
{
  RandomizeCharacterSkin();
}
```

We now need to set the data table from the Blueprint, so let's switch back to the Unreal Engine Editor.

Updating the BP_MainMenuPawn Blueprint

Now that the Pawn class is ready, you just have to assign the previously created data table to the Pawn Blueprint. To do so, open BP_MainMenuPawn and do the following:

1. In the **Details** panel, look for the **Character Skin Data Table** property.
2. From its drop-down menu, select **DT_CharacterSkins**, as shown in *Figure 13.7*:

Figure 13.7 – The character skin data table property

3. If you test the game, you will get a randomized skin for each of the characters, as depicted in *Figure 13.8*:

Figure 13.8 – The starting skin randomization

The character randomization is complete; to take full advantage of it, we just need to retrieve the data from the game level side and assign it to the playing character.

Updating the US_Character class

In this subsection, you will be retrieving the skin index data from the game instance and setting it to the player character. This process is quite straightforward once you remember that the game instance is persistent across levels and is not replicated (that is, each client has its own dedicated one).

Start by opening the US_Character.h header file from your programming IDE and declare the needed data table properties in the implicit private section:

```
UPROPERTY(EditAnywhere, BlueprintReadOnly, Category = "Character
Data", meta = (AllowPrivateAccess = "true"))
UDataTable* CharacterSkinDataTable;

struct FUS_CharacterSkins* CharacterSkin;
```

I know you are already familiar with the previous declarations, so I won't waste your time by explaining them again.

Next, in the `protected` section, you need to add the following declarations. These will handle the skin update:

```
UPROPERTY(EditDefaultsOnly, BlueprintReadOnly, ReplicatedUsing="OnRep_
SkinChanged", Category = "Skin")
int32 SkinIndex = 0;

UFUNCTION()
void OnRep_SkinChanged(int32 OldValue);

UFUNCTION(Server, Reliable)
void SetSkinIndex_Server(int32 Value);

UFUNCTION()
void UpdateCharacterSkin();
```

And in the `public` section, add the following code:

```
FORCEINLINE FUS_CharacterSkins* GetCharacterSkins() const { return
CharacterSkin; }

virtual void GetLifetimeReplicatedProps(TArray<FLifetimeProperty>&
OutLifetimeProps) const override;
```

As you may remember from *Chapter 6*, *Replicating Properties Over the Network*, whenever you need to replicate a property, you can use the `ReplicatedUsing` property specifier to notify all clients that the property value has changed. In this case, we will replicate the `SkinIndex` variable to let all of the clients update their character skins once they join a session.

Additionally, always keep in mind that, to replicate a property, it should be initialized inside the `GetLifetimeReplicatedProps()` method through the `DOREPLIFETIME` macro, which is why we declared that method.

To implement all the replication logic and skin update, open the `US_Character.cpp` file and start by adding the needed `include` declarations:

```
#include "US_GameInstance.h"
#include "US_CharacterSkins.h"
#include "Net/UnrealNetwork.h"
```

Then, add the `GetLifetimeReplicatedProps()` method implementation to implement the property replication:

```
void AUS_
Character::GetLifetimeReplicatedProps(TArray<FLifetimeProperty>&
OutLifetimeProps) const
{
```

```
Super::GetLifetimeReplicatedProps(OutLifetimeProps);

DOREPLIFETIME(AUS_Character, SkinIndex);
}
```

Next, add the OnRep_SkinChanged() method. This will be executed every time the SkinIndex value is updated from the server to the clients:

```
void AUS_Character::OnRep_SkinChanged(int32 OldValue)
{
UpdateCharacterSkin();
}
```

Then, implement the skin index update from the server side by adding the SetSkinIndex_ Server_Implementation() method:

```
void AUS_Character::SetSkinIndex_Server_Implementation(const int32
Value)
{
SkinIndex = Value;
UpdateCharacterSkin();
}
```

Note that we are calling the UpdateCharacerSkin() event from the server side; this is mandatory if you are using a listen server because the previous method will be called only on the clients and, in that case, the server will not update the skin.

The fourth method, UpdateCharacterSkin(), will take care of retrieving the data from the game instance and updating the character mesh materials. To do so, add the following implementation:

```
void AUS_Character::UpdateCharacterSkin()
{
 if(CharacterSkinDataTable)
 {
  TArray<FUS_CharacterSkins*> CharacterSkinsRows;
  CharacterSkinDataTable->GetAllRows<FUS_CharacterSkins>(TEXT("US_
Character"), CharacterSkinsRows);

  if(CharacterSkinsRows.Num() > 0)
  {
   const auto Index = FMath::Clamp(SkinIndex, 0, CharacterSkinsRows.
Num() - 1);
   CharacterSkin = CharacterSkinsRows[Index];

   GetMesh()->SetMaterial(4, CharacterSkin->Material4);
   GetMesh()->SetMaterial(0, CharacterSkin->Material0);
```

```
    GetMesh()->SetMaterial(1, CharacterSkin->Material1);
    GetMesh()->SetMaterial(2, CharacterSkin->Material2);
    }
  }
}
```

What we are doing here is almost identical to the main menu Pawn class; we are getting a row from the skin data table and assigning the materials to the character mesh. The only difference is that we are not setting the skin index to the game instance, and we are getting a replicated version of it instead.

As a last step, you will need to add the following code at the end of the `BeginPlay()` method's implementation:

```
if(IsLocallyControlled())
{
  if(const auto GameInstanceCast = Cast<UUS_GameInstance>(GetWorld()-
  >GetGameInstance()); GameInstanceCast != nullptr)
  {
    SetSkinIndex_Server(GameInstanceCast->SkinIndex);
  }
}
```

This portion of the code checks that the instance of this class is locally controlled (that is, it is a player-owned character) and gets the skin index from the game instance. Then, it calls the `SetSkinIndex()` server function to notify all the clients that they should update this character look.

As for the main menu Pawn class, you now need to update the corresponding Blueprint to declare the skin data table.

Updating the BP_Character Blueprint

Now that the character class is ready, you just have to assign the previously created data table to the corresponding Blueprint. To do so, follow these steps:

1. Open **BP_Character**.
2. In the **Details** panel, look for the **Character Skin Data Table** property.

3.   From its drop-down menu, select **DT_CharacterSkins**, as shown in *Figure 13.9*:

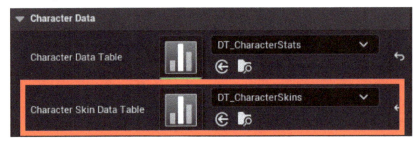

Figure 13.9 – The character skin data table property

If you test the game now, you will be able to get a randomized skin for each of the characters and keep that skin once a session is joined, as depicted in *Figure 13.10*:

Figure 13.10 – Gameplay with skinned characters

In this section, you learned how to keep data when creating or joining a session. You did this by using the game instance as a sort of data bridge to create a skinning feature; this will make each character unique and even more appealing to the players, helping you give them a killer makeover that will make the Lichlord quake in his boots!

In the upcoming section, I won't be introducing any new topics; instead, I'll give you some additional ideas to help you better manage your game sessions.

Making further improvements

In the previous sections, you did a great job of understanding how to pass data between sessions to make your multiplayer game even more engaging. Now, it's time to make your game even better by adding some additional functionalities. In this section, I'll offer some tips to help you add some excitement to your project. As always, don't be afraid to add your personal touch and make it truly yours.

Leaving and destroying sessions

In this chapter and the previous one, you have used three out of four session commands – **Create Session**, **Join Session**, and **Find Session** – but the **Destroy Session** command has been left unused. Use the **Destroy Session** command node to let the player leave a playing session.

This will be implemented in the game level (and not in the main menu one) as the player will need to leave the session after joining one. To implement this feature, you may want to create a dedicated user interface that will let players leave the game whenever they decide to do so.

As a side note, keep in mind that clients and the server behave differently regarding a session, so you will have to manage two kinds of session destruction: the one from the client – which will be almost painless – and, in the case of a client/server host, the server one – which will have to destroy all sessions from all clients (that is, all clients should leave the session as the server is not functional anymore).

Handling player death

At the moment, whenever a player is captured by a Lichlord minion, nothing will happen – you will get just a screen message and the player will keep on playing.

You can manage a player's death in many ways, but here are a couple of ideas for you:

- Destroy the player session and reload the main menu level to let the player join a new session. Just keep in mind that, if the player that is defeated is the server host, all other players will be immediately removed from the session.
- Use a respawn method, where the character will be placed in an available spawn point without the need to rejoin the session.

Selecting the player skin

In this chapter, you developed a random skin generator, but wouldn't be cool to let the players choose their own skin? You may add a user interface in the main menu level that will let the players do the following:

- Randomize the skin again if it does not suit their needs
- Select the desired skin from the full set using a dedicated selection method

Well, this could be the tip of the iceberg when it comes to creating a skin system that works like a charm and gets envious stares from your competitors. Who knows? Implementing your in-game purchases might even make games such as Fortnite weak in the knees!

Summary

In this chapter, you developed a fully functional system to pass data from one level to another during a game session. In this case, you focused on a skin system for the player character, but the use cases for this feature are almost endless.

As you may have noticed, session handling is a huge topic – it took two chapters to properly explain its main functionalities – and to succeed in the multiplayer world, it is imperative to have a strong grasp of it. If you want to ride the wave of success, then mastering this skill is a non-negotiable topic!

In the next chapter, I will guide you through a brand new topic: how to properly package your game. Get ready to dive into the exciting world of project packaging so that you can deploy your game like a boss on both server and client ends! Are you ready for this adventure?

14

Deploying Multiplayer Games

Deploying an Unreal multiplayer game can be a daunting task for any developer.

In this chapter, I will present you with the key steps involved in packaging and deploying a game – a process that needs proper planning and preparation beforehand. This will help you avoid most issues, resulting in a successful launch at deploy time.

This process will also involve a crucial task – compiling Unreal Engine from its source code and then packaging your game as a standalone server executable and client executable.

So, in the next sections, I will present you with the following topics:

- Going online for real
- Compiling Unreal Engine
- Setting up a dedicated server

Technical requirements

To follow the topics presented in this chapter, you should have completed all the previous chapters and have understood their content.

Although not mandatory, basic knowledge of Git technology (https://git-scm.com) will help in the second section of this chapter.

Going online for real

Up until now, to work on your projects, you have been utilizing an Unreal Engine official release that can be accessed through the Epic Games Launcher. However, if you aspire to enhance your skills in multiplayer development, you must take a further step to proficiently excel in this field and become an adept multiplayer game developer.

The first thing you need to know is that Unreal Engine releases are not "complete" versions of the software; they offer almost all that's needed to work on your project, but they usually miss less common and more advanced features. One of the main reasons is to keep the regular version of Unreal Engine to a smaller, more affordable size.

Regrettably, these releases lack the necessary functionality to compile a project for multiplayer deployment, which in turn means that if you plan to release your game in the wild, you are out of luck.

Luckily there is a solution available – compiling the Unreal Engine Editor yourself directly from the source code. The full Unreal Engine source code is available in a repository hosted on GitHub (`https://github.com/`) and, with minimum effort, you will be able to get it and use it for your own needs. There are many advantages in compiling your own version of the engine, including peeking through the actual engine implementation classes – such as Actor and Pawn – and stepping inside the engine code while debugging your game to get an introspection on what's happening.

A great number of individuals have made valuable contributions to the engine by identifying software glitches and taking the time to fix them. At the time of writing this chapter, the number of contributors to the engine is as many as 563 developers, as shown in *Figure 14.1*:

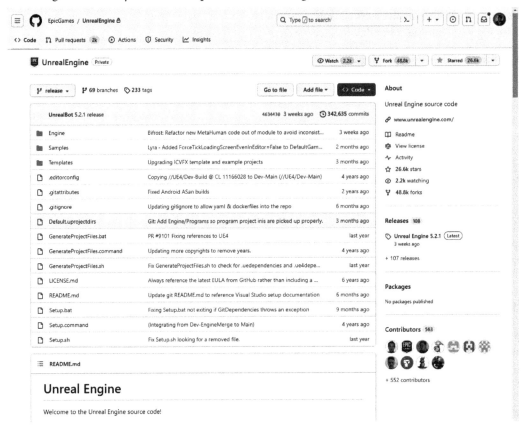

Figure 14.1 – The Unreal Engine GitHub page

Another advantage of accessing the engine source code and compiling your own executable version is that you will be able to compile your multiplayer game as a **dedicated server** – a game version that will run without rendering any visuals and that will not run on a client machine. This kind of game instance is usually referred to as a **headless** game version.

Using a dedicated server offers many advantages over a listen server:

- The size of the executable will be smaller

- The server version will mainly focus on gameplay logic and handling information from the clients

- No client will have advantages or disadvantages over the others due to hosting the game session

- You can build a dedicated server release separate from the client release and a client release from the dedicated server

- The server-side code logic can be compiled just in the server, obfuscating important code that may be available to malevolent hackers if distributed inside the client

With this in mind, let's kick off this exciting journey by creating our very own executable program for the Unreal Engine Editor using the source code.

The first thing to do is to obtain the actual source code from the GitHub repository – something we are going to do in the next section.

Compiling the Unreal Engine

In this section, you'll be downloading the engine source code and building it to get a personal, executable release that will let you create your own dedicated servers for multiplayer deployment.

This process is divided into two main parts:

- Cloning the project from the official Epic Games GitHub repository

- Setting up and building the sources with Visual Studio

Don't worry if you're unfamiliar with GitHub – I'll walk you through everything with clear and easy-to-follow step-by-step instructions.

Downloading the Unreal Engine source project

During the next steps, you will be downloading the Unreal Engine source code from the official Epic Games GitHub repository in order to have the full project in your hands. The requisites you will need to satisfy are as follows:

- Have Git installed on your computer

- Have a GitHub account

- Connect the GitHub account to your Epic Games account

> **Note**
> If you already know Git, chances are you will already have satisfied some or all of the requisites. If so, feel free to skip the following steps.

You will start by installing Git on your computer.

Installing Git on your computer

Git is a version control system that is both free and open source. It is designed to track the changes made to computer files, which it does by taking "snapshots" of a project's files whenever a commit is executed. This feature enables developers to oversee and regulate their code's evolution in an efficient, speedy fashion. Git is an excellent source code management tool for projects of all sizes, ranging from small to extremely large.

As stated before, you don't have to be proficient with Git in order to obtain the Unreal Engine repository – you will just be using its cloning capabilities to download the engine source code.

To install Git on your computer, head to the official download page (`https://git-scm.com/downloads`) and get the latest release. Once it is downloaded, simply install it as you would do with any common software. Once the installation phase has been completed, you will have the Git command line available on your machine.

> **Note**
> Some people – including me – prefer to use dedicated client software instead of using the command line, easing the pain of using the command prompt. If you feel uncomfortable with the command line, you can use a third-party client, some of which are listed on this page: `https://git-scm.com/downloads/guis`.

Once you have installed Git, you can safely proceed to create a GitHub account.

Creating a GitHub account

GitHub (`https://github.com/`) is a cloud-based service that allows software developers to store, manage, track, and control changes made to their code base using Git. It enables developers to collaborate on projects from anywhere and provides a range of features such as project management tools, documentation, issue tracking, and continuous integration and deployment. GitHub is widely used in the software development industry and has become a crucial part of the software development workflow for many organizations and developers.

To create a GitHub account, you just need to click the **Sign up** button and, after adding your email, follow the instructions you will be presented with.

Once you have got your GitHub account, it's time to get access to the Epic Games organization by connecting the GitHub and Epic Games accounts.

Connecting your GitHub account to the Epic Games account

Epic Games has a GitHub organization (`https://github.com/EpicGames`) where public repositories are stored, including the Unreal Engine project. Accessing this organization is free – you just have to connect the Epic Games account to the GitHub one. Here's how to do so:

1. Visit your Epic Games account page (`https://www.epicgames.com/account`).

2. Select the **APPS AND ACCOUNTS** page.

3. In the **GITHUB** section, click the **CONNECT** button, as shown in *Figure 14.2*:

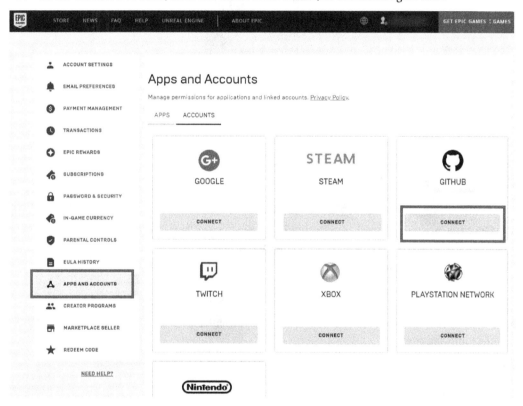

Figure 14.2 – The Apps and Accounts section

Once you have authorized the connect operation, you will be granted access to the Epic Games GitHub organization (`https://github.com/EpicGames`) and to the Unreal Engine repository (`https://github.com/EpicGames/UnrealEngine`). The Unreal Engine repository includes all the Unreal Engine versions organized in their own separate branches.

In Git, a **branch** is a separate line of development that represents changes made to a code base. Think of it as a snapshot of the code at a specific point in time that allows developers to work on different features without affecting the main code base. This way, you will be able to create your own executable with the version of your choice. In the Unreal Engine repository, the `release` branch includes the latest stable release of the engine.

You are now ready to clone the repository on your local machine:

1.   On your PC, navigate to an empty folder or create a new one.

2.   Right-click and, from the drop-down menu, select **Git Bash Here**, as depicted in *Figure 14.3*:

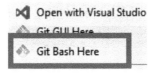

Figure 14.3 – The Git Bash Here option

This will open a command prompt and you will be ready to clone the Unreal Engine project.

3.   Type the following command:

```
git clone https://github.com/EpicGames/UnrealEngine.git
```

You may be asked to enter your credentials; in this case, use those of your GitHub account.

The download and clone process may take a long time, depending on your internet connection.

4.   Once the process has finished, you should see an `UnrealEngine` folder in your directory; this is the project source code. In the Git terminal, type the following:

```
git fetch origin
```

This command will retrieve all available branches in the remote repository.

5.   As an optional step, if you want to work with a particular release of the engine, you can type the following command:

```
git checkout -b [version number] origin/[version number]
```

For instance, if you need Unreal Engine 5.1, you will type:

```
git checkout -b 5.1 origin/5.1
```

This command will switch to the 5.1 version branch and make its sources available.

Once the process has finished, you are ready to go and compile the sources.

Compiling from the source code

Once you have downloaded the source code from the GitHub repository, you'll need to compile it, in order to get an executable out of it. This will allow you to launch the compiled Unreal Engine application and take advantage of all its features.

There are four main steps you'll need to complete in order to have a fully working executable:

- Set up your programming IDE

- Set up the project

- Generate the project files

- Compile the source files

Let's get started by checking that your programming IDE is up to date and ready to go.

Setting up your programming IDE

As you have been working with Unreal and C++ so far, your programming IDE should already be up to date to compile the source files, but a double-check is mandatory, in order to have everything properly set up:

1. Open the Visual Studio installer on your PC.

2. Select **Modify** from your own Visual Studio installation, as shown in *Figure 14.4*:

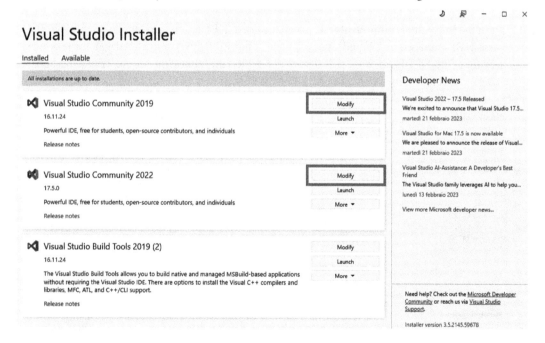

Figure 14.4 – Visual Studio Installer

3. Once the **Modyfing** window is open, select the **Individual components** tab, as shown in *Figure 14.5*:

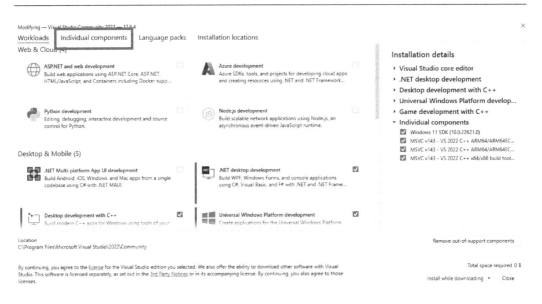

Figure 14.5 – The Modifying window

4.   From the **Individual components** tab, install the latest .NET Framework development tools, the latest .NET Framework SDK and – not mandatory, but strongly recommended – all the previous versions of the .NET Framework SDK. *Figure 14.6* depicts my setup at the time of writing this book:

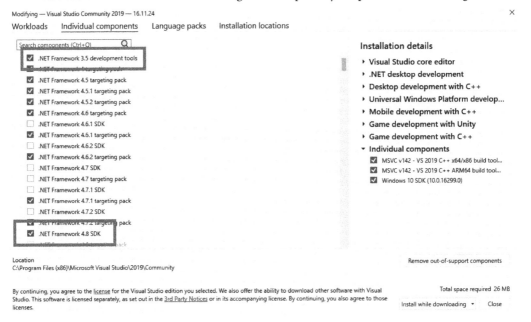

Figure 14.6 – The individual components setup

Once the installation is finished, you can safely close the Visual Studio installer and you'll be ready to set up the project.

Setting up the project

In this step, you'll be downloading the needed dependency files in order to properly set up the project. This process is pretty straightforward, but it may take some time, depending on your internet connection. Just open the source file project folder you cloned from GitHub, which should be named **UnrealEngine**, and locate the `Setup.bat` file, as shown in *Figure 14.7*:

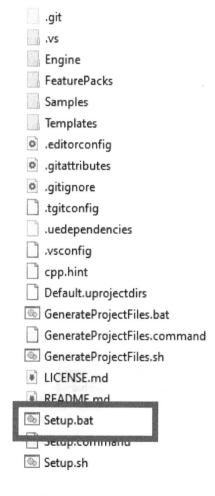

Figure 14.7 – The Setup.bat file

Then right-click on this file and select **Run as administrator**; this will open the command prompt and run the needed commands.

> **Note**
>
> For a more advanced level of customization, you may want to pre-determine the target hardware and platform. For instance, you can run the Setup.bat command excluding unneeded platforms by using the -exclude option. As an extra benefit, fewer files will be downloaded and, by the end of the build process, you will get an engine with a smaller file size.

Once the process has finished, you will have added the needed dependencies and will be ready for the next step.

Generating the project files

Once you have properly set up your project, you are ready to generate the project files, in order to open the project in Visual Studio. The process is almost identical to the previous one, but you will have to run another .bat file instead. In the sources project folder (i.e., the UnrealEngine folder), locate the GenerateProjectFiles.bat file, as shown in *Figure 14.8*:

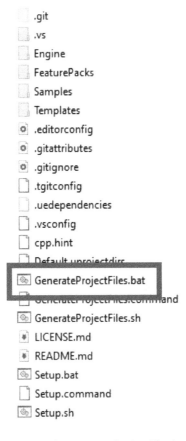

Figure 14.8 – The GenerateProjectFiles.bat file

Again, right-click on the file and select **Run as administrator**; this will open the command prompt and run the needed commands. Once the process has finished, you will have generated a Visual Studio solution and you should see a UE.sln file added to your source files folder, as depicted in *Figure 14.9*:

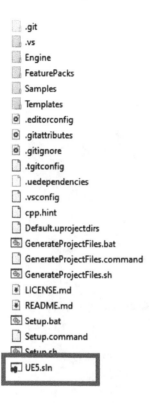

Figure 14.9 – The .sln file

> **Note**
>
> If you require a greater degree of customization for the project generation command, I recommend referring to the official documentation, which provides an exhaustive list of all available command options: https://docs.unrealengine.com/5.1/en-US/how-to-generate-unreal-engine-project-files-for-your-ide/.

You are now ready to open Visual Studio and build Unreal Engine.

Compiling the source files

We will now compile the source code in Visual Studio through the previously generated solution. To open it, just double-click on the UE.sln file and the software should open up.

> **Note**
>
> If you have more than one Visual Studio version, you may need to open the right one in order to correctly compile the project. This will depend on your PC configuration and .NET SDK installations.

The first thing to do is to set the correct solution configuration. To do so, locate the **Solution Configurations** drop-down menu in the toolbar and set its value to **Development Editor**, as shown in *Figure 14.10*:

Figure 14.10 – The Solution Configurations drop-down menu

Next, you need to check the solution platform you will be compiling for. In the Visual Studio toolbar, locate the **Solution Platforms** drop-down menu and double-check that the target platform is set to **Win64**, as shown in *Figure 14.11*

Figure 14.11 – The Solution Platforms drop-down menu

You are finally ready to start the build process. To do so, locate the **Solution Explorer** window and expand the `Engine` folder content. Then right-click on **UE5** and select **Build** as shown in *Figure 14.12*:

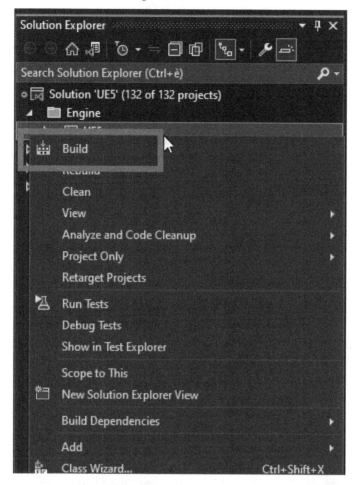

Figure 14.12 – The Build option

The build process will require a lot of time to complete (which will further depend on the capabilities of your computer), so you can relax and have a coffee break.

After completing the process, you'll have something to celebrate! You've just created your very own, fresh-out-of-the-box executable for Unreal Engine. The .exe file can be found in your source files project, in the Engine | Binaries | Win 64 folder. My own compiled binaries are shown in *Figure 14.13*:

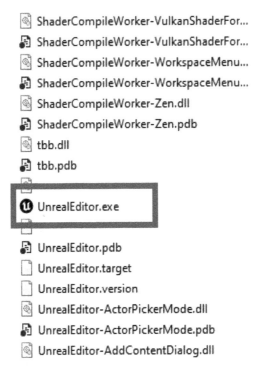

Figure 14.13 – The Unreal Engine compiled executable

When you double-click on it, Unreal Engine will launch, and you'll notice that things look pretty much the same as the regular Unreal Engine Editor. However, the difference is that, under the hood, you will have a more powerful engine with more features at your disposal.

In this section, you have accomplished the challenging task of compiling the Unreal Engine Editor from its source code – that's something to be really proud of! Now, get ready for an even more challenging task in the next section, where you'll be creating a dedicated server for a multiplayer game.

Setting up a dedicated server

In this section, you'll be compiling a multiplayer project as a dedicated server. To keep things simple, you'll be working with a simple project generated from one of the official templates, but all the topics and techniques can be easily adapted to any other project, including the Unreal Shadows project you've been working on so far.

In order to proceed with the creation of a dedicated server, your project must meet the specified requirements listed here:

- You must utilize a source build of Unreal Engine – the one you compiled in the previous section
- Your project must be created as a C++ one
- The project needs to, obviously, support client-server gameplay

Without any more delays, let's get started by creating the project.

Creating the project

In this section, you'll be creating a new project starting from an Unreal Engine template. To do this, the first thing you will need to do is to open your own compiled Unreal Engine Editor. So, locate the executable, which can be found in your GitHub downloaded directory using the following path:

```
[Your Project Folder]|Engine|Binaries|Win64|UnrealEngine.exe
```

Double-click on the file to launch the Unreal Engine Editor and, once it has started, create a new project with the following settings:

- **Template: Games | Third Person**
- **Project Name**: TP_Multiplayer
- **Project Type**: C++ (if you opt for a **Blueprint** project, just remember that, later on, you will have to convert it to a C++ one when you need to compile the dedicated server; this will be a really easy task, as you will just need to add a C++ class to the project)
- Leave **Starter Content** unchecked

My setup for this project is shown in *Figure 14.14*:

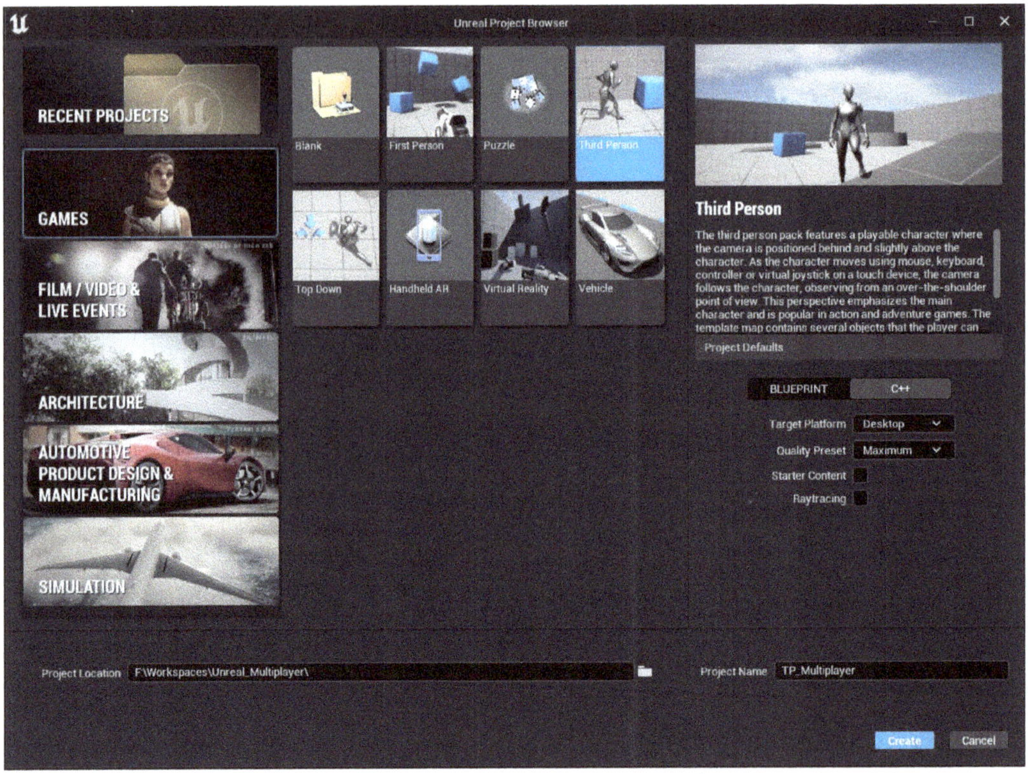

Figure 14.14 – The project setup

Once the project has been created, you are ready to set up and build the project solution.

Building the project solution

Now that you have created the project, locate the Source folder inside your project. Here, you will find two files named TP_Multiplayer.Target.cs and TP_MultiplayerEditor.Target.cs.

Target files are written in C# language and their purpose is to define how the Unreal Engine build tool will compile the target builds. In this case, the first one will be used when packaging a regular executable and the second one will be used for the Unreal Engine Editor.

We need to define a third one that will be used to package the server version of the application. In order to do this, in the same folder as the other two .Target.cs files, create a third target file and name it TP_MultiplayerServer.Target.cs.

Once the file has been created, open it with your text editor of choice and insert the following code:

```
using UnrealBuildTool;
using System.Collections.Generic;

public class TP_MultiplayerServerTarget : TargetRules
{
  public TP_MultiplayerServerTarget(TargetInfo Target) : base(Target)
  {
    Type = TargetType.Server;
    DefaultBuildSettings = BuildSettingsVersion.V2;
    ExtraModuleNames.AddRange( new string[] { "TP_Multiplayer" } );
  }
}
```

If you are not familiar with C# syntax, don't worry! There's not much to understand here – we are just defining a class named `TP_MultiplayerServerTarget` and, in the constructor, we are defining some build settings. The only thing to notice is that we have defined the built target type as `Server` as we need to create a dedicated server build.

Get back to the root folder of your project and locate the Unreal Engine project file, which should be called `TP_Multiplayer.uproject`. Right-click on it and, from the drop-down options, select **Generate Visual Studio project files**, as depicted in *Figure 14.15*:

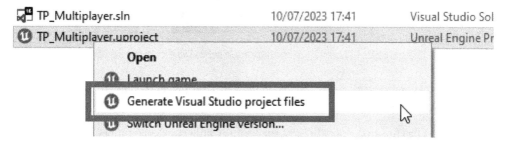

Figure 14.15 – The project file generation option

Once the generation process has finished, your project will be set to also compile a server build – something you will need to create your dedicated server.

You can now open Visual Studio by double-clicking on the `TP_Multiplayer.sln` solution file, in order to create the needed builds. Once your programming IDE is opened, create your build by clicking on the **Solution Configurations** drop-down menu in the main toolbar and selecting **Development Server**, as shown in *Figure 14.16*:

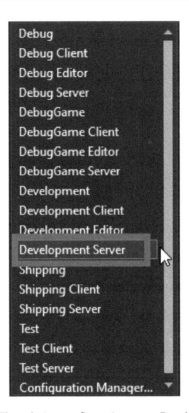

Figure 14.16 – The solution configuration set as Development Server

You can now build the project by right-clicking on the **TP_Multiplayer** item in the **Solution Explorer** window and selecting **Build**.

Once the process has finished, you will have successfully built the development server, which will allow the Unreal build tool to recognize the server build target.

Before getting back to the Unreal Engine Editor, you will have to also build the Development Editor configuration, so repeat the previous steps with the Editor configuration by taking the following steps. In the main toolbar, click on the **Solution Configurations** drop-down menu and select **Development Editor**. Then build the project by right-clicking on the **TP_Multiplayer** item in the **Solution Explorer** window and selecting **Build**.

Once the build process has finished, you can safely close Visual Studio and get back to Unreal Engine to build the dedicated server.

Building the dedicated server

In this subsection, you'll be building a dedicated server executable for your project from the Unreal Engine Editor. The first thing you will need to do is to create a new map that will serve as an entry point for the server:

1. From the main menu, select **File | New Level** and create a new **Basic** level.

2. In the Content Browser, create a `Maps` folder and save the level in it, calling it `Map_0`.

3. In the **World Setting** window of the level, set **Game Mode Override** to **Game Mode Base**; this will avoid opening this level with the default Third Person Game Mode.

    This map will be used by the client as an entry point when connecting to the server. The next step is to update some project settings before starting the server packaging phase.

4. Let's start by selecting **Edit | Project Settings** from the main menu. Then select the **Maps & Modes** section.

5. In the **Default Modes | Selected GameMode** category, expand the **Advanced** section.

6. Set the **Global Default Server Game Mode** drop-down value to **BP_ThirdPersonGameMode**, as shown in *Figure 14.17*:

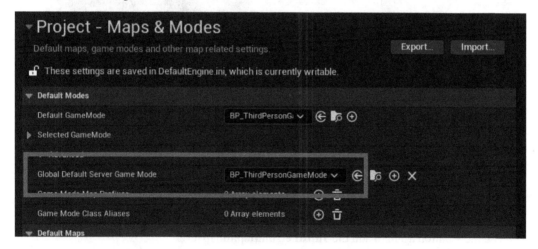

Figure 14.17 – Global Default Server Game Mode

The aforementioned setup will define the Game Mode that will be used by clients when connected to the server.

We are now going to define the game and server maps, in order to set the entry point that will be used when the clients connect. Locate the **Default Maps** category and do the following:

7. In the **Game Default Map** drop-down menu, select **Map_0**.

8. Expand the **Advanced** section and, in the **Server Default Map** drop-down menu, select **ThirdPersonMap**.

The final result for the **Default Maps** category is shown in *Figure 14.18*:

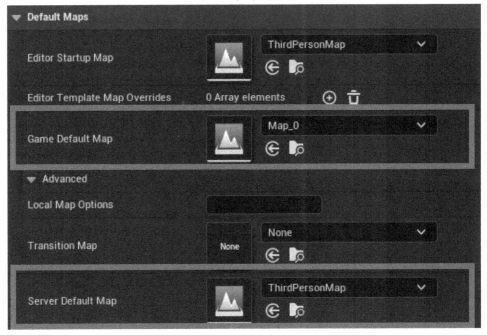

Figure 14.18 – The Default Maps category

We are done with the **Maps & Modes** settings. You will now need to define the packaging settings for your project:

9. In **Project Settings**, expand the **Packaging | Advanced** section.

10. Locate the **List of maps to include in the packaged build** array field.

11. Use the + button to add the **Map_0.umap** level.

12. Use the + button again to add the **ThirdPersonMap.umap** level.

You should now have a setup pretty similar to the one shown in *Figure 14.19*:

Figure 14.19 – The list of maps to be packaged in the build

13. As an additional step, double-check that in the **Project** category, the **Build** configuration is set to **Development**; this will allow us to connect to the server through the command line later on in this chapter.

14. Close the **Project Settings** window and in the Unreal Engine main toolbar, click the **Platforms** button and select **Windows | TP_MultiplayerServer** to set the build target, as shown in *Figure 14.20*:

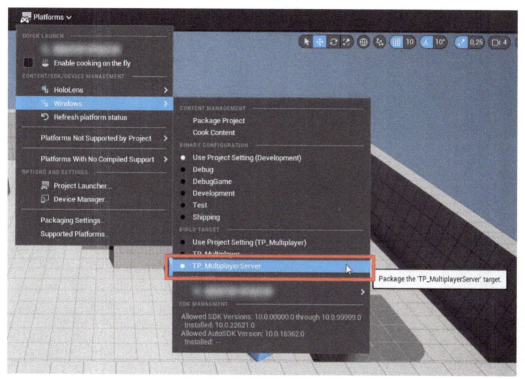

Figure 14.20 – Building the server

15. Next, click **Windows | Package Content** to start packaging the application and, once the build has finished, you will have in your hands a dedicated server executable!

16. To get a client executable, you will have to repeat the same steps as above, using a different build target. To do so, in the Unreal Engine main toolbar, click the **Platforms** button and select **Windows | TP_Multiplayer** to set the build target, as shown in *Figure 14.21*:

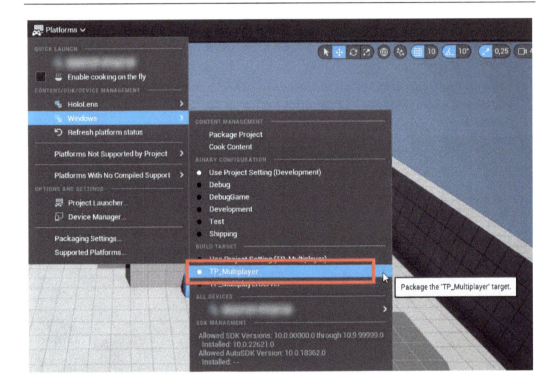

Figure 14.21 – Building the client

Then, click **Windows | Package Content** to start packaging the client build. Once it has finished, you will also have the client executable, and you will be ready to test the application.

Testing the project

Now that both the dedicated server and the client have been successfully built, it's time to test their functionalities.

To start your server locally, all you have to do is double-click on the build executable you created in the previous steps.

Alternatively, if you are interested in checking the server log, you can take the following steps:

1. Open the Windows Command Prompt.
2. Through the `cd` command, navigate to the folder that contains the server executable.
3. Insert the name of your server executable, followed by the `-log` parameter, for instance:

```
TP_MultiplayerServer.exe -log
```

Once the server has started, it will start listening for connection requests from clients.

As we have used an out-of-the-box, base template and we did not implement any session logic, we will be connecting the clients from the Unreal Engine command line. This is something you obviously won't use in a final release but that is really handy at development time.

The command line is available in the client executable because we compiled the project as a development build in the previous steps.

To start the client application, all you have to do is to double-click on the executable, which should be named `TP_Multiplayer.exe`. This will open the executable with the default starting map (i.e., `Map_0`).

As stated before, to connect to the server, we will be using the console command, which can be opened by default with the ' character (i.e., backtick). Once the console is open, enter the following command:

```
open 127.0.0.1
```

The client application with the console command open is shown in *Figure 14.22*:

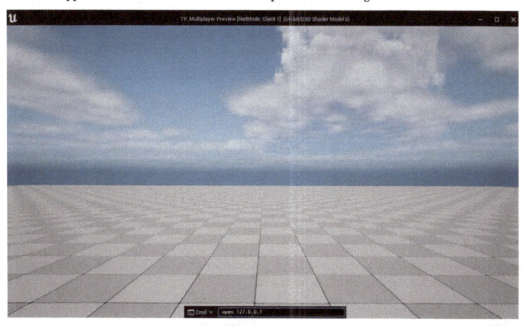

Figure 14.22 – The client application with the console command open

> **Note**
>
> If you are using a keyboard that does not support the backtick character (like mine), you can easily change the keyboard shortcut by opening **Editor Preferences** and looking for the **Open Console Command Box** field.

The client should now open the regular Third Person map and your client will be connected to the dedicated server. To double-check this, if you started the server with the `-log` option enabled, you should see a log message similar to this one:

```
LogNet: Join Succeeded: [Client Identifier]
```

And that's it – you have finally succeeded in creating your own dedicated server and connecting your clients to a LAN!

If you want an extra challenge, you can give compiling the Unreal Shadows project with a dedicated server a try. You already have some knowledge in this area, so it shouldn't take too much effort.

Additionally, if you want to go deeper into this topic, Epic Games has provided a full tutorial on how to compile Lyra Starter Game (`https://docs.unrealengine.com/5.1/en-US/lyra-sample-game-in-unreal-engine/`), a real-world project including many of the topics covered in this book. The link to the tutorial is `https://docs.unrealengine.com/5.1/en-US/setting-up-dedicated-servers-in-unreal-engine/`.

Anything is possible with a little bit of hard work!

Summary

In this chapter, you have faced the frightening task of downloading the Unreal Engine Editor source code from GitHub and compiling it into an executable application.

If you plan to make a living as a multiplayer developer, building Unreal Engine source code is a mandatory skill whenever you want to set up a dedicated server for your game or need to customize the engine's networking and multiplayer settings.

As you have discovered, building and packaging a dedicated server is not an easy task and requires a lot of time and patience – and sometimes a bit of luck!

In the next – and final – chapter, you will learn how to take a step further in multiplayer game development by using online cloud services, specifically Epic Online Services.

15

Adding Epic Online Services (EOS)

When developing multiplayer games, it is important to add online services to the overall experience in order to enable players to connect and play with other people over the internet. This is especially important for games that require a large number of players or that are played by people in different locations of the world. Adding online services allows players to enjoy a more social gaming experience and increases the overall fun and engagement of the game. Plus, it also allows the game developer to gather data and feedback from players, which can be useful for improving the game and fixing any issues that arise.

In this chapter, I will be presenting you with **Epic Online Services** (**EOS**), a cloud platform that provides developers with the tools to create, deploy, and operate high-performance gaming experiences. Developed by Epic Games, this powerful platform brings together all of its existing technologies and expertise into one unified system. With its scalable infrastructure and advanced features such as analytics and cloud hosting capabilities, Epic Games EOS allows developers to build games optimized for maximum performance on any device or operating system.

Through the next sections, I will present you the following topics:

- Introducing EOS
- Accessing the Developer Portal
- Getting started with the EOS SDK

Technical requirements

To follow the topics presented in this chapter, you should have completed all the previous chapters and have understood their content.

Introducing EOS

EOS (`https://dev.epicgames.com/en-US/services`) is a powerful suite of services and tools designed to help developers create the most immersive online experiences possible. With EOS, developers can easily manage user authentication, matchmaking, leaderboards, achievements, and more – all from one centralized system. Whether you're working on an MMO or a single-player game with online features such as multiplayer mode or leaderboards, EOS has something to offer every developer looking to take their games further. One thing to mention is that all services are free to use, even if you don't use an Epic Games account.

EOS can be categorized into three distinct sets of services:

- **Game Services**, which covers multiplayer functionalities, such as sessions, lobbies, or achievements
- **Account Services**, which covers player identity, such as authentication and profile handling, and friend management
- **Store Services**, which covers Epic Games store transactions, including catalog management and verification

Game Services can also be used with any identity provider, such as Discord, Steam, Google, and, of course, Epic Games; this means players won't need an Epic Game account in order to get access to these services. On the other hand, Account Services and Store Services can only be used with an Epic Games account.

> **Note**
>
> In case you are wondering, EOS does not include a cloud machine to host a Dedicated Server (like the one you built in *Chapter 14, Deploying Multiplayer Games*). To host your server in the cloud, you will need to use services such as **Amazon Web Services** (**AWS**) or **Microsoft Azure**. The official Epic Games documentation has a dedicated section on this topic and can be found on this web page: `https://docs.unrealengine.com/5.0/en-US/unreal-engine-cloud-deployments/`.

EOS is accessible via the **Epic Games Developer Portal**, which is a browser-based tool that enables users to configure and set up their games through a list of developer resources. In addition to the EOS, the Developer Portal also offers the functionality to manage the games that you may have made available in the Epic Games Store.

Upon successful registration for a Developer Portal account, you will gain the capability to manage your products, configure services, and establish settings for identity providers and available platforms. Additional features provided within the Developer Portal include the ability for users to update game information, provide support for players, manage game finances, and access usage reports and statistical data.

It is also worth noting that the Developer Portal is intended to be cross-platform-compatible, giving developers the capability to deploy their games across an array of different platforms – such as consoles, desktops, and mobile devices – while utilizing a single service for managing gameplay across all of these platforms. This functionality helps to provide a cohesive and seamless experience for players across these different platforms.

> **Note**
>
> As the Developer Portal and EOS are web-based, they remain in a perpetual state of development. Consequently, it is possible to encounter inconsistencies or variations in the features and functionality described in the following sections. Despite any discrepancies, you should still be able to navigate and engage with these services effectively and with minimal disruption to the overall experience.

As EOS is a huge topic on its own – and not meant to work just for Unreal Engine but with many developer platforms – having a full understanding of it is out of this book's scope; however, in the following sections, I will guide you through the main parts of the Developer Portal, EOS, and their peculiarities, so you will have a solid base to use them in your games.

The first thing to do is to start creating your own organization in order to grant you access to all the features available in the cloud service.

Accessing the Developer Portal

In this section, I will guide you through the creation of a Developer Portal account in order to properly set up and manage your own projects, whether they are multiplayer or not. The steps you will need to complete to get your game ready are as follows:

- Setting up an Epic Games account (you should have one already) and creating an organization for the Developer Portal

- Creating a Product

- Configuring the Product

So, let's get started.

Accessing the Epic Games Developer Portal

The first thing you need to do in order to access and use the Epic Games Developer Portal is to create an **organization** – this is a group that holds the responsibility for both creating and owning Products within the Epic Games Developer Portal.

Start by accessing the dedicated web page, which can be found at this link: `https://dev.epicgames.com/portal`. After logging in with your Epic Games account, you will be presented with a registration form where you will need to insert an organization name and an email, as shown in *Figure 15.1*:

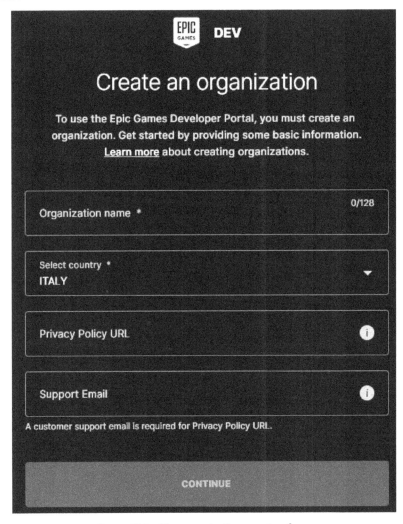

Figure 15.1 – The organization creation form

Once you have registered, you will be granted access to the Developer Portal, where you will be able to manage your organization, download the EOS SDK, create your projects, and, most importantly, set up them.

As the creator of the organization, you will be responsible for setting up all the needed information for it, such as tax and payout information if you plan to generate some revenue from your games.

Additionally, unless you plan to work as a one-man army, you'll be able to invite additional members to the organization itself. This feature is available in the **Organization | Members** section. Each member can be assigned a role, to get access to some, or all of, the features available in the organization. You can create your own roles, each with its custom access level, but Epic Games has already created some for you; some of these roles are listed here:

- **Admin**: This role will grant the member access to all functionalities in the Portal. It is the role automatically assigned to the organization creator (i.e., you).

- **Community Tools**: This role will give the member access to all community-related features, such as game analytics, accounts, and the ticketing system.

- **Payout**: This role will give the member access to all finance-related sections, such as payout and reports.

If you're working in a game studio – even if it's a small one – having this kind of member access is going to be really important to make everything work perfectly.

Once the organization has been properly set up and you have a well-organized team, the next thing to do is to create your first Product, be it a multiplayer game or anything else.

Creating a Product

Once you are inside an organization, you will need to create a **Product** – this is a game or a software project that contains some EOS logic. Once a Product has been created, it will be assigned a default **Sandbox**, which is a development environment that will contain the distribution data, such as store-related or specific deployment information. At the time of writing this book, Epic Games provides the following default Sandboxes:

- **Dev**: Used for editing and configuring a Product at development time

- **Stage**: Used for testing a Product for readiness

- **Live**: Used to distribute a Product on the Epic Games Store

Inside a Sandbox, you will be able to create one or more **Deployment**, a specific distribution that will store all gameplay and player data, such as achievements and current matches.

As an example, let's imagine you want to implement some services for the Unreal Shadows game, and you don't want to make things too complicated. First of all, you will need to create a dedicated Product and then you will work with a single Sandbox; inside the Sandbox, you will use the aforementioned deployment environment depending on your needs. For example, see the following:

- In the **Dev** environment, you will conduct development and internal testing for your project

- In the **Stage** environment, you will test the game

- In the **Live** environment, you will ship the game as an official release

Let's now imagine that, during your game development, you (or the game design team) decide to add a new experimental feature, such as a voice chat for all the players. You'll create a new deployment, called **Dev-Experimental-VOIP**, and test its functionalities internally. Once this feature is solid and ready for a release, you will simply have to add it to your **Stage** deployment and, once it is solid enough, to the **Live** deployment.

As a practical example, we'll create a demo Product. Inside your **Developer Portal Dashboard**, click the **Create Product** button, as shown in *Figure 15.2*:

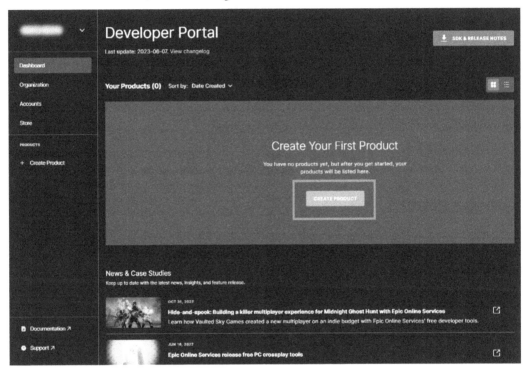

Figure 15.2 – Creating a new Product

You will get a pop-up window where you will need to insert the Product name. In my case, I opted for EOS Demo, as shown in *Figure 15.3*:

Figure 15.3 – Naming the Product

> **Note**
> Once created a Product, you won't be able to change its name, so choose wisely!

If this is the first Product you have created with your organization, you'll be asked to review some agreements with Epic Games, involving topics such as store distribution and marketing subscriber lists; read them carefully and, if you agree with the terms, click the **Accept** button. Once accepted, you will probably be asked to pay a submission fee; just skip this as it's about the Epic Games Store and not related to the Game Services we are interested in at the moment – you may need in the future once you decide to publish your games on the Epic Games Store.

Now that you have created your own Product, you are ready for the next step, configuring the services you will be using.

Configuring the Product services

To access your project page, all you have to do is click on your Product link – in my case, the **EOS Demo** Product – in your Developer Portal, as shown in *Figure 15.4*:

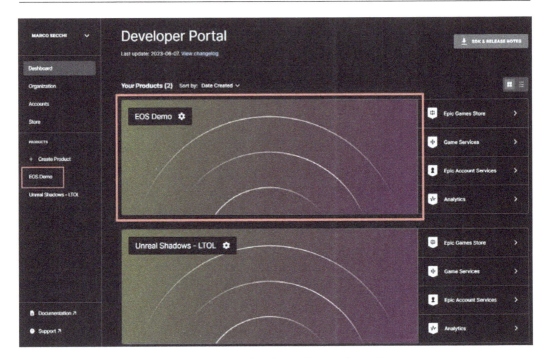

Figure 15.4 – Selecting the product configuration

Once you are on the Product page, you can access its settings by clicking **Product Settings**, as shown in *Figure 15.5*:

Figure 15.5 – The Product Settings section

You are now able to create an EOS Client for your application.

Creating an EOS Client

In the context of Epic Online Services, the term **Client** refers to a program that utilizes the functionality of EOS for a particular Product. This can encompass locally installed game builds that end users operate on their systems, dedicated servers maintained by the Product's owners, or any other program that necessitates access to the backend services that EOS provides. Each Client will have its own ID and secret password for authentication.

Each Client will also have its own **Client Policy**, which will determine the level of access for the features that will be implemented. This means that, if you are creating a multiplayer game using EOS, your dedicated server will need its own EOS Client, and the player's clients will have their own dedicated EOS Clients. On the other hand, if you plan to distribute a listen server version of your game, you will need just one EOS Client for your game.

If you're feeling a bit confused by the term "Client" in this context, don't worry – I felt the same way the first time I read the official EOS documentation! To help with this, let's actually create a Client:

1. Click the **Clients** link in the main page toolbar, as shown in *Figure 15.6*:

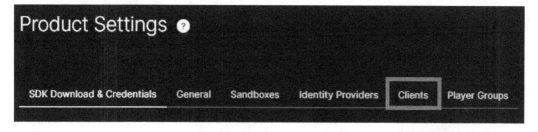

Figure 15.6 – The Clients section

Click on the **Add New Client** button; this will open the **Add New Client** window (shown later in *Figure 15.8*).

2. In the **Client Name** input field, insert a name for your Client; I opted for EOS Demo Client.

3. Click on **Add New Client Policy**. This will open a new window where you can configure your policy:

    I. Insert a name in the **Client policy name** input field; in my case, I choose EOS Demo Policy.

    II. In the **Client policy type**, you can choose one of the pre-made configuration or you can create a custom one. For the purpose of this example, I chose the **GameClient** options, which are configured to manage untrusted Client applications and, as such, will require an authenticated user.

III.   The previous selection will enable a list of additional options, such as **Leaderboards**, **Matchmaking**, or **Lobbies**, which you will be able to change, depending on your own needs.

IV.   Once you are happy with your Client's configuration, click **ADD NEW CLIENT POLICY**, as shown in *Figure 15.7*:

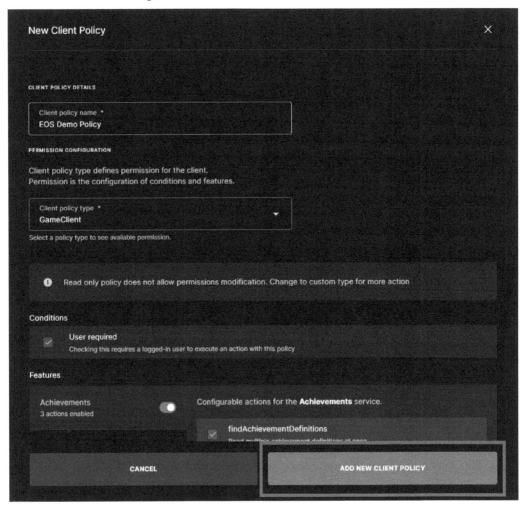

Figure 15.7 – The Client policy creation

4. Once the Client policy has been created, you will be brought back to the Client creation. Click the **Add New Client** button, as shown in *Figure 15.8*:

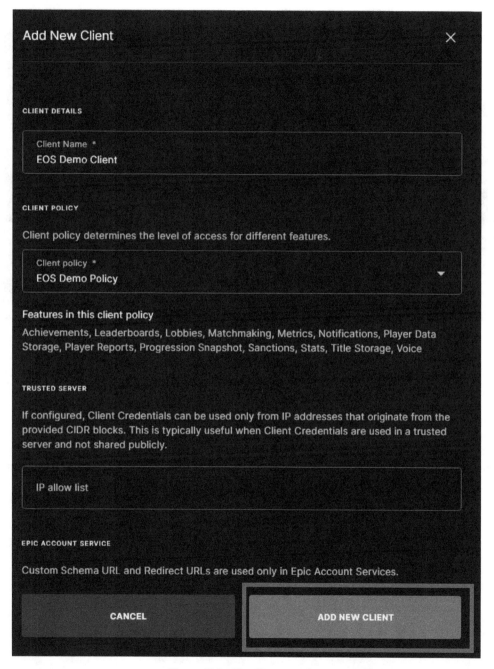

Figure 15.8 – The Client creation

Once the Client has been created, you will be brought back to the Product page and you should see listed both the Client and the Client policy, as shown in *Figure 15.9*:

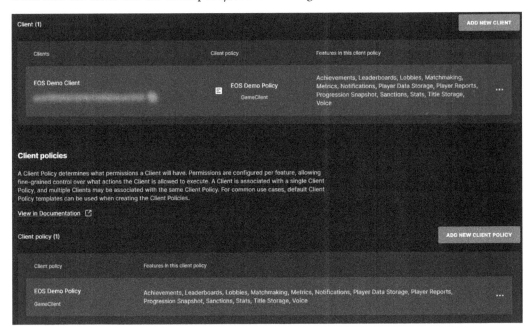

Figure 15.9 – The Client and the Client Policy on the Product settings page

In the **Client** section, you will notice the features that have been enabled for this Client and its ID, which will be used when connecting to the services.

Accessing Epic Account Services

Now that the Client has been created, you need to access the **Epic Account Services** section of your Product page, in order to finalize the EOS configuration. To access this section, click the **Epic Account Services** button, as shown in *Figure 15.10*:

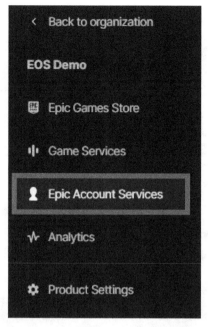

Figure 15.10 – The Epic Account Services section

The first thing to do is to configure the permissions for the Client so, click the **Permissions** button in the **EOS Demo** application section, as shown in *Figure 15.11*:

Figure 15.11 – The PERMISSIONS section

Unless you want to add some custom configuration, you will just need to click on the **SAVE CHANGES** button, in order to initialize the permissions configuration. This will set this section as **CONFIGURED**, as depicted in *Figure 15.12*:

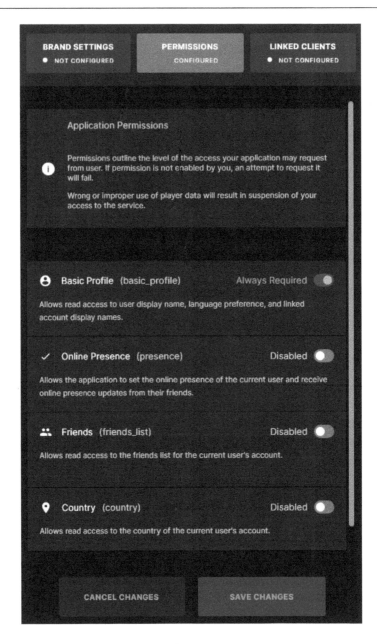

Figure 15.12 – The configured PERMISSIONS section

Next, you need to select the **Linked Clients** section in order to set the previously created Client as the selected one. Once you are in the **Linked Clients** section, all you need to do is to select your Client – in this case, **EOS Demo Client** – from the drop-down menu and click the **SAVE CHANGES** button. This will set this section as **CONFIGURED**, as shown in *Figure 15.13*:

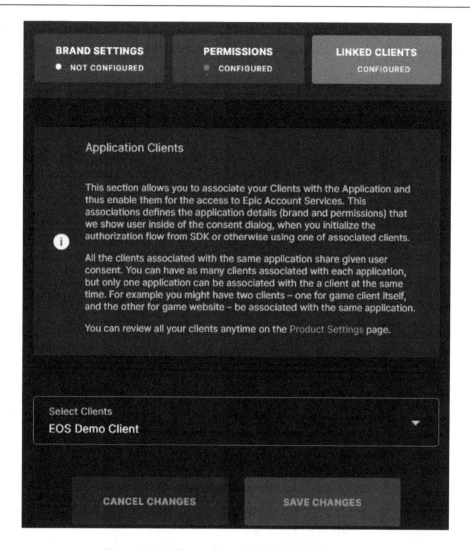

Figure 15.13 – The configured LINKED CLIENTS section

The **BRAND SETTINGS** section can be left unconfigured at a development stage because it will be required only once you are in a release phase and your application will need to be reviewed and approved by Epic Games.

Once you are done with this, your application is ready, and EOS can be connected with your game or application.

In this section, you have been introduced to the Epic Games Developer Portal and its online services. As you have seen, you will need to access the portal in order to initialize and configure the cloud features you will implement in your game. In the next section, I will give you a brief introduction to the tools that you'll use in your game, to integrate it with the EOS environment.

Getting started with the EOS SDK

The **EOS SDK** is a tool that's independent of any particular game engine, providing developers access to several cross-platform services that can be integrated into their games. Depending on the game engine being utilized, the level of integration options available to incorporate the EOS SDK into the game will vary. Nonetheless, the method of integration is at the discretion of the development team, and they may even use a combination of integration options.

In order to start using the EOS SDK you will have to:

- Download it from the Developer Portal
- Integrate it into your game

In this section, I will give you a brief walkthrough on how to get the SDK and to understand the basic concepts on how to integrate it in your project.

Downloading the EOS SDK

To download the SDK, go to your **Developer Portal Dashboard** page and click the **SDK & Release Notes** button, as shown in *Figure 15.14*:

Figure 15.14 – The download SDK button

As stated before, the SDK is meant to target multiple developer platforms and so you will get multiple download options (i.e., the SDK for C, C#, iOS, or Android), as shown in *Figure 15.15*:

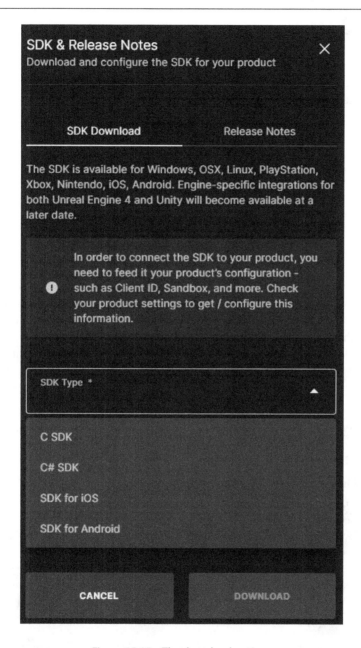

Figure 15.15 – The download options

After choosing your preferred platform, the download will start. Once it's finished, you will be able to start integrating the SDK with your own application.

Integrating the system into your game

No matter which game engine you decide to use, you can totally use the EOS SDK in your game! All you need to do – after having configured the Product in the Developer Portal and having downloaded the SDK – is to write your integration to your game engine of choice.

If you plan to integrate the SDK with an Unreal Engine project, there are two options to integrate the EOS SDK:

- Use the EOS **Online Subsystem (OSS)** plugin
- Use a third-party plugin or write one on your own

Let's look at both options.

Using the EOS Online Subsystem

As you have already seen in *Chapter 12, Managing Multiplayer Sessions*, the OSS in Unreal Engine is a tool that provides a uniform way of accessing the numerous online features provided by different online services by means of a set of plugins. This includes Xbox Live, Steam and, finally, the Epic Online Services – through the dedicated EOS OSS plugin – making it immensely valuable in game development workflows that support multiple platforms or online services. With this in mind, you will be able to easily configure your game's EOS settings within the Unreal Editor without the need for coding.

To access the EOS OSS, you will have to enable the plugin in Unreal Engine. This is quite easy to achieve. Once you have opened your Unreal Engine project, all you will have to do is:

1. Select **Edit | Plugins** from the main menu.
2. Enable the **Online Subsystem EOS** and **EOS Shared** plugins.
3. Restart the Unreal Engine in order to initialize the plugins.

Once the plugins have been enabled, you will need to setup your project, to connect it with the EOS Product you have previously created. This setup is pretty long but quite straightforward; you can find instructions on how to do this in the official documentation, found here: `https://docs. unrealengine.com/5.1/en-US/online-subsystem-eos-plugin-in-unreal- engine/`. You can also find more information about the OSS plugin, which is out of the scope of the book.

It is worth noting that at the time of writing this book, some of the EOS SDK interfaces haven't been developed yet in the EOS OSS plugin and so they will not be available out-of-the-box. The interfaces that aren't still available are as follows:

- Anti-cheat interface
- Reports interface

- Sanctions interface

- Custom Invites interface

This means that if your game needs these features, you will have to write your own plugin, or use a third-party one.

Using a third-party plugin

As stated before, the other option for integrating your game with the EOS SDK is to develop your own plugin in Unreal Engine.

> **Note**
>
> The EOS SDK needs to be initialized inside a plugin – writing your own implementation inside your project may result in unexpected behaviours or some interfaces not working at all.

Developing your own plugin in Unreal Engine is a wonderful way to hone your skills and bring them to the next level. To get started, the best advice is to read the official documentation that thoroughly describes the process of developing and managing plugins in Unreal Engine. The documentation page can be found by following this link: `https://docs.unrealengine.com/5.1/en-US/plugins-in-unreal-engine/`.

However, if you feel uncomfortable with plugin development, you can take advantage of the Unreal Engine Marketplace (`https://unrealengine.com/marketplace`) and look for a commercial solution. As an example, a couple of amazing integration tools are **EOS Online Subsystem** (`https://unrealengine.com/marketplace/en-US/product/eos-online-subsystem`) developed by Redpoint Games and **EOS Integration Kit** (`https://unrealengine.com/marketplace/en-US/product/eos-integration-kit`) developed by Betide Studio. Both offer seamless integration with EOS and almost all service interfaces are exposed, in order to make your multiplayer game easier and more efficient to develop and maintain.

It is also worth noting that both plugins offer some sort of free or open source license, so you can test them out in order to check if they are the right tool for you. Buying them will, of course, help the development team maintain the plugin and add new features as time goes by.

Now that you have the basic knowledge on EOS, it's time to start working on your soon-to-be successful game and integrate it with some (or all!) of the services offered by Epic Games.

> **Note**
>
> To learn about all the features that come shipped with EOS, you can start by checking the official documentation that can be found on this web page: `https://dev.epicgames.com/docs/epic-online-services`.

Summary

In this final chapter of the book, I have presented you to the Developer Portal and the EOS platform. You accessed the Developer Portal in order to create your own Product and to connect it with any kind of application or game. You have also seen how the basic structure of an EOS application is made and initialized with some basic and default settings.

Finally, you have learned that you can integrate these services with any development platform, including Unreal Engine; this can be achieved by using the official – but, at the moment, incomplete – plugin, you can use a third-party integration system, or you can even write your own code so that you will focus on what you really need.

As you guessed, there's a lot more on this and you have just started scratching the surface of this environment. My final advice is to try the services and explore all the interfaces offered by the SDK. Experiment by writing your own code and – if you feel courageous enough – create your own plugin; I assure you, if you are a game programmer, this will be super-fun! (But, maybe, this topic might be best left for another book!)

And that's the end of *Multiplayer Game Development with Unreal Engine 5*. It has been a pleasure to share my knowledge and experience with you, and I am confident that you now know how to create amazing multiplayer games for your soon-to-be players.

Thank you for joining me on this journey and may the odds be ever in your projects' favor!

Index

Packtpub.com

Subscribe to our online digital library for full access to over 7,000 books and videos, as well as industry leading tools to help you plan your personal development and advance your career. For more information, please visit our website.

Why subscribe?

- Spend less time learning and more time coding with practical eBooks and Videos from over 4,000 industry professionals

- Improve your learning with Skill Plans built especially for you

- Get a free eBook or video every month

- Fully searchable for easy access to vital information

- Copy and paste, print, and bookmark content

Did you know that Packt offers eBook versions of every book published, with PDF and ePub files available? You can upgrade to the eBook version at Packtpub.com and as a print book customer, you are entitled to a discount on the eBook copy. Get in touch with us at customercare@packtpub.com for more details.

At www.packtpub.com, you can also read a collection of free technical articles, sign up for a range of free newsletters, and receive exclusive discounts and offers on Packt books and eBooks.

Other Books You May Enjoy

If you enjoyed this book, you may be interested in these other books by Packt:

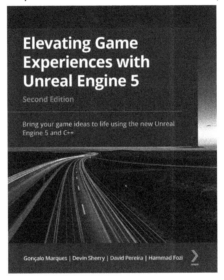

Elevating Game Experiences with Unreal Engine 5 - Second Edition

Gonçalo Marques | Devin Sherry | David Pereira | Hammad Fozi

ISBN: 9781803239866

- Create a fully functional third-person character and enemies.
- Implement navigation with keyboard, mouse, and gamepad.
- Program logic and game mechanics with collision and particle effects
- Explore AI for games with Blackboards and behavior trees.
- Build character animations with animation blueprints and montages.
- Polish your game with stunning visual and sound effects.
- Explore the fundamentals of game UI using a heads-up display.

Blueprints Visual Scripting for Unreal Engine 5 - Third Edition

Marcos Romero | Brenden Sewell

ISBN: 9781801811583

- Understand programming concepts in Blueprints.
- Create prototypes and iterate new game mechanics rapidly.
- Build user interface elements and interactive menus.
- Use advanced Blueprint nodes to manage the complexity of a game.
- Explore all the features of the Blueprint editor, such as the Components tab, Viewport, and Event Graph.
- Get to grips with OOP concepts and explore the Gameplay Framework.
- Work with virtual reality development in UE Blueprint.
- Implement procedural generation and create a product configurator.

Packt is searching for authors like you

If you're interested in becoming an author for Packt, please visit `authors.packtpub.com` and apply today. We have worked with thousands of developers and tech professionals, just like you, to help them share their insight with the global tech community. You can make a general application, apply for a specific hot topic that we are recruiting an author for, or submit your own idea.

Share Your Thoughts

Now you've finished *Multiplayer Game Development with Unreal Engine 5*, we'd love to hear your thoughts! Scan the QR code below to go straight to the Amazon review page for this book and share your feedback or leave a review on the site that you purchased it from.

`https://packt.link/r/1803232870`

Your review is important to us and the tech community and will help us make sure we're delivering excellent quality content.

Download a free PDF copy of this book

Thanks for purchasing this book!

Do you like to read on the go but are unable to carry your print books everywhere?

Is your eBook purchase not compatible with the device of your choice?

Don't worry, now with every Packt book you get a DRM-free PDF version of that book at no cost.

Read anywhere, any place, on any device. Search, copy, and paste code from your favorite technical books directly into your application.

The perks don't stop there, you can get exclusive access to discounts, newsletters, and great free content in your inbox daily

Follow these simple steps to get the benefits:

1. Scan the QR code or visit the link below

https://packt.link/free-ebook/9781803232874

2. Submit your proof of purchase
3. That's it! We'll send your free PDF and other benefits to your email directly

www.ingramcontent.com/pod-product-compliance
Lightning Source LLC
Chambersburg PA
CBHW080609060326
40690CB00021B/4628